PAN AMERICAN

 KUWAIT

 U.S. AIR FORCE

 WESTERN

 EL AL

 AIR INDIA

 AIR MADAGASCAR

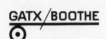 GATX-BOOTHE

 ICELANDAIR

 MEXICANA

 CHINA AIR

 ANSETT-ANA

 IRAN AIR

 KLM

 ALLEGHENY

 IRISH

 SWISSAIR

 AIR ASIA

 UNITED

 FLYING TIGER

 DETA

 WORLD

 BWIA

 AIR FRANCE

 AIRLIFT

 FAUCETT

 FRONTIER

 BOAC

 IBERIA

 ARGENTINAS

 ALASKA

 WARDAIR

 VASP

 QANTAS

 AVIANCA

 UNITED ARAB

 NAC-NEW ZEALAND

 FAA

 SCANDINAVIAN

 PIE...

 MIDDLE EAST

L-1011 TriStar and The Lockheed Story

DEDICATION

To my wonderful wife, Mary Sue, without whose support, faith and love this book could never have been written.

OTHER BOOKS BY THE AUTHOR

"The Plane That Changed The World—Story of The Fabulous DC-3."

"Tin Goose—The Fabulous Ford Trimotor"

"747"—Story Of The Boeing Superjet

and

The Lockheed Story

by Douglas J. Ingells

AERO PUBLISHERS, INC.

329 Aviation Road Fallbrook, Cal. 92028

Library of Congress Catalog Card Number
73-83065

ISBN 0-8168-6650-3

Printed and Published in the United States

FOREWORD

Lockheed and its people generally look ahead, not back. But there are times when a reflective glance back is a good thing. So we feel honored and grateful that Douglas Ingells has done that for us in this book. It seems particularly fitting that the year of publication, 1973, marks the 60th anniversary of the first flight of the first airplane to bear the Lockheed name—even before there was a Lockheed corporation.

Mr. Ingells has carried the story of the Lockheed Winged Star forward to the present, including an account of our development of the new L-1011 TriStar luxury jetliner, and speculates about our future.

As to the future of air travel itself, I am tremendously optimistic. At this time, air travel has accounted for three-fourths of the total growth in all commercial transportation during less than 15 years from the start of the jet transport era.

The volume of today's air passenger travel is truly impressive. About 1.5 million people are airborne every day—60,000 every hour. And this is only the beginning. Present projections show that total airline revenue passenger miles will triple from 1970 to 1980—and the outlines of how widespread air travel finally will become are still not clearly in sight.

Probably the dominant reason for the great growth of air travel is that an airplane seat remains one of the world's greatest bargains for the traveling public.

Mr. Ingells has told the story of Lockheed's aviation activities in detail. Left for later telling are equally interesting stories behind the company's achievements in other exciting fields—including pioneering in missiles and space exploration, propulsion, electronics, the oceans, land transportation, shipbuilding, and international operations.

In the preparation of this book, Mr. Ingells interviewed Lockheed people and was supplied with photographs and other information to the best of our ability. But the book is entirely the product of his own enterprise. He was not subsidized by Lockheed in any way.

For aviation enthusiasts, and there are many of us, I am sure his story will serve as a useful and informative reference volume.

Daniel J. Haughton
Chairman of the Board
Lockheed Aircraft Corporation

PREFACE

It is always difficult as with life itself, to pinpoint the exact moment when a book is born. In this case, however, the author's memory recalls his first flight in a Lockheed-built aircraft.

The pilot was famed aviator Colonel Roscoe Turner, he with the snappy blue uniform and the diamond-studded wings, the man who became legend in a thousand skies. As I remember, Roscoe brought his glistening new Lockheed *"Air Express"* named THE GILMORE LION to Dayton, Ohio for an Air Show there. Through a mutual friend, Bill Mayfield, who incidentally, was Orville Wright's official photographer, I met Roscoe and he took me for a ride that was unforgettable.

We had another passenger aboard, a lion cub named "Gilmore" and when you have flown with Turner and with "Gilmore" you don't forget—pilot, plane or passenger. I was only in my teens, then, but I had a desire to be a writer, and I vowed to myself that someday I would write a book about Roscoe Turner and "Gilmore" and that beautiful red and blue and gold Lockheed *"Air Express"* high-wing monoplane.

Things didn't turn out quite the way I had them figured. Roscoe died before we got a chance to complete a manuscript we had started so long ago called "THE MAN WHO FLEW WITH THE LION." But through the years I followed closely the exploits of the famous Lockheeds from the fabulous *"Vegas"*—flown by such greats as Wiley Post, Jimmy Mattern, Art Goebel, Frank Hawks, Amelia Earhart and others—and the evolutionary process which produced today's most advanced technology jetliner, the L-1011 *"TriStar."* For more than three decades I have watched Lockheed wings grow stronger.

It has been my privilege to have flown as a passenger in the *"Electra"* and the *"Lodestar"* of the thirties. I rode in one of the first *"Hudson"* bombers at Wright Field on its way to the RAF. I flew "piggy-back" in the P-38 *"Lightning."* My first jet ride was in the second seat of a *T-Bird,* trainer version of the P-80 *"Shooting Star"* our first combat jet. The list can go on—up front with Jack Frye in the cockpit of the first TWA *"Constellation;"* a guest of the Navy aboard a *"Constitution"* demonstration flight; aloft in the *"Super Connies,"* the second generation *"Electra"* turbo-prop jetliner. I have flown in the *"Hercules,"* *"Starlifter,"* *"Galaxy"* and now *"TriStar."* But there is much more to it than just having "flown" in this marvelous family of Lockheed aircraft.

It has been my pleasure to have talked with many of the men and women who designed and built them. And I have seen virtually every one of these planes in their factory "nests;" and watched them grow from shop to sky. To me, each has its own "personality" of purpose; each having contributed something in its own way to the building of today's airpower and the best air transportation system in the world.

My files are filled with notebooks and photographs, hundreds of anecdotes and stories, gleaned from personal interviews and experiences. With so much material, the book had to be written. If for no other reason, but to put down on paper a well deserved tribute to the Lockheed family, who turned so many dreams into realities.

Indeed, in the history of our great aircraft manufacturing industry, there never was and probably never will be, a more dedicated group of men and women and a company spirit that has produced so much progress for this winged world.

"L-1011 TriStar and The Lockheed Story" is my effort to capture that "spirit" and with words and pictures give the reader an accurate account of the history of the Lockheed Aircraft Corporation, its trials and triumphs, past, present and future.

It is my hope that in presenting this volume, the reader will also sense this feeling, as did the author, and that the material so graciously made available to me, does justice to one of the great sagas of the sky.

To me, at least, it is the stuff of which stars are made.

Douglas J. Ingells
Ludington, Michigan
July, 1973

ACKNOWLEDGEMENTS

The author wishes to express deep gratitude to all of those who gave so much of their time in interviews, helped to document facts and dates, and provided so much interesting background during the months of research to gather material for this book. Space does not permit listing all their names, much as I would like, but in most cases, they appear in the story itself, and I hope the way it is presented will suffice to show my appreciation. It is much more their story than it is mine.

Most especially, I want to thank Phil Jurgens and his staff who wrote the splendid Lockheed history "OF MEN AND STARS" which provided so much historical data and anecdotes.

Then, there is one individual who probably more than anyone else is responsible for my completing the book, which like *"TriStar,"* itself, had many ups and downs. He is Jim Ragsdale, Publicity Manager for the Lockheed-California Company. Jim's moral support, friendship and understanding kept this project "alive" more than once, when it was heading down the runway in the wrong direction.

Sharing this role are two others: Dick Martin, who checked and doubled checked the manuscript with so many sources, and Bob Ferguson, photographer, who was never too busy to fulfill a request, and whose pictures really make the book.

I also want to thank Lockheed management and all concerned for the splendid cooperation in making the material available, the freedom of touring through the great Lockheed complex, the many courtesies, pleasant flights in *"TriStar"* and most of all for the opportunity to tell their story as I saw it. The association has been a memorable one.

Douglas J. Ingells

PHOTO CREDITS

Lockheed-California Corporation, Lockheed-Georgia Corporation, AVCO Corporation, Rolls-Royce, British Aircraft Corporation, Pratt & Whitney Aircraft, United Aircraft Corporation, United States Air Force, The Boeing Airplane Company, McDonnell/Douglas Aircraft Corporation, The National Smithsonian Institution (Air Museum), Eastern Airlines, Trans World Airlines, General Electric Company, The Henry Ford Museum, Dearborn. All photographs appearing in this book were supplied by these companies and organizations.

Table Of Contents

The Lockheed Model-G hydroplane, first of a long line of aircraft that would make the name Lockheed famous in aviation and aerospace, taxis on the waters of San Francisco Bay, June 15, 1913, the day the plane made its maiden flight. Ironically, at the time, few people realized that the Cruiser U.S.S. Wisconsin and ocean liner in background, would be relegated to secondary roles in warfare and commerce by Lockheed wings for war and peace which would change the course of history.

CHAPTER ONE

Birth Of The Winged Star

Imagine a young red-haired teen-ager roaming through the exhibit halls at the University of Santa Clara near San Francisco. His name is Allan Loughead. Like most boys his age he is interested in mechanical things; ships, trains, the crude, but brand new horseless carriage. This latter holds his avid attention. He has been thinking about building a race car. Now, suddenly, he is completely captured by something else—a flying machine. The race car is forgotten. This is really what he wants: To soar through the air like the birds!

He is looking at the strange aircraft constructed by James Montgomery, a professor at the university. Before the youth's eyes is the man-carrying glider which Montgomery many times had ridden to earth on the currents of air after being released from a hot-air balloon. "What sport it must be!" young Loughead is thinking. "What craftsmanship it must take to build so frail a thing of wood and cloth that it should weigh only 45 pounds but support the body of a full grown man!"

Allan Loughead was fascinated as he read the placard describing details about the glider. His mind, quick to grasp mechanical theories, flashed from the automobile in one corner of the exhibit hall to the glider in another corner. He linked the two together. If you could just take the motor in the horseless carriage and put it in the glider. That would be the ideal way to travel. This combination would produce a powered flying machine. He left the museum-like shop of the university and walked home. But the idea of a power-driven glider went along with him.

It was the early part of 1904. A few weeks later with the memory of his visit to see the glider still fresh in his mind Allan heard about the Wright Brothers. He read, how, on a gusty day—December 17, 1903—from the sands of Kitty Hawk, North Carolina, they had flown their glider with the motor on it. It was the first power-driven, heavier-than-air, man-carrying flying machine in history. The Wrights had turned Loughead's dream about flying into a reality.

By the time the news reached his ears young Allan already was hard at work building a speedy auto racer. The townsfolk of Alma, California, a small town south of San Jose where he lived, complained that he would "kill himself in that race-about." They said, that boy Loughead had speed in his blood and goo-grease in his veins. Naturally, his racer was the fastest thing on wheels. But it wasn't fast enough. It wasn't what he really wanted. He wanted wings.

It was not easy to get them. The Wrights kept their secret to themselves, and for more than a year after the first historic flight at Kitty Hawk, they were the only ones to fly in an heavier-than-air machine with any degree of success. But soon others caught on. It was really quite simple, this thing called powered flight—once you knew how. The trick was to get the right airfoil to produce the right amount of lift, decrease drag or resistence wherever possible, devise a means of control to attain stability. Orville and Wilbur Wright were the first to fly successfully because of their unique control method. It amounted to an elevator-aileron-rudder combination. They achieved it first by simply warping the tips of the wings, and making the elevator and rudder surfaces moveable. This gave them lateral and vertical control of their flying machine. It was something the other pioneers, even Professor Montgomery had overlooked. Others didn't take long to apply similar control techniques to their own designs. A fellow named Glenn Curtiss did it. So did Alexander Graham Bell, finally. By the end of 1907 only seven men in America had flown powered planes. But interest was spreading rapidly.

The Mongtomery glider which caught Allan Loughead's eye, and got the youth interested in the problems of flight.

The following year, the U.S. Government became interested when the Signal Corps contracted with the Wrights to build a military aeroplane. The requirements called for a craft capable of carrying two men at 40 miles per hour for 125 miles. In demonstrating the craft during trials at Fort Myer, Virginia, Orville Wright suffered a severe back injury when the machine crashed. Lieutenant Selfridge was killed as a result of the accident. It was the airplane's first tragedy.

The Wrights built another plane which a year later successfully passed the rigid Army trials and was accepted by the Signal Corps. The United States was the first major power in the world to have an Air Force.

Meanwhile, aviation came to California. Glenn Curtiss was building a seaplane at San Diego and Glenn Martin, another pioneer, was working on an aircraft of his own design in an old abandoned mission near Santa Ana.

In January, 1910, America's first flying meet took place at the Dominguez hills south of Los Angeles. While thousands of spectators quieted their horses, a French pilot, Louis Paulhan, took off to set a new altitude record of 4,165 feet—two-thirds as high as Mount Wilson. He also carried out a series of weight-dropping experiments—with California oranges—that gave a hint of the future military value of the airplane for bombing.

There was plenty right in his own backyard to further excite the interest of the air-minded Loughead. Allan was 20 years old now, and a "hot-rodder" by modern definition in the first decade of the 20th Century. He was picking up prize money as a race driver going from one track to another. And whenever he could, he visited locales where the earlybird "barnstormers" were flying their planes. A racing car driver and a pilot—both speed demons and dare-devils in the public eye—had a lot in common.

Furthermore, Allan's interest in aviation had been sharpened by a book which a half-brother—Victor Loughead, a Chicago writer-engineer—had written about flying machines. The book, called "Vehicles Of The Air", was a technical best-seller for years. Reading Victor's detailed descriptions about the future of flying, Allan decided to go to Chicago, get better acquainted with this relative, and pick up more knowledge about the new sport of wings. He

worked his way crosscountry, racing at various tracks along the route and further enhancing his fame as a speed king.

Arriving in Chicago, Allan promptly got himself a job as a mechanic for Jim Plew, who owned an old Curtiss pusher biplane. The plane was based at the now famous Hawthorne Race Track just outside of Chicago.

Snow was still on the ground that chilly morning in 1910 when a group of curious spectators gathered at the track to see the airplane put on another demonstration. Anxious eyes watched as the flimsy biplane struggled through the snow of the infield trying to get off the ground.

Two men tried and failed. Then, they saw the mechanic take his place at the controls. It was Allan. The engine—a 35-horsepower motor—sputtered and coughed; the plane staggered, wobbled, picked up a little speed and then mushed down in the snow. It wouldn't lift.

"Help me turn it around, I know I can fly it," Loughead yelled. "I've got a twenty dollar gold piece that says I can get it off the ground!"

They turned the machine around. This time, after mechanic Loughead had made a carburetor

Allan Loughhead's interest in aviation was furthered by these books authored by a half-brother, Victor Loughead, best sellers in their period, about 1910.

adjustment, the motor burst forth with a throaty roar. The machine, in a flurry of snow, whizzed across the field, wobbled a little, then rose into the air. It circled the track once and came down to a rather bumpy landing. Allan Loughead had taught himself to fly. This was his first solo flight!

The old Curtiss pusher, however, was too slow. It was far from what he had in mind that an aircraft should be—only framework and wires, wood and glue, little more than a motorized kite. His mechanically inclined nature worked overtime as he rode aloft on the cloth-covered wings. At night, he lay awake dreaming of a new design. When he had the opportunity he put his dreams on paper. With the money he picked up as mechanic and racing, he had some parts built and shipped them to San Francisco where he was determined he would build his own airplane.

Back in California again, he had little trouble convincing his brother, Malcolm, to join him in the enterprise. "I expect to see the time when aviation will be the safest means of transportation, at 40 to 50 miles per hour, and the cheapest," he predicted. "And I'm not going to have long whiskers when that happens. The airplane will take over land and water travel—flying has no barriers!"

Together the two brothers put up $1800 of their savings. It was quite a chunk of money at a time when room and board cost only fifty cents a day. They also interested a local taxicab company in putting up another $1200 in the project. With this capital they started work on their new plane in a small garage at Pacific and Polk streets in San Francisco.

By day they worked at odd jobs, and Allan occasionally picked up some extra money at the race tracks with his racing car, to pay for food and lodging. Every night and week-end found them busily hammering, glueing and stitching at work on their plane. They called it the Model G.

Years later, Allan confessed, "We called it the

This is Curtiss-type plane in which Allan Loughead learned to fly. Allan took plane on "barn-storming" tour of midwest. When he narrowly escaped serious injury in a crash that demolished plane, he decided to build one of his own design.

Model-G with Allan Loughead in cockpit is poised on the ramp ready for launch. Rudder, above and below fuselage, and ailerons between upper and lower wings were unusual features.

Model G purely for psychological reasons. We were new in this business, and we wanted to give the impression that we had built airplanes before. This was just another model to come out."

It was a biplane with the engine in front. There was only one propeller, driven by a Kirkham 6-cylinder water-cooled engine. They decided to make it a seaplane because of the availability of the large water areas for take-offs and landings. It had a flat float type undercarriage with the covered fuselage resting on struts attached to the float.

The craft had an upper wing span of 46 feet. Its lower wing was ten feet shorter. The fuselage was 30 feet in length. It weighed 2200 pounds and could carry a useful load of 584 pounds; two passengers and a pilot. It was to have a cruising speed of 51 miles per hour, a top speed of 63 mph, extremely fast for that period.

The big question was—would it fly? Up to that time only 750 airplanes had been built by aviation enthusiasts in their backyards and home workshops. Only a few of them ever got into the air.

Allan and Malcolm Loughead's first airplane did.

It was June 15, 1913 when they trundled the Model G. onto a ramp slipping down into the Bay for its trial flight. Allan was at the controls. A small group of on-lookers, mostly skeptics and scoffers, were on hand. The betting was that

the contraption wouldn't fly.

In the pilot's seat Allan cracked the throttle. The plane bumped down the ramp, swung around into the wind and began to skim across the blue waters of San Francisco Bay. The spray shot up from the sides like snow from the plow of a locomotive. Faster and faster it picked up speed, its wake splashing waves across the launching ramp. Then, it shook itself free and, still dripping, began to climb steadily. Rounding Alcatraz, Nob Hill and Market Street, Allan remained in the air for 15 minutes.

The flight was important in the annals of aviation. It was one of the very few successful planes using a tractor propeller mounted ahead

Allan and wife, Dorothy and daughter Flora pose in front of Model-G. Horseshoe-shaped radiator and Kirkham engine were later replaced with Hall-Scott powerplant.

14

Birth of The Winged Star

Model-G with passengers at Pan Am Exposition in San Francisco, 1915. Plane was one of largest of privately-designed aircraft of that era.

of the engine. There were only two or three other designs capable of carrying two passengers. And the plane could fly at a mile-a-minute!

The Loughead Brothers had an airplane, and a good one, in the Model G. Next, they started a long Loughead tradition. They were not just in this flying game for the thrill or sport of it. They were in it to make money.

Other fields came first. The two brothers went prospecting for gold. They "made beans" as Allan put it. The Model-G lay collecting dust in storage. Then, ironically, they found a gold mine in the sky.

It was 1915 and February of that year the historic Panama-Pacific Exposition opened in San Francisco. Opportunity was knocking; the Lougheads bid for the flying concession. They lost the bid to a more famous "Barnstormer", Bob Fowler, but when Fowler's plane cracked up on its first flight, the Model-G got its chance. Allan Loughead started flying passengers ("$10 a head for a 10 minute ride") in September, and during fifty flying days the business grossed $6,000!

In this venture the Lougheads had a new partner, a man named Meyer, who had hit it rich as a baker and restaurant owner in Alaska during the Gold Rush days. The Lougheads and Meyer had bought the Model-G from the Alco Hydroaeroplane Company, which had grown out of the relationship with Max Mamlock, owner of the Alco Cab Company of San Francisco. The company was dissolved soon after, and the new partners started in the aerial sight-seeing business at the exposition.

Altogether, the Model-G carried 600 passengers during the Pan Am Exposition—two at a time, *provided their total weight didn't exceed 320 pounds!* The Model-G couldn't carry any more weight plus the pilot. Nobody cared, it netted its owners $4,000. Everybody was happy.

More important, the flights at the exposition were a main attraction. Visitors from all over the world saw the plane perform; saw the skill of Allan's pilotage, and spread the word to the four far corners. Californians, in particular, recognized the Loughead name, and the Model-G made headlines everywhere it flew.

After the exposition, the Lougheads moved back to Santa Barbara. They shipped the Model-G because it didn't have the fuel capacity to fly that far, reassembled it on the beach, and started an "aerial charter" service, probably one of the first of its kind in the country. Almost immediately the business showed a modest profit. "Anyway, it kept us going," Allan Loughead said, "and it kept us interested in aviation."

There was money in the bank. The Lougheads intended to stay in aviation. They decided to build another plane. This one would be larger, capable of carrying at least ten passengers. It would be the largest seaplane in the world. With it, they reasoned, they could earn money and turn the passenger business into a bonanza.

Already, they had plans for the new plane, designated the F-1. It would be a giant: An upper wing span of 74 feet; lower wing, 47 feet from tip to tip—powered with the popular liquid-cooled Hall-Scott 160-horsepower engine—two of these engines driving twin propellers. A hull-type seaplane with a length of 35 feet, an enclosed cabin, the machine would weight 7300 pounds, carry 3100 pounds payload, cruise at 70 mph.

To build the giant, they decided to form an aircraft manufacturing company, birthright of present day Lockheed Aircraft Corporation and its many subsidiary companies. "The true pronounciation of our name (Loughead) is L-o-c-k-h-e-e-d," Allan once explained. "But so many people called it 'Loghead' that we decided to legalize the phonetic spelling." Ever since, the name LOCKHEED has emblazoned itself across the heavens, proudly lettered on some of the finest aircraft to roar aloft in a thousand skies. The latest, of course, is the fabulous *"TriStar"*, L-1011.

Wooden hull of F-1 flying boat was designed by Jack Northrop. Note plane's two engines and cooling vents in casings.

But let's go back to the beginning. The original firm was called the LOUGHEAD AIRCRAFT MANUFACTURING COMPANY, organized in the summer of 1916, and it was located in the rear of a garage on State Street in Santa Barbara. The owner of a machine shop, Berton R. Rodman, subscribed a quantity of the initial investment monies, and was elected President of the organization. Allan Loughead became first vice president, and Malcolm Loughead, secretary and treasurer. Norman S. Hall was made manager of Sales, and a Czechoslovakian mechanic, Anthony Stadlman, who had worked with Allan in the Chicago "barnstorming" days, was made factory superintendant. It was a small staff, but everybody knew his job, and they were all "sold" on the future of aviation.

Shortly after the factory opened its doors, it had a frequent visitor, a 21-year old garage mechanic and draftsman, who said he wanted a job, "any job just to get into aviation." His name was John K. Northrop, a self-taught engineer. He told the Lougheads that he understood stress analysis, and they hired him to shape the hull of the F-1 (Flying Boat No. 1) and whose dimensions at that time made it the largest seaplane in the world. The plane's performance was proof of his talents.

Brochure announces formation of Loughead Aircraft Manufacturing Company and explains reason for change in spelling of name to LOCKHEED.

Birth of The Winged Star

Jack Northrop would go on to become one of the most famous names in the aircraft industry; president of his own aircraft manufacturing company, prime mover in the concept of the Douglas DC-1, "granddaddy" of the famous DC-3, fast mailplanes, World War II night fighters and the highly revolutionary "flying wing" bomber.

Of him it was once said, "There's a little bit of Jack Northrop in just about every good airplane ever built."

He certainly played a major role in the design and development of the F-1. Allan Loughead took the big flying boat up for its first flight on March 28, 1918.

Like their first attempt at plane building, the F-1 seaplane was as big a success as it was just

King and Queen of Belgium were among world figures who flew in Lockheed F-1 flying boat.

The F-1 had triple rudder arrangement (shown here) which would make its appearance 20 years later in configuration of famous Lockheed "Constellation" airliners.

big. The big plane, incidentally, inaugurated a design configuration that years later was to become distinctive on the modern Constellation airliners—*it had a triple finned tail,* mounted on metal booms attached to wings. As a result the plane had unusually steady flying characteristics for those early days and, despite its great size handled easily.

Allan Lockheed did most of the piloting and built up an enviable safety record. He carried aloft as many as 12 passengers at a time without a single mishap. King Albert and Queen Elizabeth of Belgium were among the many noted passengers who flew in the ship. It gained recognition everywhere. The Navy soon heard about the plane because of its good flight performance and asked that it be submitted for evaluation tests at North Island, San Diego. The Navy was even then thinking about its Trans-

Second Lockheed design, F-1 flying boat, on its maiden flight.

17

The F-1 "construction gang" Allan Loughhead (third from left) and brother Malcolm (second from right) in Santa Barbara factory. Their fine attention to craftsmanship is evidenced in detail of flying boat's hull and wing rib structures.

Atlantic ferry service.

When Allan Lockheed heard the Navy was interested, he didn't waste any time. Uncle Sam might be a good customer. He decided to show off the big plane. So, despite low ceiling and poor visibility, he climbed into the cockpit and took-off, heading for San Diego. He landed there, setting a new world's record—180 miles in 181 minutes!

The Navy was greatly impressed. For three months it kept the big plane, putting it through a rigid test program. But the Navy never ordered any F-1s built.

The F-1 later was used extensively for passenger and charter service. It also participated in some early tests for aerial cameras; some of the first photos made from an airplane were made by cameramen flying in its massive hull which provided ideal "shooting" accommodations.

Because landplanes were becoming extremely popular, Allan and Malcolm Lockheed redesigned their big flying boat and converted it into a landplane—the F1-A. Wheels and a tail

Hall-Scott advertisement exploiting record-breaking flight of F-1 to demonstrate plane's performance for Navy.

Movie actress Mary Miles Minter bids "bon voyage" to pilots Swede Meyerhoffer and Bob Ferneau at start of transcontinental flight attempt in F-1A landplane version of F-1 flying boat.

Converted back to flying boat, F-1 wound up as "star" of early air epics. In cockpit, are Allan (left) and Malcolm. The large wheel-controls and dual arrangement were new features.

skid replaced the wing tip floats.

The F1-A demonstrated extreme performance capabilities and to demonstrate its full utility the Lockheeds hired two pilots, Swede Meyerhoffer and Bob Ferneau, to fly the plane across the continent from California to New York and attempt to break the record of 84 hours flying time held by Calbraith Perry Rodgers. The flight ended when Pilot Ferneau made a bad landing at Gila Bend, Arizona, and the ship was damaged. The F1-A was rebuilt as a flying boat again and ended its days performing for early flying movies.

Ironically, however, more than a quarter of a century later it was another Lockheed plane that was first to make its debut as a specifically-designed transcontinental non-stop airliner. It was called the Lockheed *Constellation*. Its triple-tail, a trademark the world over, reminds historians that the triple-tailed F-1 and F1-A were certainly far ahead of their time in 1916-17.

Under a Navy contract, obtained because of their experiment with the F-1, Lockheed was to build (For $90,000) a Curtiss-designed, three-man, single-engined pusher scout seaplane. It put the Company in business. The Lockheeds set out to prove to the Navy that they could meet schedules and the company grew to 83 employees; work went on seven days a week. There was a War on.

The Navy officially followed the progress of the work and the first of the planes, designated the HS2L, was christened with appropriate

Bad landing brought end to F-1A's cross-country flight.

The F-1A hops off on cross-country record attempt.

The S-1 Sportplane designed by Allan Loughead and Jack Northrop to promote sport flying in the early '20s. The plane was sleek and streamlined and pioneered many innovations in construction and design.

Allan, Anthony Stadlman and others designed this two-cylinder, 25-horsepower, water-cooled engine for the S-1 Sportplane.

ceremonies on the beach of Santa Barbara in early 1918, well ahead of schedule. Pleased with their new Scout Plane, the Navy ordered 50 more. But before the new contract was begun the Armistice was signed and the fleet never was built.

With no further need—so the ground-bound military brass believed—for fighting airplanes, the bottom fell out of the sky. Aircraft production collapsed. Companies bravely converted to peacetime models. The Lockheed brothers, determined to stay in aviation, faced a gloomy future. But they had an idea they could keep their company alive if they could come up with a new type plane.

Allan Lockheed summed up their plan nicely when he said: "Flying is the greatest sport in the world. We just build a small airplane for private flyers. Certainly, there will be a market with all the war aviators returning."

Allan Lockheed and Jack Northrop teamed up to design a sportplane which was years ahead of its time. They called it the S-1. The little plane even judged by today's standards was an outstanding performer. A biplane with tractor propeller, two wheels and tail skid, the little ship could zip along at 70 mph! It could carry a pilot and one passenger with an operating cost of only two cents a mile! The wings were only 28 feet in span (upper) 24 feet (lower) and the

Birth Of The Winged Star

The S-1 on first flight. Plane was excellent performer, but not a single one was sold. War surplus planes flooded the market.

Fuselage framework (covered with plywood halves) was bullet-shaped and looked like wing-tip tanks on today's jet fighters.

fuselage was 20 feet in length. It weighed only 825 pounds. They even designed their own engine—50 miles per gallon.

The S-1 introduced many other new features which pioneered aviation in aerodynamics and in manufacturing techniques. The Lockheeds had watched seagulls bend back their wings to slow down when landing on the beach. So they developed a "wing brake" system similar to that of the seagull. It was the beginning of wing flaps. The entire lower wing of the little S-1 could be

turned to a semi-vertical position and slow the ship down in flight!

In addition, the plane was built differently from any other. It had a molded plywood fuselage. The two halves were glued together under heat—you stamped out the fuselage shape in halves and put the two together like a waffle iron. The effect produced an extremely smooth, bullet-like shape, which proved highly efficient aerodynamically. And it introduced an entirely new method of aircraft construction.

The S-1 had another pioneering feature, too. Its wings could be folded so that the plane could be stored in an area only 10 by 20 feet. The same idea is used today on most carrier-based fighters.

Despite its many innovations, however, there was no market for the S-1. The Lockheed brothers were unable to sell a single airplane. It

Concrete forms were used to mold plywood fuselage halves of S-1, a process that the Lockheeds patented. Certainly, it was unique in aircraft fabrication techniques.

Wings on S-1 folded back to permit ease of parking on airports. Expectancy was the company would sell "thousands".

was not the little plane's fault. It was simply that the market after World War I was flooded with war-surplus Curtiss JN-4 "Jennies", old DH-4 deHavillands and other warplanes no longer needed. For as low as $100 you could buy a Jenny brand new!

The Loughead Aircraft Manufacturing Company was forced to suspend its operations. It was the year 1920. For six years the Santa Barbara factory lay dormant following the failure to find a market for the S-1 Sport Plane.

The brothers separated. Malcom Lockheed left the company to develop an invention of his own for the automobile world. It was an idea for a superior brake. He worked out a method for putting brakes on all four wheels of an automobile. The system worked by hydraulic pressure from a small pump mounted on the brake pedal pushing the fluid to work the brakes in each wheel. Basically it is used today—with minor variations—on virtually every automobile. The company he founded, Lockheed Hydraulics, became a world-wide subsidiary of the Bendix Corporation.

Meanwhile, Allan Lockheed stayed with his dream of building a better airplane. But he had no money and he had no airplane to build. More discouraging was the fact that nobody wanted any new airplane. But he still had faith that the right kind of an airplane would catch the public's fancy. At least, he believed from talking with flying men that there could be a market developed if a designer could come up with the right kind of a product.

Fred S. Keeler, a Burbank, California, businessman, who had also invested in Malcolm Lockheed's brake venture, was one of those who expressed a great deal of interest. He offered to put up all but $2500 of a stock subscription for $25,000. Allan Lockheed himself put up the other $2500, and they formed a new company known as the Lockheed Aircraft Company in

Designer Jack Northrop (left) inspecting engine of first Lockheed "Vega" before initial test flight. Thick cantilever-type wing and absence of struts were streamline features of new design.

Birth of the Winged Star

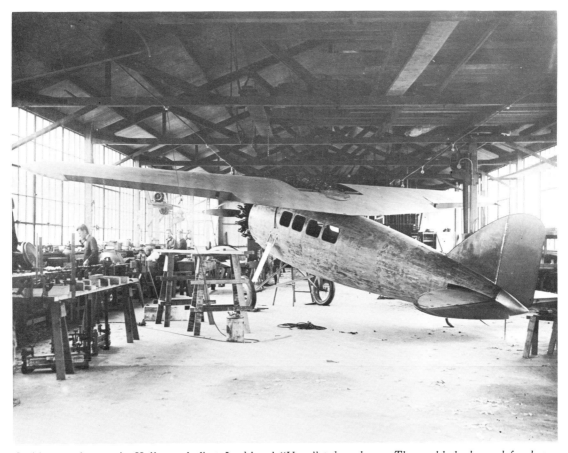

Inside new factory in Hollywood, first Lockheed "Vega" takes shape. The molded plywood fuselage, adapted from S-1 fabrication technique, with sleek finish would help give plane superior speed.

December, 1926. Operations began in a small building at Sycamore and Romaine Streets in Hollywood.

Keeler became President, Allan Lockheed, vice-president and General Manager. They immediately hired back Jack Northrop, who had left to join Douglas Aircraft Company, as Chief Engineer. Together Allan Lockheed (the name had been officially changed) and Northrop worked tirelessly on a new concept which they felt would create its own demand.

In the factory on Romaine and Sycamore construction was started on the new Lockheed-Northrop design, a high-wing, ultra-streamlined monoplane built around a molded plywood monocoque fuselage, similar to the construction used in the S-1 sportplane.

The single-spar wooden wing of the new plane was a radical design departure. There were no struts to support it. Engineers seriously considered adding struts "just for window dressing" to reassure doubtful pilots who had never seen anything without strutting before. But the idea

was abandoned. Let the plane stand on its own new revolutionary design and concept.

On the Fourth of July, 1927, the new plane, decked out in a coat of orange paint with red trimmings and a large, red winged star on its rudder, waited in the corner of a large hay field in Los Angeles. The site today is that of the mammoth Los Angeles International Airport. The trim little ship was called the *"Vega"*, named after one of the brightest stars in the heavens.

The *"Vega"* was something revolutionary in

Lockheed "Vega" No. 1 takes off on first flight.

The Lockheed "Vega" series (No. 1 shown here) would fly into immortality. Record breakers, earth-shrinkers, speed "kings" and airliners, the planes would make the Winged Star insigne heralded the world over.

aircraft design even to look at. It was one of the few planes of this period to use the radial air-cooled engine (a Wright J-5, 225-horsepower engine) whose nine exposed cylinders ringed the bullet-shaped nose like a collar. The cockpit was enclosed, mounted in the nose very similar to the modern airliner. Eight windows in the fuselage framed its cabin. It had a wing span of 41 feet, weighed 3,470 pounds and could carry 1800 pounds payload. It had a top speed of 145 miles per hour!

This was the plane that stood ready to try its wings as a couple of farmers in overalls, several knicker-clad gasoline salesmen, and the inevitable gang of goggle-eyed youngsters watched anxiously. Mechanics and engineers made final adjustments. Watch dials showed 4 o'clock as Edward A. "Eddie" Bellande, an airline pilot hired for the tests, flexed the controls and then

poured the coal to the powerful engine.

Like a meteor the *"Vega"* flashed across the ground, then fairly leaped into the air. It climbed like a fighter plane. Observers never had seen anything so fast in the skies.

Bellande stayed up an hour before coming down for a perfectly smooth landing.

"Boys," he turned to Allan Lockheed and Jack Northrop. "She's a dandy. You'll sell this airplane like hotcakes."

The plane would sell itself. But only two months before something else had happened which opened up a whole new frontier for aviation.

A young unknown Air Mail pilot named Charles A. Lindbergh, alone, in his Ryan monoplane "The Spirit of Saint Louis" had flown non-stop from New York to Paris!

CHAPTER TWO

More Stars In The Sky

The flight of the Lone Eagle—Lindbergh—took aviation out of its rompers and put it into long pants. Flying the Atlantic, 3600 miles non-stop, proved the reliability of aircraft engines. The fact that the little Ryan monoplane could weather the beating of ocean storms and the rough salt air for more than 33 hours showed decided progress in aircraft design and structures. Beyond this, the flight demonstrated the utility of the airplane as a means of safe and speedy travel over long distances. The flying machine, Lindbergh had exploited as more than just a puddle-jumper for short hops around an airfield. Why, someday, airliners would be plying their way across the ocean just like the big ocean-going ships. New York to Paris in an airplane—it was an epochal beginning of a new era!

Roaring into the very center of the spotlight came the Lockheed *"Vegas."* The project which Allan Lockheed and Jack Northrop had worked on for so long had remained very secret. Even Lindbergh, looking everywhere for a plane which he believed could fly the Atlantic, hadn't known about it. There had been only the Bellanca monoplane and the Ryan monoplane which attracted his attention. The latter he helped to design and build specifically for the ocean flight. The *"Vega"* came along two months too late, or surely, its demonstrated performance might have seen it in the race to fly the Atlantic. No matter, the *"Vegas"* were to break every record in aviation before the dies that stamped them out of molds would wear out.

The prophecy of "Eddie" Bellande when he told Lockheed and Northrop that they would easily "sell" their new plane was to come true

"Vega" No. 1 was bought by Hearst Newspapers and entered in the famous Oakland to Honolulu Dole Race. Named the "Golden Eagle", craft and its pilot Jack Frost, (left) were lost at sea. Huge star on rudder was first Lockheed emblem. Plane set record Los Angeles to Oakland in less than three-and-a-half hours carrying pilot, three passengers and 1500-pound payload.

"Vega" No. 2 named the "Los Angeles" is shown fitted with skis for hop across North Pole. At left is pilot Ben Eielson with Sir Hubert Wilkins, knighted for the flight which New York Times called "the greatest feat in all aviation." Publicity put Lockheed name and the "Vegas" into world spotlight.

almost before the engine stopped on the first flight. The initial *"Vega"* was purchased by the Hearst newspapers. Named the "Golden Eagle", it was fitted with flotation gear and extra gas tanks and was entered in the famous Dole Race to Hawaii. The plane was lost in the Pacific. But *"Vega"* No. 2 went on to win undying fame.

It was the choice of Sir Hubert Wilkins, the famous Arctic explorer for a series of polar flights. Wilkins and his pilot, Ben Eielson, made the first flight over the top of the world in the ship which was fitted for skis for the snow regions. They flew non-stop for 2200 miles across the Arctic Sea from Point Barrow, Alaska, to Spitzbergen in 20 hours and 30 minutes. And a few months later the same team made the first flight over the continent of Antarctica and its mountainous areas where they mapped more than 100,000 square miles of the unknown territory. Before they were a year old the *"Vegas"* had been at the top and the bottom

of the world. They were to go on to wrap a flight line belt around its middle.

It was the era of a thousand record-breaking flights. Everybody was fired up with interest in aviation as a result of the Lindbergh thing. Airports mushroomed up in communities where people never heard of airplanes before. The "Barnstormer" suddenly became a very dignified owner and operator of a flying school. Small airlines began to appear here and there. Any designer with a good idea and even those with "crackpot designs" was able to get financing. Aviation money was as free as a prospector's pay after his first strike. Aviation stocks soared higher than the planes could fly.

Veteran pilots, sportsmen and business firms bought the *"Vegas."* An improved model of the first plane powered with the just-coming-out Pratt and Whitney *Wasp* radial, air-cooled engine pushed the ship's top speed upwards of 165 miles per hour! It made the plane so fast, nothing in the skies could catch·it. During the first National Air Races held at Cleveland in 1928, the *"Vega"* walked away with all the speed trophies.

It was here that the famous racing pilot, Colonel Roscoe Turner remarked: "All you have to do is to point it at a distant destination and there's another new record—good only until some other pilot comes along in another *"Vega"* and picks up a more favorable tail wind!"

Business was so good that the Lockheed Aircraft Company had to move from its location in Hollywood. It located in Burbank, and this was to become the permanent site of today's huge Lockheed Aircraft Corporation's main plant operation. From this small plant—in the beginning—there came all together more than 144 *"Vegas"* which were to set more than 34 World's Records, making the famous Winged Star insignia a familiar trade mark in the four far corners of the earth.

Names that will live forever in Aviation History made the *"Vega"* a shining star in the heavens.

Flying in his all-white *"Vega"*, "Yankee Doodle", Colonel Art Goebel roared across the continent in 24 hours and 20 minutes, New York to Los Angeles with only one stop at Phoenix. And less than three months later, Goebel with a

Part of New York Air Associates' order for 20 "Vegas" moves down assembly line at new Burbank factory. Totaling $250,000, order was largest ever placed for a commercial plane up to that time.

passenger on board, Harry Tucker, took advantage of the westerly winds and pushed his *"Vega"* non-stop across America in 18 hours, 58 minutes—Los Angeles to New York. Such coast-to-coast time nobody had ever dreamed of before.

But Allan Lockheed and Jack Northrop still weren't satisfied with such startling performance. They brought out a new airplane, a modified *"Vega,"* using the same fuselage but having a strut arrangement for the wing making it a parasol type. The same fuselage was used, however, with the only major change being the location of the cockpit in the aft section, an open

Popularity of "Vegas" led to move to new factory headquarters in Burbank. Aerial view shows plant buildings in 1928; factory force numbered about fifty men. Site is today that of Lockheed-California Company. Some part of virtually every plane to bear Lockheed name was built here.

Following famous "Vega" line came his Lockheed "Air Express", fastest commercial-type in late twenties. Plane featured "parasol" wing and redesigned rudder with more dorsal fin. Note the first appearance of the Winged Star insigne on vertical fin. "Air Express" ships set many records.

cockpit of more conventional design. They called the ship the *"Air Express."* It pioneered another innovation, too. The *"Air Express"* was the first plane to try out the NACA engine cowling.

For years the National Advisory Committee of Aeronautics at Langley Field, Va., a Government agency set up by Congress for aeronautical research, had been exploring new means of streamling aircraft to cut down on air resistence and provide greater speeds. They knew, from hundreds of tests in their wind tunnel, that the big frontal area of the popular radial engines was cutting down on speed. But, by wrapping the big engine in a streamline cowling, they proved in the wind tunnel that the drag, or resistance

Another view of the "Air Express" and closer look at the Winged Star.

More Stars In The Sky

Famous speed flyer Frank Hawks poses beside the Texaco Oil Company's "Air Express" fitted with new NACA cowling for streamlining. Hawks set new transcontinental record in plane. Cowling was later fitted to "Vegas" and one flown by Colonel Roscoe Turner was test bed for first 1,000-horsepower engine!

could be reduced by as much as one-third.

Lockheed, working with the NACA, decided to try the idea on its new *"Air Express"* model with famous flyer Frank Hawks at the controls, A lot was at stake that day that Hawks climbed into the plane at Burbank, roared into the sky and pointed the "ringed nose" eastward. But when he landed 18 hours, 21 minutes later at New York—non-stop—nobody had any doubts about the cowling idea.

Meanwhile, the *"Vegas"* blazed new sky trails. Lieutenant Herbert J. Fahy, chief test pilot at Lockheed took one aloft and remained up there for 36 hours and 56 minutes, longer than anyone had previously stayed in the air in an heavier-than-air machine. At Detroit in Air Race competition a woman flyer, Amelia Earhart, flashed past the grandstand over a 100-kilometer course in the blazing record time of 174.897 mph! Another famous aviatrix, Ruth Nichols, high over Jersey City set a new altitude record for women—28,743 feet aloft in a new 420-horsepower engined *"Vega"*. The following year, 1932 Amelia Earhart became the first woman to fly the Atlantic non-stop, alone, making the trip in 15 hours, 48 minutes from Harbor Grace, Newfoundland, to Londonderry,

Amelia Earhart, first woman to fly solo across the Atlantic. She made the trip Harbor Grace to Londonderry in "Vega".

Probably one of the most famous "Vegas" was the "Winnie Mae" which Wiley Post and Harold Gatty flew round the world in eight days, 1931. Post made trip solo again in 1933. The plane today rests in Smithsonian Institute, Washington, D.C. along with Wright Brothers first airplane and Lindbergh's "Spirit fo St. Louis".

Ireland. Her plane was a specially-equipped *"Vega"*. A month later Jimmie Mattern and Bennett Griffin made the fastest Atlantic Crossing in *"Vega"* No. 6—non-stop from Harbor Grace to Berlin in 18 hours and 41 minutes. Then came Wiley Post in his *"Winnie Mae"* flying solo around the world in 7 days, 18 hours and 49½ minutes!

Another famous woman flyer, Laura Ingalls, soloed 17,000 miles around South America in Lockheed "Air Express" in 1934.

Women's "libber" vintage 1931, aviatrix Ruth Nicholas set new altitude record for women in special "souped-up" VEGA.

Carl B. Squier (left) was World War One pilot. He became General Manager of Lockheed in 1929, "sold" the Lockheed name to the world.

It got so everytime a *"Vega"* took off with a "big name" pilot at its controls there was a record of somekind in the making. With each headline came newly created public interest. The effect was electrifying to the entire aviation industry. The boom was both good and bad for the small aviation companies. Get-rich-quick schemes expanded the industry like a giant bubble. Financiers sought to consolidate the scattered smaller companies along the lines of the mergers in the automobile industry. One group, aiming at a "General Motors Of The Air" in July, 1929, purchased Lockheed and 11 other companies including Ryan and Parks Air College. They called their merged companies the Detroit Aircraft Corporation.

A World War I pilot, Captain Carl B. Squier was made General Manager of the new company at Lockheed and in 1929 during the height of the boom the company continued production of its famous *"Vega"* and the *"Air Express"*. Significant was the sudden transition from a sportplane to a utility transport plane which both these types pioneered. There were orders for the Lockheed *"Vega"* and the *"Air Express"* from newly formed airlines such as Western Air Express, American Airways, Braniff, Continental Airways, Pan American, Transcontinental-Western Air, Inc., Swiss-Air and operators in Canada, Alaska.

On the engineering side Lockheed went ahead with development of the *"Sirius"*, the *"Altair"* and the "Orion"—all low-wing designs, each destined to make a name for itself in the annals of aviation. It was in a float-equipped Lockheed

Squier's efforts interested Army Air Corps in buying "Vegas" for utility transport. This one shows off striped tail and Air Corps' star and circle insignia on wing tip. It was one of first Lockheed planes sold to the military, beginning of a long relationship.

L-1011 TriStar and The Lockheed Story

Charles A. Lindbergh, first to solo across the Atlantic New York to Paris in 1927, chose the low-wing Lockheed "Sirius" to pioneer new air routes in the 1930s. Here Lindbergh is about to take off on record-breaking transcontinental flight. Insert is rare picture of "Lone Eagle" in cockpit of highly streamlined "Sirius" as evidenced by "wheel pants" and faired landing gear struts.

"Sirius" that Lindbergh and his wife, Anne, blazed new air routes around the world when the famous flyer was pioneering for Pan American and TWA. Sir Charles Kingsford-Smith and Captain P. G. Taylor flew a Lockheed "Altair", 7365 miles from Brisbane, Australia, to Oakland in 54 hours 49 minutes flying time.

But the last of the molded-fuselage "old line Lockheeds" was the "Orion", and it was the brightest star of them all in the wooden-ship

galaxy. Faster than many military fighters of that period, it streaked across the sky at 225 miles per hour—far and away the fastest commercial airplane of its day. More important than its speed, however, were some of its improvements in design which it introduced to aviation.

With the advent of the "Altair" and the "Sirius" models Lockheed designers had started a new fad—low-wing airplanes. Project engineers, Jimmy Gerschler and R. A. Von Hake, who worked on both the "Altair" and the "Sirius", pointed out—"Low-wing monoplanes were becoming stylish. The high-wing "Vega" was starting to look old-fashioned. So, we just switched the wing from top to bottom and did a little redesigning, cleaned up the airplane with

Equipped with floats, Lindbergh's plane named "Tingmissartoq" was used in history-making route survey flights.

Another low-wing design was this "Altair." Sir Kingsford Smith flew sister ship from Australia to California.

More Stars In The Sky

The old and the new. One of the first model "Vegas" without NACA cowling escorts new "Sirius" with Lindbergh and his wife, Anne, at start of one of their survey flights. "Vega" was last high-wing Lockheed commercial design until "Saturn" came along. The "Sirius" was first of long line of low-wing configurations.

some streamlining, and there was the *"Orion"."*

The low-wing design let them do something else which virtually revolutionized aircraft design and certainly put a lot of miles of increased speed on the *"Orion"*. It gave them room to experiment with a retractable landing gear. The *"Orion"* was the first commercial plane equipped with wheels that folded-up and hid themselves away. Gerschler, Von Hake and Gerard Vultee, another engineer, had worked out a method of retracting the gear. It was cranked up by hand. And they tried it out on the *"Orion"*.

The retractable gear added 30 mph an hour speed to the airplane which as Von Hake put it—"was some cleaning up job!" But the new type gear also produced a lot of problems. On delivery of the first *"Orion"* to a Midwest airline, Temple-Bowen the pilot, brought the airplane in for a perfect landing. So he thought.

Then, he sat there red-faced at the last minute—he had forgotten to put the gear down! The plane, however, skidded in for a belly landing.

Other pilots experienced the same forgetfulness. The problem brought the first of a multitude of airplane safety devices which Lockheed pioneered. Engineers rigged warning horns, lights, plungers and mirrors on the *"Orion"* so

that the pilot could tell whether the gear was up or down, locked or whatnot. Many of these devices are on today's planes. The *"Orion"* showed us the know-how.

There was a sad story connected with the *"Orion"* when Wiley Post, a former Lockheed test pilot, built up a "half-breed" airplane using an *"Orion"* fuselage and a *"Sirius"* set of wings. One day he came to Lockheed with the bastard-built ship and wanted the company to put floats on it. He was going to do some over-water flying in the Alaska region with his good friend and aviation enthusiast, Will Rogers. Actually, they were going to make another round-the-

VARNEY SPEED LANES pioneer West Coast airline made low-wing Lockheed "Orion" one of most popular, certainly, the fastest of airliners in the early thirties. Walter T. Varney would play important role in future Lockheed re-organization.

world trip.

At Lockheed, engineers said they didn't want to fit the *"Orion-Sirius"* with floats; the plane would be nose heavy. They refused to make the modification. Engineering studies indicated that the plane, with a slight loss of power from the engine on take-off, would tend to go in on its nose. Lockheed didn't want anything to do with the float-equipped model which, otherwise, was a good airplane.

But Post was determined. He took his plane to another aircraft company which was more than eager to put the floats on it. Then, near Point Barrow, Alaska, tragedy struck. The engine sputtered on take-off. The plane staggered and tried to pull itself up to a safe altitude to permit returning. They never made it. The nose was too heavy and the plane plunged into the water. Wiley Post and Will Rogers were killed. The world lost two of its most famous men.

Despite the accident, Lockheeds continued to set new records everywhere. Pilots extolled their splendid performance with such remarks as—"It takes a Lockheed to beat a Lockheed."

But in a way there was irony in the praiseful

Float-fitted "Orion-Sirius" half-breed in which Post and Will Rogers were killed. Post had been warned of plane's trickiness.

saying which was to become a company slogan for years.

The company was making money, as long as Allan Lockheed had retained control. And it had a good man in Carl Squier to run it under the Detroit Aircraft Corporation establishment. But the money interests completely disregarded Squier's recommendations. Mercilessly, stockholders began to milk the thriving company of dividends. The treasury ran dry. No money was provided for research. Its engineers and designers, who had built the reputation with continued improvements and new designs were

This view of "Orion" shows retractable landing gear which folded up into wing roots. That's famous racing pilot and later historic "Tokyo Raider" James H. "Jimmy" Doolittle standing by plane.

Bob Gross as he looked when he took over helm at Lockheed in 1932. He and his brother, Courtlandt, would build company into a giant.

not allowed to maintain the pace. And in aviation there is a axiom that has never failed to prove true—"keep five years ahead of the times or you lose your shirt." Lockheed had its "five years ahead" with its *"Vega"* series and the other stars that followed the line—for all came from the same basic molds. But for five years it stood still. Engineers had stretched to the limit the basic wooden fuselage common to the *"Vega," "Sirius", "Air Express", "Altair"* and the *"Orion"*.

During this period there was also the big Market Crash of 1929. Aircraft stocks took a tailspin. There was no more money available for "old" ideas. Small and large aviation companies suddenly found cob-webs growing in their factories. Everything was shut down. Lockheed survived until 1931 when it went under in a wave of bankruptcy suits.

Even in the hands of federal bankruptcy receivers, the company managed to continue for while producing its old line of aircraft. But there was that big frightening barrier—it had no new designs to offer to new investors. Its research was dead. Engineers tried. They mocked up a projected observation biplane for the Army and an exceptionally clean flying boat, but even Congress' military appropriations were broke. There was no money in the treasury, either. There was simply no money at all.

Orders dwindled. At Christmas time, 1931, Squier had to mortgage all his personal possessions to pay his workers. By April, the following year, employment had dropped to four workers. A Federal receiver took inventory, valued the assets at $42,456 and offered them for sale. The Winged Star, brilliant as it was, seemed to be dying out.

But a man who didn't believe it came winging down from San Francisco in a Varney Speed Lanes Lockheed *"Orion"*.

His name was Bob Gross.

Americans were standing in the breadlines when Bob Gross came down to Los Angeles to look at the fading Lockheed Aircraft Company's assets. Economically, the nation was at its lowest ebb in June of 1932. Everything was down—business, employment, even peoples' spirits. It was no time, exactly, to go off half-cocked and put money into an aviation enterprise with planes all over the country rotting on airfields and pilots starving to death. But young Robert E. Gross believed in the future. Experience-wise, he had a lot to offer any company, especially an aviation manufacturer that had made the name for itself that Lockheed had achieved.

A native of Boston, Massachusetts, Bob Gross had stepped out of college into the investment business, putting to use his Harvard degree. In 1928, at the height of aviation's Lindbergh "boom" he had invested in the Stearman Airplane Company and later formed the Viking Flying Boat Company with his brother Courtland. In 1932 he was associated with Walter T. Varney in operating the Varney Speed Lanes which was flying West coast passengers in the fast Lockheed *"Orions"*. When they heard of the Lockheed situation, Gross, Varney and Stearman decided to raise capital and buy the Lockheed Company. So it was that day in July of 1932 that Gross appeared in a Los Angeles Federal Courtroom and heard the judge confirm purchase of Lockheed for $40,000!

Part of Bob Gross' background in aviation was heading Viking Flying Boat Company which produced this amphibian vintage 1928.

The FOUNDING FATHERS, left to right, Carl B. Squier, Robert E. Gross, Cyril Chappellet, Lloyd Stearman and Walter T. Varney, five of them at least, who put it all together at Lockheed Aircraft Corporation in 1932. Picture was taken at a reunion in 1956.

Gross was made Chairman of the Board and Treasurer. Lloyd Stearman became President. Carl Squier was retained as vice-president in charge of sales. Cyril Chappellet became secretary. The entire group—all aviation-minded businessmen—were well aware of Lockheed's reputation as a builder of high-performance airplanes. Their interest went deeper than just the acquisition of $40,000 worth of assets of a small rented factory. They believed sincerely in the products of the past, but more important, they believed in the future of aviation. It was really the same old story and the same old problem that had faced Allan Lockheed and Jack Northrop when the Loughead Aircraft Manufacturing Company had suffered its first failure, and had to close its doors back in the early twenties. There was nothing wrong except Lockheed needed a new type of design to present to money people and the public. The big question was: *What kind of a new plane to build and still maintain the company's already established reputation?*

Shortly after taking the helm, Bob Gross brought in a young Massachusetts Institute of Technology aeronautical engineer named Hall Hibbard who for some time had been a consultant for Gross. Hibbard was full of ideas. So was Lloyd Stearman, Gross' other partner. A "brainchild" both Hibbard and Stearman had been working on was a new twin-engined all-metal transport airplane design. They also had sketched out a large single-engined transport plane. Together they had tried to convince Gross that one or both of these designs would be marketable to the expanding airline industry. But they needed a facility to build the "on-paper" airplanes. When Gross bought Lockheed, part of their problem, at least, was solved. Maybe the new company would manufacture one or the other of their designs.

For a while, however, the directors of the new

More Stars In The Sky

Lockheed Aircraft Corporation spent their time getting the house in order. But the time was drawing near when they had to start shooting for a new target. That meant a completely new airplane design. The *"Vegas"* and the fabulous *"Star"* series could no longer support the company. This was a certainty. There were too many newer designs flying.

The decision as to what to do was up to Gross. One day he sat idly dunking a doughnut in a cup of coffee at the Coffee Shop in the Union Air Terminal at Burbank. He was grappling with the problem—what kind of a plane to build—as he sat there watching passengers board their planes.

There were three planes waiting out on the ramp and taking on passengers. Gross smiled to himself as he looked at the trim little single-engined Lockheed *"Orion"*. It was a Lockheed doing the job of an airliner. His ears started ringing all over again as he glanced at the silvery Ford, all-metal trimotor—remembering the time he almost went deaf from the vibrations and the roar of its trio engines. But the other

plane, a sleek, twin-engined Boeing 247, he couldn't get out of his mind. It was an entirely new configuration.

"Let's see," he mused to himself, "if I were going to make a trip which one would I choose?" Of course, he was prejudiced to the *"Orion"*. But, face it. The single engine wasn't as safe—didn't have the reserve that the multi-engined ships had if something went wrong. The "Tin Goose" (Ford Trimotor) was much too noisy. No doubt about it. He'd pick the little Boeing; two-engined safety, modern design, sturdy, comfortable looking.

Then suddenly, he remembered something. He'd seen a design something like it before somewhere. Sure, in young Hall Hibbard's office. That sketch which Hibbard and Stearman had shown him awhile back. This new design could be the answer to Lockheed's problem.

He gulped down his coffee, walked rapidly as he went to Hibbard's office. "Hall," he said, "forget all about that single-engined transport and let's build the little twin-engine plane. We

One of airliners Gross mused over was this twin-engined Boeing 247 which in 1933-34 introduced a new dimension in luxury and speed to U. S. air transportation. Boeing's cut coast-to-coast flying time in half over cumbersome Ford and Fokker trimotors.

L-1011 TriStar and The Lockheed Story

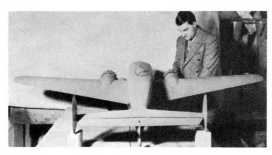

Clarence L. "Kelly" Johnson studies model of Lockheed "Electra" with twin-tail configuration, which he designed. From this moment he would play stellar role in putting the Winged Star ahead of all others with notable contributions advancing the state of the art.

may lose some engineering time, but I think it will pay off later."

Lockheed was going to build a small twin-engined transport plane. Work was started in a little farmhouse. Engineers Gerschler and George Prudden were charged with the job of turning the Hibbard-Stearman airplane into a reality. They called it the *"Electra"*. Another star was born.

There were plenty of birth pains. One disappointment followed another. But finally the engineers had worked up a model to send to the University of Michigan for wind tunnel tests. They thought they really had something. But bad news came back from Ann Arbor.

"Your design needs some more work," a young aeronautical engineer working in the Wind Tunnel at the University wrote to Lockheed. "That single rudder doesn't provide sufficient control with one engine out."

The engineer's name was Clarence "Kelly" Johnson. Shortly afterward he came to work for Lockheed. At Lockheed he designed a twin-tail for the *"Electra"*, loaded a scale model in the trunk of his car, drove back to Ann Arbor and did some further testing. This one worked. The *"Electra"* had built-in safety. You could conk out an engine on take-off and it still had good control. That is, it worked that way in the Wind Tunnel. The big test was to come—in the sky.

The *"Electra"* was flown for the first time on February 23, 1934. Performance was excellent. It cruised at an honest 190 miles per hour, had a top speed of 200 mph—the first multi-engined aircraft to boast such speed. The plane went through a rugged series of tests with Marshall Headle, test pilot, at its controls, to pass Civil Aeronautics Authority certification tests as a passenger airliner.

The tests were carried out at Mines Field, now Los Angeles International airport. After the last test had been completed Headle phoned Hall Hibbard back at Lockheed: "We're in. It passed. We're certificated for commercial. See you in a few minutes."

The test pilot climbed into the sleek all-metal ship with a CAA inspector and a mechanic aboard and took off, heading back to the Burbank Airport. But the flight took longer than "just a few minutes". Headle came in over the field and made a low pass to show off the new *airliner* to the plant workers who had built it. Then he made a large circle and started to put the gear down. One "down" light didn't blink. The wheel was stuck!

Hall Hibbard was watching. He swallowed hard. "I felt sick to my stomach," he recalled. "One minute we were all set to do business and fill all those orders that Carl Squier and his salesmen had been getting for the new fast transport plane—and the next minute—all we had was a sick prototype up there, showing all the signs of coming in for a crash landing."

The crippled plane "up there" meant everything to Lockheed. By the time the first *"Electra"* had flown the Company had $139,404 tied up in its investment. And it had borrowed most of the money!

A lot depended on the actions of the pilot in a situation like this. But Headle was doing his best to get the gear down. He repeatedly ran the gear motor up and down, but the drive shaft to the left-hand gear had sheared off. The motor worked all right. But without the shaft it was just a whirring noise.

An early "Electra" in airline service in the middle 1930s. Design launched Lockheed as a contender in commercial airliner race.

More Stars In The Sky

Al Zeiner, the mechanic, taking his first airplane ride came up forward and talked to Headle. He had an idea. Why not let him cut a hole in the fuselage and try to get to the broken shaft and tap the wheel loose?

"Okay, go ahead," Headle said.

Seconds later Zeiner's pet chisel was biting into the aluminum skin of the fuselage wall just behind the box beam of the wing. He cut a gaping hole in it and tried desperately to reach the wheel. "There isn't enough room, by inches, to get to it," he reported to the pilot. "It's no use."

What to do? Headle made another pass over the field and dived the plane to try and shake the gear loose. Nothing happened. Then, he scribbled a note explaining the plight, wrapped it around one of Zeiner's wrenches and threw it out the door to the group on the ground asking instructions what to do. Should they "bail out" in their parachutes or attempt a crash landing? It being a test flight everybody aboard had parachutes.

A few minutes later a black and gold *"Orion"* came squawling up from the field and pulled in alongside of the *"Electra"*, wig-wagging its wings to get attention. On the ebony fuselage of the ship was scrawled a message—"TRY LANDING AT UNION. . .GOOD LUCK."

Union Air Terminal had a lot more space. And it had a lot more fire-fighting equipment which might insure greater protection to the crew aboard the *"Electra"*. Sometimes, terrible things happened when a plane came in on its belly. Although the trick was getting to be rather common after the introduction of the retractable gear. For a time, pilots across the nation had a "Wheels Up" Club which came near having as many members as the famous "Flying Dumb-bells" organization—a club for pilots who made boners, and lived to profit by their mistakes.

Headle asked the two men aboard if they were with him in the one-wheel landing attempt. It was more tricky than a belly landing, far more

dangerous. Zeiner and the CAA man said they were for trying to save the airplane. They pitched in to ready the *"Electra"* for the emergency.

The plane was loaded with "dead men"—lead weights to simulate a full load of passengers—which had been put aboard especially for the trials. The CAA man held open the door and Zeiner threw the weights overboard as quickly as possible.

While the two men were lightening the plane by throwing the weights overboard, Headle dumped all the gasoline in the tanks to reduce the fire hazard. Then, he circled the Union field once and started his approach.

The little plane slipped out of the sky like a feather floating to earth. Gently, ever so gently, the one wheel touched and the ship maintained its balance like a unicycle. It rolled for several hundred yards balancing like a tight-rope walker. Then, with most of its momentum gone, it flopped down on the left wing and ground looped. It was safe. You might say it was almost a normal landing.

But that landing saved the Lockheed Aircraft Corporation. Its treasury was at such a low ebb that, had the plane crashed, the company once more, might have been forced to dissolve. As it was, the plant had to lay off most of its force, keeping only a skelton crew to repair the slightly damaged *"Electra"*.

Back in the air again, the *"Electra"* proved to be a wonderful new airliner, fast and true. Pilots and passengers liked its comfortable interior with passengers seated five on each side of the aisle, and each seat having a large window for sightseeing. Pilot and co-pilot occupied a glassed in "front office". And performance-wise the ship was the fastest airliner in the skies. Airlines grabbed it like a woman at a bargain counter during a big sale because it was not only a good performer, but the price was right.

Overnight, Lockheed became a leader as a manufacturer of a commercial airline transport plane.

CHAPTER THREE

Under Pressure

It all started with a strange little procession making its way up the narrow, winding trail leading to the summit of Pike's Peak—14,210 feet above sea level. In early September, 1918, the barren flat surface of this mountain was the highest spot in the world accessible by roadway. Even a railroad ran to the top. Slowly moving along the world's highest highway were several trucks loaded with strange paraphernalia. A group of engineers and scientists were going to test a new kind of an engine in the rarified air of the upper mountain regions. They called it the turbo-supercharger.

One of the men was Dr. Sanford Alexander Moss, a native of San Francisco who had worked his way up from a four-dollar-a-week machinist's apprentice to one of the top scientists at General Electric. The supercharger was Moss' invention. He described it thusly—"A mechanical device that kids engines at high altitudes into thinking they are at sea level!"

It's a strange thing about engines. They're almost human. They have to have food and that's gasoline and oil. You have to give them plenty of water because they get hot and thirsty. And they have to breathe. They need oxygen just as does a human. They suck in just the right amount of air into their cylinders or "lungs" and then, they mix it with just the right amount of gasoline. This mixture is ignited by a spark that causes an explosion which is the force that makes things go round. Every combustion

Inventor of the turbo-supercharger was Dr. Sanford A. Moss, shown here holding model of DC-2 which, ironically, never did have a pressurized cabin. Other photos are of planes that tested Moss' turbo-supercharger. Moss also worked on early gas turbine engines. (Photo courtesy General Electric Co.)

Test installation atop Pike's Peak in 1919. Army truck with chains and disk wheels hauled test rig up winding, gravel-dirt road to peak's summit. Turbo-supercharger was mounted on World War I Liberty engine. Note wide-bladed wooden propeller.

engine works the same way whether it's in an automobile or an airplane. But when you take an engine up to high altitude where the oxygen is thin and scarce, it starts to gasp and choke because it can't breathe normally. So, for a long time airplanes couldn't get up very high, because their engines chocked to death from lack of oxygen.

Doctor Moss' device was another kind of an engine attached to an engine that would let it breathe normally in the thin air. It was simply a fan-like principle that blows a lot of air into a small chamber and compresses it to make it weigh more—the difference between grape juice and grape jelly. The parallel is that an engine could run on jelly but not on juice. The heavy sea-level air lets it burn to create power; the thinner air upstairs burns up too quickly.

An engineer would put it this way: "The proper mixture of gasoline and air at sea level is about sixteen parts of air to one part of gasoline. The air comes from the atmosphere which at sea level has a pressure of 14.7 pounds per square inch. It mixes well in the carburetor, never varying much from the 16 to 1 ratio of mixture. But when you take the engine up to higher altitudes, the carburetor, unaided, finds it difficult to keep the proportion the same. The air pressure decreases with increased height. When you get up above 20,000 feet the air weighs only about half as much as it does at sea level. So, in order to keep the right mixture in the carburetor you have to get double the amount of air to the same amount of gasoline. If you don't keep this

mixture, then your engine will quit. A supercharger insures getting the proper mixture.

The question in the minds of the little group—Dr. Moss, his assistant, Waverly Reeves, an Army Sergeant and four other enlisted men—as they climbed to the top of Pike's Peak, was whether or not the device would actually work at high altitudes like it did in the laboratory.

For six weeks they stayed on the summit testing the turbo. The location provided similar conditions to those an airplane would encounter at like altitudes. It was cold and their hands suffered frostbite more than once as they worked on the machinery. But it was worth it. They learned a lot. The engine which back in the laboratory had produced 350 horsepower dropped to 230 horsepower rating in the high atmosphere *without the turbo-supercharger*. But the same engine with the turbo connected developed 365-horsepower. The invention was considered a success!

Unfortunately, it didn't come in time to be used in World War I and the turbo-supercharger literally died with the famous in-line Liberty Engine. Nobody thought there was any need for it any more during aviation's lean years—the early 20's—and the whole idea was buried among the dead. Then, suddenly, someone remembered it, and the engine people adopted the turbo-superchargers to the higher-horsepower engines which came along in the thirties and the airplane had its ceiling lifted. It

Turbo's first flight was made in LePere biplane at McCook Field, Dayton, Ohio, 1919. Dr. Moss (left) Lieut. G. W. Elsey, observer, and pilot, Major R.. "Shorty" Schroeder, just before take-off.

41

had the power to go way, way, way up into the heavens. Flight moved into an entirely new arena miles above the earth where you could ride on favorable wind currents and most of the storms and roughness were far below.

Like that day in 1935 when Wiley Post climbed into his famous *"Vega"*—equipped with a supercharger—and pushed the little white ship up to 30,000 feet, levelled off over Los Angeles and then streaked toward Cleveland. He landed there in 8 hours flying time. The *"Vega"* averaged 235 miles an hour. Without the turbo-supercharged engine its top speed was 165 mph. His feat proved the value of high altitude flying—when you get up high, you go like Hell.

But there was another problem. An Air Corps major, R. W. "Shorty" Schroeder, ran into it when he tried Doctor Moss's supercharger out for the first time in a French LePere pursuit plane. He climbed up to 38,180 feet, higher than any human had ever been before. But something went wrong and for a brief second or so he lost his oxygen supply. His senses blanked out. The plane fell into a dive. Only luck spared him. There was no oxygen up there for humans to breathe. But, fortunately, he recovered in time to clamp on the mask and pull his diving plane out

of its fateful plunge. But it was also cold up there, and he was bundled up like a Teddy Bear in a cumbersome flying suit. He could hardly move inside the cramped cockpit. Something had to be done about the pilots of planes to let them go where the engines could go—and live comfortably.

Wiley Post had the right idea when he made his famous flight in the substratosphere. He had invented what he called a "pressurized suit". What it amounted to was a supercharged pair of pants and jacket and helmet. The latter looked like a deep sea diver's headgear. When he wore it, Post looked like a Man from Mars. The story goes that once during his trials he had a forced landing in the desert. A prospector who saw him got frightened and reported an invasion from another planet. Law agencies combed the desert for the "mysterious stranger."

About the time that Post was running his experiments with the pressure suit, a young, curly-haired, fire-ball Air Corps Major, Carl F. Greene, full of aeronautical engineering and bursting with energy and ideas, strolled into the office of commanding general at Wright Field, the research and development center for the Army Air Corps. He talked so fast and so

The man who looks like an ocean diver is famed flyer, Wiley Post in cockpit of his Lockheed "Vega" just before take-off on high-altitude cross-country flight. Post pioneered pressure suit idea. His high flying "Vega" set many records.

Under Pressure

TWA which introduced first pressurized-cabin airliner in Boeing 307 "Stratocruisers" did a lot of pioneering with this Northrop designed "Gamma". D.W. "Tommy" Tomlinson was test pilot. Plane designed by Jack Northrop bears resemblance to Lockheed "Sirius"

enthusiastically about an idea he was nursing that even rough, gruff, Brig. Gen. A. W. Robins had to listen. "Look at these sketches," Greene said laying out some papers on the General's desk. "It's a new fighter plane, only it's different from anything we've ever tried. The cockpit is a hermetically sealed container. The pilot can fly in his shirtsleeves. He won't need any oxygen masks. There's plenty of room. We can heat it like an oven and he won't have to wear that itchy, heavy fur suit. The plane will be faster than anything we've got with those new engines and the superchargers. We can get all kinds of publicity with a record-breaking flight. God knows, we need something to excite people. They don't even know we exist."

The General was impressed. "I'll think it over," he said. "I'm going to Washington day after tomorrow and I'll talk it over with the brass down there. If they like it, maybe we can do something. I'll let you know."

Greene was chief of the Aircraft Laboratory at Wright Field at the time. His word meant a lot. For the next ten days he called Robins every day after he learned of the General's return. But the secretary always brushed him off. Then, one day he was summoned into the General's office. "No soap", Robins told him. "They turned down that fighter idea cold."

"But why. . .that's our business. . .to keep ahead with new designs," Greene said.

"Don't blow your top", Robins joked. "I said they turned down the idea for a fighter plane. But they think it's all right to put that drum idea of yours on a bigger plane. Maybe, then it will be worth the try."

"You mean we can go ahead?"

"Better make it a transport plane," Robins said. "a pressurized cabin transport. And you

better do it with something off the shelf. We can't build a whole new plane."

Back at his office Greene looked through his design file trying to pick a type airplane that would be suited to his purpose. He needed a sturdy fuselage to withstand pumping it up and pressurizing the air inside it; a fuselage that had to be more like a submarine construction that an airplane's. It had to be a shell-type cabin preferrably of monocoque construction, because this seemed to offer the lightest, strongest and most desired shape.

He decided to fly down to the NACA at Langley Field, Virginia and talk with the scientists and the evaluation experts at this big research center. Landing at the NACA laboratory field he was walking across the flight line to operations and check-in when he spotted a neat little ship inside one of the hangars. It was a modified Lockheed *"Electra"* Model 10 with a strange triple tail arrangement.

"What ship is that?" he asked a mechanic.

"Oh, that's the special hot-wing job."

"Hot-Wing?"

"Yeah. They're working on some system where they pipe the engine exhaust hot air through channels in the leading edges of the wing. The idea is supposed to make the wing so hot that ice won't form on it. If it works, this thing may start a whole new offensive against icing conditions. Sure would help."

"It certainly will," Greene said, looking closer at the Model 10 *"Electra"*. And, suddenly, there it was. The plane he was looking for. The *"Electra"* had just the right shaped fuselage. It was just big enough. And it was an inexpensive aircraft as transport planes go. He didn't wait any longer but turned on his heel, yelled to his pilot, flew back to Wright Field, and told General

Robins he had the airplane in which he wanted to put the pressurized cabin.

A few weeks later, Lockheed got a contract for a modification program on one of its *"Electra"* Model 10's to make it into a pressurized cabin airplane. It was a top secret project. The Air Corps called it—the XC-35.

Back at Lockheed, a close-mouthed group of engineers and workers began building the new airplane which became the first pressurized cabin airplane in the world. One of aviation's basic advances was being riveted together. It was to make possible "over-weather flying" a boon that was to hit the airline industry like Lindbergh's flight to Paris exploded the whole aviation picture less than 10 years before. It was the year 1936.

The prime problem was how to build the fuselage. Engineers laid out a circular cross-section cabin with heavy doors and internal bracing. It looked strong enough. But what would happen when you pumped it up like a balloon tire was another question. Just the idea of pressure in the fuselage gave engineers the whim whams.

Small wonder. Specifications called for a cabin fuselage that would hold a 10 pound per square inch differential between inside and outside pressure. It meant that nearly three-fourths of a ton of force would be exerted on each square foot of cabin area. In a way, it was like riding inside a torpedo. The fuselage might blow up at any minute under such pressures. Unless they made it strong enough— which meant almost boiler-plate construction. So, they used double thickness skin, and actually put a fuselage within a fuselage to accomplish the desired strength and safety.

An idea of the beefing engineers did to the Model 10 *"Electra"* when they turned it into the XC-35, is gleaned from weight figures. The finished substratosphere airplane weighed 1,486 pounds more, empty, than did the standard *"Electra"*. That extra weight was all beef—thicker aluminum formers and frame, thicker skin.

When you looked at the fuselage as it was taking shape, there was only one thing you could call it. Here, if ever there was one, was a winged boiler. Workmen dubbed the XC-35—"The

Fuselage of XC-35 was sealed tight. This is aft view of interior. The cabin was pressurized, insde air bleeding off engine turbo superchargers through series of auxiliary turbos.

Boiler."

During an early phase engineers built a test cylinder to check their sealing methods. The cabin had to be completely hermetically sealed. A leak would ruin the whole principle. They put strips of cloth soaked in marine glue between each riveted section as they assembled it. But as air was pumped in the thing leaked like a seive. This type sealing compound simply wouldn't work. It was like trying to blow up a punctured innertube.

Nobody could come up with a satisfacotry sealing method until a fellow named Pete Beck from Dupont showed up on the scene. His suggestion was a new neoprene sealing tape. You just sealed all joints with the new tape and you had a fuselage as airtight as a bottle with a waxed cork in its throat. He was right. When they pumped up the fuselage this time, it no longer hissed.

But there were other problems. The design of the fuselage nose called for a spun section more than three feet in diameter, more than two feet deep and formed from a single sheet of aluminum. Nobody had ever attempted such a king-sized spun aluminum job before. It took learning the skill with big aluminum sheets and

several failures before the nose finally emerged just right and okayed by Government inspectors.

Then one day, when the nose and the fuselage had been joined and the whole thing began to look like a fat *"Electra"* (some called it a pregnant *"Electra"*), they were ready to try pumping the fuselage under pressure. Ferris Smith, a project engineer, turned the air valve.

"Lookout!" Someone yelled. "The thing's going to blow sky high!"

It sounded that way. Air hissed from cracks around the doors, loose fittings, ragged gasket holes. The ship screamed, whistled, squealed and shrieked. It sounded like a pig pen at the stockyards with a couple of garage men turning air hoses on the pigs to quiet them down. The din created an illusion—the XC-35 looked like it was puffing itself up like a balloon. Workmen scattered in all directions.

But nothing happened. Smith turned off the pressure. They patched up the little cracks and pinpoint holes, and then, they pumped up the fuselage again. This time everything was quiet. The pressure was at its maximum. The plexiglass cabin windows bulged half an inch, but nothing popped. Men were inside, too. It was comfortable and very normal.

The Army's experimental high-altitude XC-35 Lockheed. It had "double skin" fuselage like submarine. Note the turbo-superchargers on engines. Plane shared in 1938 Collier Trophy award. It gave Lockheed head start in development of pressurized "Constellation" airliner.

The rest was simple. They put wings on the "Boiler" and it was ready for its test flight. The XC-35 was a big airplane. It had a wing span of 55 feet and a fuselage length almost that of a DC-3 airliner. It was powered with two Pratt & Whitney engines equipped with the GE superchargers. It weighed more than five tons.

The airplane flew on its initial flight on May 7, 1937. It was delivered to the Air Corps three months later. Back at Wright Field, Carl Greene and Captain Alfred H. Johnson, a test pilot, both of whom had bird-dogged the project from its very beginning, took the plane up to see what it would really do.

Johnson climbed the ship to 12,000 feet and turned on the superchargers, which in addition to supplying new air to the engines served as the "pumps" to put the cabin under pressure. The plane climbed higher—15,000, . . .20,000. . .up. .up. . up. . to 28,000 feet. Inside the cabin men worked in their shirtsleeves, recording data, watching a hundred and one spinning dials and needles. For the first time in history they were riding in the sub-stratosphere in an airplane without oxygen masks.

Although the early tests were successful, things did go wrong. Frost formed on the windows and the pilots couldn't see. They fixed that, using small automobile windshield fans—each fan keeping a portion of the glass clear. Sometimes, even these didn't work and ice formed on the outside of the windows, built up into a solid sheet and the pilots had to descend to lower altitudes. Later they remedied the frost problem and ice problem with new heating devices and windshield wipers.

The high altitudes took their toll on the plane's instruments, too,—observers found errors in air speed meters, rate-of-climb indicators and other necessary flight instruments. It was due to instrument case leakage; the casings couldn't stand the pressure changes. So, they sealed in the instrument cases just like they sealed the cabin—another innovation.

Another problem presented itself in the sluggishness of hydraulic mechanisms operating off engine oil pressure systems. Propellers and supercharger governors were particularly affected by the cold temperatures at high altitudes. They cured this by heating oil lines. Once again, the hydraulically operated flaps and landing gear worked faultlessly. XC-35 just wouldn't be whipped. It overcame the technical detail problems that had held back pressure cabin aircraft for years. The *"Electra"* as a

modified super-charged, pressure cabin airplane showed designers and engineers how to overcome one of aviation's biggest bugaboos. It provided the "know-how" for all pressurized aircraft of the future, including Lockheed's forthcoming *"Constellation"*.

In a dramatic flight on February 13, 1938, the XC-35 demonstrated its full capabilities and the practicability of over-weather flying—a key to the future of air travel. The flight didn't just happen. It was an emergency.

The XC-35 was at the airport in Chicago, getting some instrument work done. The weather was stinko. Planes were setting on the ground. There wasn't an airliner operating.

In Chicago at the time was Assistant Secretary of War, Louis A. Johnson. The Secretary was called to the White House. He had to get through. When he contacted the Air Corps to get him a plane, someone suggested the XC-35. The ship was there. It had been boasted as an "over-weather" craft. Let it prove itself. The Air Corps' top test pilot, Major Stanley M. Umstead, could bring it through if anybody could. They decided to try it, weather or no weather.

Louie Johnson was game. He told Umstead as he boarded the plane—"Let's set a record that everybody will have to shoot at for a long time."

"We'll try", Umstead told him.

It was rough going the first ten minutes. Touch and go, as the plane roared down the runway and headed right into the center of an electrical storm that hung over the entire area. But, suddenly, it was climbing up through the rough air to a height of 22,000 feet where it broke out into the bright sunshine. There, with the sun's brilliant rays bouncing off its silvery wings, the XC-35 began to show its stuff. Umstead poured on the throttle. With the aid of a tailwind the Army's Substratosphere baby—Lockheed's pressure-cabin *"Electra"*—hit over 300 miles an hour—100 mph faster than any airliner had ever been known to fly before. The Secretary landed in Washington almost before he had a chance to settle down in the comfortable seat.

"Ump", he congratulated the pilot, "that flight was out of this world!"

The XC-35 became the forerunner—in principle at least—of the pressurized cockpits and other crew stations that let the B-29 Superfortresses raid Tokyo. It put airpower on stilts into a battlefield miles above the earth. Perhaps, more important for world peace—it clipped the

Under Pressure

tops off the treacherous mountains, and opened a new and safer highway in the sky for future airliners.

About the time that the XC-35 was setting one high-altitude and high-speed record after another for planes in its category, Hall Hibbard, "Kelly" Johnson and Bob Gross, back at Lockheed, were doing a little of "out of this world" thinking by themselves. On paper, they were making more sketches. With their pencils, they were thinking about a much larger airplane than the XC-35—an airliner capable of carrying 40 or 50 passengers. They called it the *"Excalibur"*.

At the same time, down in the shops, workers were busy on a very secret project, modifying another *"Electra"* Model 14, for a millionaire oil man named Howard Hughes. One day not too far off Hughes was to climb into the plane

with a three-man crew and blaze a new trail around the world.

"I'll be back in a couple of days", Hughes, himself a veteran pilot, told the hotel clerk in New York. He didn't say where he was going.

Three days, 19 hours, 8 minutes and 10 seconds later the world heard all about it. Headlines told of Hughes globe-girdling flight that had covered 14,791 miles from New York to Paris, Moscow, Omsk, Yakutsk, Fairbanks, Minneapolis and back to New York!

Big things were happening in aviation. The first pressure-cabin airplane. The big new *"Excalibur"* on paper and in mock-up stages. The earth shrunk to a week-end trip around the world.

Strange enough all three were to fit nicely into the jig-saw puzzle of the future. Pressure-cabin

High above the clouds, Army XC-35 roars toward Washington on record-breaking flight carrying Assistant Secretary of War Louis Johnson. Crew and passengers rode the sub-stratosphere in pressurized cabin without individual oxygen masks, in their shirtsleeves.

airliners had to come because the public would demand their comfort and speed. Likewise, if the airlines were going to make money there was need for bigger planes to carry more passengers. Hughes and Lockheed were destined to meet again.

Another view of Wiley Post and his famous "Winnie Mae." His Lockheed Vega was not suitable for pressuriza-tion, so Post used a pressure suit for high altitude flights. See photo on page 42.

CHAPTER FOUR

The Airliner And The Bomber

Northwest Airlines' "Electra" one of first to go into scheduled service takes on passengers. Note the slanted windshield which was popular with the Boeing 247 and the Ford Trimotors. It appeared only on the early Model-10s, later was reversed for more streamline effect.

Before the first *"Electra"* Model 10 flew, Carl Squier and Bob Gross had "sold" the new transport to Pan American World Airways and Northwest Airlines. Other air carriers followed suit—Braniff, Mid-Continent, Delta. Within a year, forty of the *"Electras"* in one version or another had joined the growing family of scheduled airlines. The sales put Lockheed in the black. The company was off and running with a whole new line of fast, safe, medium-range airliners ideally suited for the smaller short-haul feeder lines.

Bob Gross, who got his feet wet in aviation

with Varney Speed Lanes, a small California inter-state airline, brought with him to Lockheed a winning philosphy about the role Lockheed should play in the commercial air transport field. His plan to pull the company out of its doldrums was this: "Don't just go after the Big Boys (American Airlines, United, Transcontinental & Western Air, Inc., Eastern Airlines), Douglas has them pretty well tied-up with the popular DC-2 and the DC-3 that's on the boards. Build a good utility airliner for the smaller airlines and internationals, a smaller plane, more economical. And hit 'em where it

British Airways' "Electra." The cockpit windshield is noticeably different from original design. BA was one of first foreign customers.

Lockheed Model 12 "Electra Junior" was very popular as executive aircraft. Army and Navy both placed orders for limited number.

hurts; go for speed. In air transportation, that's the name of the game!"

The *"Electra"* Model 10 turned the philosophy into practice. It was smaller than the DC-2; wing span 55 feet as against 85 feet. The fuselage was about two-thirds as long as the DC-2's. Yet it could still carry 10 passengers (as against 14) although, admittedly, in more cramped quarters. But more important, the *"Electra"* Model 10 was powered with two 450-horsepower engines, while the DC-2 depended upon two 750-horsepower engines, a big difference in operational costs. At the same time the smaller ship provided 200-mile-an-hour transportation, almost identical with the bigger, more powerful Douglas. With such performance, it appealed to the smaller carriers. And above all, the price was right; about one-third less than the Douglas.

Following the success of its *"Electra"* Model 10, Lockheed brought out a similar but smaller plane identified as the Model 12, *"Electra*

junior". This was the fastest airplane of its size and type ever constructed in the U.S. up to this period, and was intended for executive, corporation, feeder airline or sportsman pilot use. It had a top speed of 219 mph. The ship carried six passengers, pilot and co-pilot.

The Model 12 found favor throughout the world because of its excellent flying characteristics, maneuverability, ease of handling, speed and low-cost maintenance. It is interesting to point out that *"Junior"* kept Lockheed's hand in the executive plane, sportsplane market which it had dominated for years with the *"Vega"*, *"Orion"*, *"Altair"* series.

In short, the low-wing, all-metal *"Electra"* configuration let the company keep a lot of its old customers, while at the same time generating new business in the airline category. Both the Model 10 and the Model 12 were sold to the

Navy Model 12 was used to test tricycle landing gear. Another "Junior" was used by Army Air Corps at Wright Field to try out early automatic-landing and auto-pilot systems.

Douglas DC-2 was "Electra's" chief competitor. It was larger plane but the Model-10 was faster. Douglas Aircraft Company (Now McDonnell Douglas) and Lockheed through the years were neck-and-neck for the commercial airline business. The leader always had somebody right on his tail.

The Airliner And The Bomber

"Electra Junior" with triple-tail was used for "hot-wing" experiment at NACA Langley field facility. This is plane Major Greene (Chapter Three) saw and picked for XC-35. Later it was decided to modify larger Model-10 for the sub-stratosphere experiment.

Army Air Corps and to military forces of other countries to be used as a command type personnel transport. The U.S. military versions were called the C-36 and C-40 (the C stands for Cargo) respectively.

In yet another role, "Junior" was modified to become a tactical high performance warplane. As a bomber it was manned by a crew of three, and it could carry up to eight 110-pound bombs, hung externally under the center section of the wing. Armament consisted of a .30 caliber fixed machine gun in the nose and an identical gun flexibly mounted in a rotating, retracting turret atop the fuselage amidships. Ironically , in this configuration the Model 12 was faster than most of the pursuit planes of that era. It was so well received in some countries that Lockheed engineers started looking at the larger Model 10 and what it would take to make it a bomber type.

It was the summer of 1938 and all Europe was astir with the actions of a man named Adolf Hitler whose Nazi armies and Luftwaffe seemed bent on over-running the continent, indeed, on world conquest. About this time Bob Gross sent Brother Courtlandt to England hoping to sell the British some military versions of the popular *"Electra"* series. Already the British were familiar with the name Lockheed; an *"Electra"* Model 10 had been chosen as the King's personal plane.

In England, the RAF people said they weren't interested, that British Aircraft Industry was capable of meeting that nation's needs. Perhaps, Gross' timing was off. Prime Minister Neville Chamberlain had just returned from Berlin (in a Model 10 *"Electra"*) with a signed pact that

Prime Minister Neville Chamberlain steps from British Airways "Electra" after historic meeting with Adolph Hitler (September 30, 1938) when German Dictator signed "Peace Declaration" with Britain. Eleven months later Hitler attacked Poland, and "Electras" as converted "Hudson" bombers were first American-built planes to carry the war to Germany. (Photo from Lockheed files)

Stretch version of original "Electra" was this Model-14 which could carry 12 passengers. Note the mid-wing configuration. It was real competitor of DC-2s although interior arrangement was more cramped. The Lockheed, however, was much faster than Douglas.

guaranteed "peace in our time."

Meanwhile, back at Burbank, the *"Electra"* line was going through some modifications. The Model 14 *"Electra"* appeared, and the company picked up new airline customers all over the world with the larger capacity airliners.

Although very much the same configuration as the original *"Electra"* with the familiar twin-rudders, engineers added about 10 feet to the wing span, and stretched the fuselage six feet on

Hughes' modified Model-14 named "World's Fair 1939" (July, 1937) at Floyd Bennett Field, L. I. after historic globe-girdling flight. Resultant publicity made "Electras" famous and boosted sales in many foreign countries. Insert shows Howard Hughes (left) with Lockheed's Carl Squier discussing plans for round-the-world trip.

The Airliner And The Bomber

the Model 14. The main cabin seated six along each side of a center aisle, and the plane carried a crew of two. It was powered with two 750-horsepower Pratt & Whitney "Hornet" engines, permitting a useful payload of over 7,000 pounds, very compatible so far as airline operations were concerned with the DC-2 airliners. The Model 14 was also a mid-wing airplane, an easily recognizable change from the low-wing Model 10 design.

It was a modified version of this Model 14 that Hughes chose to use for his record-breaking around-the-world flight. The resultant publicity helped boost sales of the Model 14 to the airlines, making the larger *"Electra"* one of the most popular airliners of the day. The plane also was slated for another role, as we shall see, that would win for it undying fame in the skies over Europe.

So popular was the Model 14, that they stretched the basic design once more to come out with the Model 18, the *"Lodestar"* had a longer fuselage and could accommodate a crew of two upfront, with 16 passengers and 1 stewardess in the main cabin. Indeed, the *"Lodestar"*, gave

the popular DC-2 a real run for its money; many air travelers preferring the Lockheed because of its faster schedules.

Then it happened. Northwest Airlines, first to introduce the Model 14 on its St. Paul to Seattle route, lost one of the planes and one of its veteran pilots, Nick Namer, in a crash atop 9,000-foot Bridges Peak, north of Bozeman, Montana. Namer and nine others were killed and the airline after 72,000,000 passenger miles of fatality-free flying, suffered its first serious accident. All hell broke loose when crash investigators determined the cause of the crash—*structural failure!*

According to aviation historian Henry Ladd Smith, writing in his book AIRWAYS (Alfred A. Knopft, 1942)—"Inspectors found the new ships were subject to 'tail flutter.' When wind tore away the H-shaped double rudder, there was nothing for Namer to do but brace himself for the crash." The then government regulatory agency, The Bureau of Air Commerce, grounded all Lockheeds for structural weakness.

Overnight, Lockheed, second only to Douglas in the building of safe, commercial airliners,

Royal Dutch Airline (KLM) was one of first foreign carriers to buy Lockheed equipment. This is "Super Electra" another stretched version (eight windows) which also had high-speed wing with integral fuel tanks. Trailing edge extensions are guide rails for Lockheed-Fowler flaps. Insert shows flaps fully extended which shortened take-off run and cut runway landing distances. Lockheed pioneered this development.

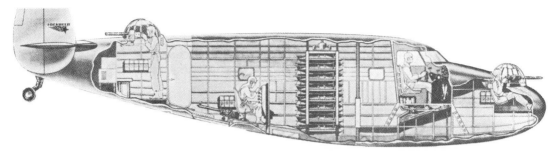

Artist's cut-a-way side view shows what engineers did to Model 14 to convert it into bomber.

suddenly found itself in the same position as that of Tony Fokker after the tragic crash of a Transcontinental & Western Air Inc. Fokker trimotor that killed famed Notre Dame football coach Knute Rockne in 1931. The wing had come off Rockne's Fokker, and the Bureau had put the blame on *structural failure*. It imposed such rigid inspection requirements that airlines flying the planes, could no longer afford the rigid restrictions and expense. The famed Fokkers disappeared from the scene.

Were the wonderful Lockheeds doomed to the same fate? Back at Burbank they solved the "flutter" problem with counter-weighted rudders, got the Model 14s back in the air again, came out with the bigger and better Model 18 *"Lodestars"*, but things weren't the same, anymore.

Moreover, the Douglas DC-3, 21-passenger airliner had virtually captured the air transport market.

Things weren't going well for Britain, either, as war clouds gathered over Europe with Hitler seeding them. It became more and more evident the Nazi dictator disdained the Chamberlain "peace in our time" formula. Military observers in the U. S. and abroad warned that war was imminent. At home Roosevelt announced a 5,000-plane program for the Army Air Corps. For the first time in a decade the purse strings were loosened on the Air Corps' pocketbook, and just about every aircraft designer and manufacturer frequented the Air Corps' Materiel Division at Wright Field, near Dayton, Ohio, procurement center and test facility.

Bob Gross carried the ball for Lockheed, spending more time in Dayton than he did at Burbank trying to get orders for the military versions of the Model 14 and Model 18 as Air Corps cargo planes. He did sell a few, one version of the *"Lodestar"* to be used as a troop carrier and paratrooper.

But it was evident Lockheed wouldn't get rich

in this area; the Douglas' were more suitable for such missions, especially as cargo planes in the Air Corps' rapidly expanding air freight operations.

On one of his visits to Dayton, however, Gross picked up a choice bit of information. He learned that a special purchasing commission from Britain was arriving in the U.S. to look at designs which might be suitable for bombers, just in case the RAF might one day have to strike back. The British Commission would soon be in California, he was told, and he kept the telephone lines hot getting his people in Burbank geared-in so they would have something to show the RAF crowd.

There wasn't much time. And Lockheed didn't have anything along the bomber line to show, not even any "on-paper" designs. Cyril Chappellet, corporate secretary, would recall later that the only thing on the books at the time was an order for some Model 14s from a Japanese airline. If they hadn't had this business, the British visitors might have seen a "pretty bare factory." As it turned out, the British saw a bustling assembly line, and good business stature for the small company.

The engineering department and shop gang also had cooked up a surprise for the prospective customers. In a record five days, after notification from the British Attache in Washington of the commission's arrival in Caliornia, they had designed and constructed a full-scale mock-up of a Model 14 *"Electra"*, converted to meet certain requirements for a *medium bomber!* The members of the commission liked what they saw, and told Gross of their favorable impression. But the idea still had to be sold to the British Air Ministry back in England.

Courtlandt Gross, "Kelly" Johnson, Carl Squier, R. A. VonHake, factory superintendent and Robert Proctor, a contract attorney, formed the sales team that went to London. For sixty days they made their pitch to the British. It was rough going. The British wanted a lot of changes, details, some of which changed daily. "Kelly" Johnson recalled—"Almost every night I had to rough out some new blueprints in the hotel room."

The "team" stuck with it, and on June 23, 1938, the British signed a contract for 200 airplanes plus as many more as could be delivered by December, 1939, up to a maximum of 250. Total value—$25,000,000!

The contract made history. It was the largest single order in numbers of aircraft and dollar-value ever placed with any American aircraft manufacturer up to that time.

More important, Chappellet declared, that it marked the turning point in Lockheed's history.

Bob Gross had another way of putting it when he told the author years later—"There were a lot of guys in the industry who thought we were NUTS for taking on the British order. We had to prove to the world we weren't crazy."

Lockheed leadership, know-how, confidence and guts made the skeptics eat crow. Gross shifted into high gear: He hired a young banking expert. Charles A. Barker, Jr., made him a vice-president in charge of finance, and together they tapped the credit market, and raised new capital for plant expansion.

Management had other ideas, too. It innaugurated a new apprentice training program that benefited not only Lockheed but the entire aircraft manufacturing industry, a kind of "model" program to train new workers in the specific trades and crafts peculiar to the airframe manufacturing business.

In the final tally sheet of the war effort, the program adapted by many others in the industry probably would be ranked as Lockheed's greatest contribution. "Big Bill" W. S. Knudsen, head of General Motors and a Lt. General in charge of the wartime Air Material Command's aircraft production program summ-

First "Hudson" bomber minus turrets is rolled out of hangar. It was daring gamble for small company, but paid off with big dividends.

Women on the assembly line was part of Lockheed's novel wartime training program. "Rosie The Riveter" even made popular song hit.

ed it up—*"machine power* without *manpower* is like wife without husband!" Lockheed's far-sighted program proved a very happy marriage. In the long run, it cemented a worker/management philosophy and loyalty that would produce great benefits.

At the time it was started one saw immediate results. In January 1939, the first three "bombers for Britain" came off the assembly line. By June only 48 had been completed. There was some doubt if the company could meet the December deadline of 250 planes. Maybe, the skeptics were right all along? Gross and company came up with another pioneering step, unprecedented inside the highly competitive airframe manufacturing industry. In a bold move, Lockheed *subcontracted* a substantial amount of parts assembly for the bombers (the British called them *"Hudsons"*) to Rohr Aircraft in San

Diego. Production stepped up to one plane a day, then two a day, and it never let up.

The 250th plane rolled out of the factory seven and a half weeks ahead of schedule. By year's end (1939) Lockheed had 7,000 on its work force another turning point. Lockheed Aircraft Corporation, formed in 1932, seven years young, was now up there in the Major Leagues. It would produce many stars.

Indeed, in a surprisingly short time, the *"Electra"* Model 14 assembly line had become the *"Hudson"* bomber assembly line. They couldn't build the *"Hudson's"* fast enough. A few months later, after Hitler invaded Poland in September, 1939, the British placed another $65,000,000 order. *"Hudsons"* flowed out the door and overseas faster than the current in the Hudson River. And before the war was over the company would turn out more than 3,000 of the

"Hudsons" with protective coating against salt water were shipped by surface transport to Britain. Others (right) spread their wings and flew across north Atlantic, a route future airliners would follow.

The Airliner And The Bomber

First "Hudsons" often flew escort for convoys. In 1942 "Hudson" made history by capturing German U-boat caught on the surface.

"bomber that grew from the airliner."

In external appearance, the bomber was similar to the commercial airliner, certainly in profile, minus gun mounts and turret protuberances. It had the same wing span as the Model 14, but they chopped two feet off the fuselage length. For military performance the planes were fitted with 1,100-horsepower Wright "Cyclone" engines. Besides increased speed, the added power permitted carrying more than a 2,000-pound bombload. The *"Hudson"* also had a revolving turret near the tail and mounted forward firing .30 caliber guns. The plane made history as the first U.S.-built aircraft in World War II to see combat.

Early in the war the planes, piloted by RAF flyers, did reconnaissance duty with the Coastal Command. Later, fitted as bombers, they took part in the initial air strikes in Norway, at Kiel, the Dieppe Raid, and they were numerous in the skies over Dunkirk. When it was needed most the *"Hudson"* became a "jack of all trades."

Flying in virtually every theater of operations, *"Hudsons"* wore the markings of the British, Canadian, Australian, Chinese and Dutch air squadrons. They performed as dive bombers, skip bombers, medium-range bombers, sub-busters, escort fighters and ambulance ships. Churchill is reported to have told Roosevelt—"They helped save our neck."

The *"Lodestar"*, too, emerged in 1941 in a military version called the *"Ventura."* A few of these planes saw service with the U.S. Navy as patrol bombers. Others were modified as tactical

Commercial Model-18 ("Lodestar") emerged as "Ventura" bomber bigger, faster and packing more firepower and bomb load than the "Hudson". British ordered limited number. U.S. Navy version (right) also saw action in Pacific as reconnaissance bomber.

bombers, originally designed to replace the slower *"Hudsons,"* but few ever saw action in the performance of this type of mission. Others were adapted as tow ships for gliders, hospital planes, and troop carriers. With a fuselage slightly longer than the commercial *"Lodestar,"* the *"Ventura"* was also fitted with more powerful Pratt & Whitney twin *"Wasp"* engines, and was able to attain speeds in excess of 275 mph. After the war many were reconverted as executive phanes. They were still the fastest commercial transport flying until the four-engined airliners came along.

The *"Hudson"* and *"Ventura"* programs had indeed changed the whole complexion of the Lockheed Aircraft Corporation. The company which had made a great name for itself building commercial airliners, and doing very nicely financially, with the war emergency became a giant in the warplane production program.

Like all the other U.S. plane makers which became the "arsenals of airpower," Lockheed went through a terrific expansion program. "We didn't expand," Bob Gross would say, "we exploded! Like a bomb hit Burbank."

The company, whose commercial transports had upped its work force to about 2,500 workers in 1939, in the peak war period reached a payroll of 94,300. The facility at Burbank grew and grew and grew. There was built a whole new plant, a wholly-owned Lockheed subsidiary, the Vega Airplane Company near the original Burbank factory site where Lockheed built Boeing-designed B-17s when the famed "Flying For-

Wartime plane program resulted in new Vega Airplane Company plant built at Burbank. During war plant turned out "Hudsons", "Venturas" and in "pool" arrangement with Douglas-Boeing had assembly lines rolling with B-17 "Flying Fortresses" Insert shows one of first B-17s to come out of Vega plant.

Lockheed-Vega employees donated their time and talent and the company the materials to build this "Hudson" which promptly joined RAF Coastal Command on patrol in Iceland area. The name of the plane typified spirit of entire Lockheed organization.

tresses," four-engined bombers, were needed to carry the war deep into Germany.

Before World War II ended Lockheed was the nation's largest aircraft producer turning out 23 planes a day. "Altogether during the war years," Bob Gross would report, "nearly 20,000 military aircraft of assorted types rolled out of our factory doors."

Among these was a completely new and radically-designed pursuit, whose exploits in the wartime skies would become legend.

CHAPTER FIVE

Lightning In The Sky

In the City Room of the Dayton, Ohio *Daily News* the first report came from two sources: An informant at nearby Wright Field called in a "tip" that one of the Field's pilots was in the air at that moment flying a revolutionary new pursuit plane from California to New York in an attempt to set a new coast-to-coast speed record. About the same time the Associated Press teletype in the wire room clicked off a query—"CHECK WRIGHT FIELD PILOT MAKING CROSS-COUNTRY FLIGHT. PLEASE."

Minutes later, before anyone had had time to check too thoroughly, the AP answered its own request. The teletype printer clacked out—B-U-L-L-E-T-I-N—AMARILLO, TEXAS (dateline)—"A SILVER STREAK FLASHED OUT OF THE WEST AND LANDED AT THIS AIRPORT HERE TODAY LESS THAN THREE HOURS AFTER IT HAD TAKEN OFF FROM MARCH FIELD, CALIFORNIA.

"THE ARMY'S LATEST FIGHTER PLANE, LOCKHEED XP-38, WITH LIEUTENANT B. S. KELSEY AT THE CONTROLS WAS ON THE GROUND HERE ONLY 20 MINUTES FOR REFUELING. THE PLANE IS HEADING EAST FOR DAYTON, OHIO. . ."

It was February 11, 1939.

General Henry H. "Hap" Arnold, Chief of the Army Air Corps and Brig. General A. W. Robins, Commanding Officer at Wright Field were on the flight line there to meet Kelsey when he landed a couple of hours later. The author was also there. Everyone was in high spirits; the XP-38 was better than 1900 miles from its starting point and only 5 hours 43 minutes in the air. No wonder they gave her the name *Lightning!*

Standing next to General Arnold I heard him ask Kelsey—"Ben, are you tired?"

"Not a bit, sir."

"Want to go on and try for a record?"

"It's up to you."

"Get crackin' and good luck!"

We watched the plane take off and vanish into

The XP-38 poses for her portrait just before Army Test Pilot Ben Kelsey flew it from Burbank to Mitchell Field for new coast-to-coast record. Plane carried no armament; gun portals in nose were sealed.

Lightning In The Sky

Lieut. Ben S. Kelsey, later to become Brigadier General, deputy chief USAF Research & Development, examines model of "Lightning".

the eastern sky, and Arnold remarked—"That's the fastest damn thing with wings I've ever seen!"

There was little doubt that Kelsey wouldn't set a new record. It would be great publicity for the Army Air Corps. But things turned sour. Kelsey made it to Mitchel Field, Long Island in little more than 2 hours, but coming in to land he nicked a tree with a wing tip, crash landed in a creek bed near the golf course. XP-38 was sprawled all over the ground; a total washout. Luckily, Kelsey escaped injury.

He had set a record—seven hours, 48 minutes, flying time, coast-to-coast!

More important, the flight had proved the XP-38 was one helluva good aircraft. Back at Wright Field a few days later, Ben Kelsey confided—"There was nothing wrong with the ship. It was just that damn fool pilot." The truth was, he admitted, he was a little tired at the end of a long, long journey with a tiger on a leash all the way. And the tiger got away from him for just a brief minute.

I asked him how it felt flying the fastest plane. (At times he had averaged better than 400 mph.) And I'll never forget the answer.

Puffing on a new Kersten metal air-cooled pipe, an idea as revolutionary as the twin-boomed XP-38 design, Ben answered—"It feels like you've got 2,000 horsepower in your lap and a dozen feathers in your tail and you're going like Hell."

Ben liked the Lockheed XP-38 and his official report as the Army's project test pilot recommended that the Air Corps buy this experimental design and develop it as a front-line combat fighter aircraft. Thirteen YP-38s were ordered as service test models. Results showed the design had great potential, but there were a lot of growing pains. Perhaps, because of its twin-boom profile so radically different from other contemporary fighter designs, the plane was in for a lot of criticism before it would prove itself in the skies over Europe, Africa and the Pacific in World War II—one of the most famous and legendary fighting machines of the great Air War.

Beyond this contribution, the P-38 would also play a major role in changing the whole atmosphere of the Lockheed Company. Bob Gross once told the author—"It not only put us in the

One of thirteen YP-38 Service Test models with Test Pilot Ben Kelsy at controls. Short time later he had to "bail out" when plane ran into "compressibility" phenomona and disintegrated.

Design team of J. J. Johnson (left) Hall Hibbard, C. L. Johnson and James Gerschler came up with revolutionary twin-boom XP-38.

fighter plane business, but the superb wing design gave us a head start in the development of the *"Constellation"* series of post-war airliners."

We will discuss this in a later chapter. But, first, let's go back to the very beginning of the P-38 story. It was almost two years to the day before Ben Kelsey's cross-country dash in the XP-38 that the concept for the fighter was born. Mid February, 1937, Bob Gross received an Army Air Corps bid specification for a new fighter plane.

The Spec called for a pursuit (the *fighter* designation came later) that would have a *20,000 foot ceiling and a top speed of 360 mph.* Further, the Spec stated that the plane must be capable of

a *range in access of 750 miles with a crew of (1) and a minimum of four machine guns to perform effective tactical intercept missions of hostile aircraft at high altitudes.*

Such a request was "way out" by comparison with the then in-service Curtiss P-36 pursuits. The P-36s were lucky if they could hit 300-mph, and at higher altitudes this performance fell off considerably. The challenge facing Lockheed and competitive bidders on the latest Air Corps proposal was to design a plane at least 50-mph faster with substratosphere capabilities. There were those who said it couldn't be done with the present state of the art.

Lockheed's design team of Kelly Johnson and Hall Hibbard went to work. They came up with a variety of ideas: They tried a conventional design that looked not unlike a single-tailed streamlined *"Electra"*, engines in nacelles on the wing. Then, they tried mounting two engines in tandem arrangement inside the fuselage driving twin propellers one on each side of the fuselage in the leading edge of the wing by a system of shafts and gears. Another sketch had tandem engines inside the fuselage driving a pair of pusher propellers on the trailing edge of a wing,

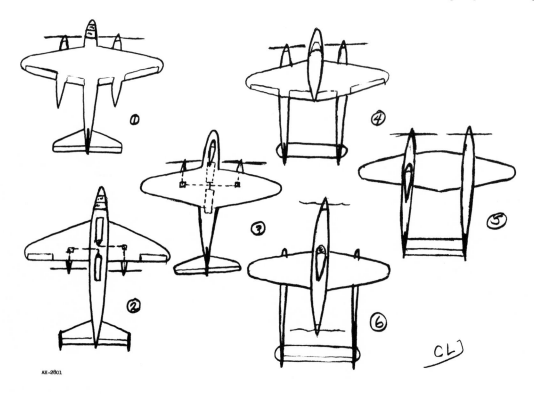

AH-2801

Lockheed's XP-38 wasn't designed "on the back of an envelope" but these sketches drawn by "Kelly" Johnson show an interesting evolution of the various configurations considered. No. 4 became the XP-38.

with a twin-tail empennage. They even tried a twin-boom, pusher-puller arrangement. But finally, Lockheed's "mystery plane" emerged with an entirely new wing configuration supporting a pod-like cockpit arrangement in its center section, a pair of engines mounted, one on each side of the pilot's "bubble" in a long twin-boom arrangement supporting a double tail. It would make the P-38 the most easily recognized of all World War II fighters.

This was the proposed design that Bob Gross took to Wright Field early in 1937, and which won the Air Corps competition with Lockheed being awarded a contract to build the prototype in June of that year. They started to build the plane in July, 1938, and on January 27, 1939 the prototype made its first flight. It almost ended in disaster because of a wing flap malfunction. Engineers were satisfied, however, there was nothing drastically wrong with the design aerodynamically. XP-38 was simply a radically new design that had to prove itself. There was a lot to learn.

XP-38 weighted over 15,416 pounds, almost twice the weight of the Curtiss P-36 pursuit. It was powered with two Allison in-line, liquid-cooled engines, the first of this type to develop 1,000-horsepower and over. The plane's life was short-lived—16 days (11 hours and 50 minutes flying time)—and it lay a twisted mass of wreckage after Ben Kelsey's record-breaking transcontinental flight. It was the first plane to exceed 400-mph, and the first aircraft to encounter the phenomenon of "compressibility", a preview of the problems to be encountered in transonic flight.

The "compressibility" problem wasn't really new. Engineers all along had known it would occur; they had seen it happen in wind tunnels. As the speed of the airflow was increased to 400. .500. .600-mph, the transonic range, air piled up on the leading edge of the wing, a kind of "eddying action" distorting the normal smooth flow and lift characteristics. Its lift thus minimized, a plane could fall out of the sky. The disturbing forces could also tear it apart.

Indeed, that's what happened one day high in the skies over San Fernando Valley when Test Pilot Ben Kelsey ran into "compressibility" with another P-38, and the ship disintegrated. He parachuted to safety, and his detailed report of what happened led engineers to make the addition of a dive-brake on the underside of the wing and other changes. This change whipped the problem. Just in time, too, for the P-38 was already going into production when World War II broke out.

Before Pearl Harbor, in August, 1941, thirty-six P-38Ds were delivered to the Army Air Corps. Before the war was over a total of nearly ten thousand of the famous *"Lightnings"* were built with 18 different model designations performing as interceptors, skip bombers, camera planes, fighter-bombers, tank-busters, troop

Altogether more than 10,000 of the famous Lockheed "Lightning" series were built in some 18 different model designations. Here is scene at Burbank factory P-38s moving down production line. At extreme top of photo can be seen the first four-engined "Constellation" nearing final assembly. Lockheed was lucky it could be so deep in fighters and still have "Connie" moving ahead. It would be highly important to postwar future.

Fourteen rockets slung under wing provided firepower equal to Naval cruiser's six-inch broadside. Armament also included four .50 caliber machine guns and one .20mm rapid-fire cannon in nose.

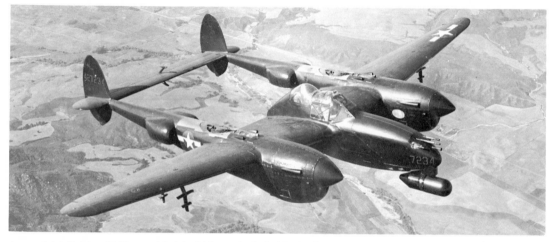

As a night fighter P-38 provided bubble cockpit behind pilot for radar operator. Torpedo-like capsule beneath nose housed radar.

"Droopsnoot" version had elongated nose section for bombardier. As bomber P-38 could carry 500-pound, 1,000-pound bombs slung under wings. Note bomb racks between fuselage and engines.

Lightning In The Sky

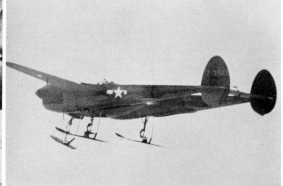

External fuel tanks, fitted with stretchers turned P-38 into "Flying Ambulance." Plane's high speed helped save many lives. On duty at far north bases, P-38s were fitted with tricycle ski-gear.

strafers, glider tow planes, night fighters, ambulance planes and rocket-carriers. The latter version with 14 rockets slung under its wings had firepower equal to a Naval cruiser's broadside of six guns. As a bomber the P-38 carried more bombpower than the early B-17 "Flying Fortresses!"

The P-38s were everywhere, did just about everything, earned the acclamation of being probably the "most versatile fighter plane of the air war." They flew across the North Atlantic and the South Atlantic. They saw action in the skies over Italy, in the Aleutians, over Germany, the Mediterranean, in North Africa, New Guinea, the South Pacific, with the Flying Tigers in China flying over the Hump, and operated, island-to-island, in the final assault on Japan.

A P-38 was the first American plane to down a Nazi aircraft after the U.S. declared war on Germany, shooting down a Focke-Wulf patrol bomber off Iceland. The P-38s were in on the beginning, and in on the end, after four years of the conflict.

Strangely, in the early days of the War, the first "*Lightnings*" didn't really flash too rapidly into good favor. The British, who ordered 143 of a special Model 322 before the first YP-38 ever had flown, didn't like the plane at all. But there was good reason; the special export version was equipped with a mechanical supercharger, not the turbo-superchargers which went into the Army Air Corps models. Result: the RAF version couldn't get up to 20,000 feet and above, where the plane was most capable of high-speed performance. Moreover, the early models—even

Army Air Corps for training purposes adopted "Piggy-back" version. Student literally "rode the shoulders of pilot". The two-place jobs were also used for gunnery training. •

65

those delivered to the Army Air Corps—were subject to "growing pains", mainly, a "flutter" problem which until remedied put on a 350-mph restricted speed. And when the *"Spitfires"* came along, the RAF didn't have much use for the P-38. Britain turned its P-38s back to the U.S. and the Army Air Corps quickly converted them into a "piggyback" trainer.

Inside the small bubble-like pilot's canopy, they jerry-rigged an arrangement which enabled a passenger to "ride the pilot's shoulders". The author remembers such a ride with one of Wright Field's pilots. He squeezed in, and boy, what a ride. She leaped off the runway and climbed straight up! No other plane could do that. It took your breath away.

The "piggy-backers" were ideal gunnery trainers. And what firepower even the original P-38s packed in their nose—a 20mm cannon, two .50 caliber and two .30 caliber machine guns. Small wonder Nazi pilots, when they first encountered the P-38, called it *"Der Gabelschwanz Teufel"*—the fork-tailed Devil!

Although P-38 pilots accounted for a goodly share of enemy aircraft in Europe's skies, the plane as a photo-reconnaissance aircraft recorded its greatest claim to fame. Because of its great speed, the P-38 was ideal for low-flying photographic missions. In Italy, for example, P-38 photo-recon ships photographed 80 per cent of the entire country before the invasion began. And P-38 recon squadrons photographed Tokyo areas that pinpointed targets for the B-29 raids on Japan.

It was in the Pacific theater, incidentally, that the *"Lightnings"*—vastly improved versions—really came into their own and flew into immortality. American aces like Major Richard Bong, Major Thomas B. McGuire, Jr., Colonel Charles H. MacDonald and Colonel Gerald R. Johnson racked up their scores flying P-38s. They made the vaunted Jap Zero live up to is name. The Zero might outturn a P-38, but it could never outfly one.

In New Guinea, Charles A. Lindbergh on a top secret mission (a civilian observer studying pursuit plane performance) gave the P-38 a much-needed shot in the arm. Lindbergh worked out a flying technique for long over-water missions. He showed other pilots how to use power-settings that greatly increased the radius range of the *"Lightning"*. "It was like a gift from heaven," General MacArthur declared. It made the P-38 an even greater threat in the island-to-island, long overwater path to Japan.

It was on one of his experimental missions

Test Pilot Jimmy Mattern (at controls) with U.S. Army pilot show how cramped cockpit was in "Piggyback" P-38.

Air Force Sgt. Vaughn A. Bass in this painting captures the last moments of Japanese Admiral Yamamoto. The Admiral's "Betty" bomber, one engine afire from guns and cannon of Captain Thomas G. Lamphier's P-38 minutes later exploded in a ball of fire. The action took place in the skies over Bougainville Island. (Photo reproduction courtesey USAF).

that Lindbergh, flying with pilots of the 475th Fighter Group, was attacked by a formation of Jap Zeros. The famous flyer shot down one of the Zeros in self defense.

But, perhaps, the greatest P-38 exploit of the war came on April 18, 1942 the same day that General Jimmy Doolittle's B-25 bombers took off from the Aircraft Carrier *Hornet* (FDR's Shangrila) and bombed Tokyo. What happened unfolds like a Hollywood cliff-hanger script.

The U. S. had cracked the Japanese code. As a result a message was intercepted by the Navy which made known that Admiral Isoroku Yamamoto, commander-in-chief of the Japanese Navy (the man who planned the attack on Pearl Harbor and boasted he would "dictate the terms of peace from the White House.") was planning an inspection tour of Japan's bases around Bouganville. Navy Intelligence had the exact date and time that the Admiral would be in that area. If the trip went as planned, it would put the Admiral within range of U. S. Guadalcanal based P-38s. What an opportunity!

Secretary of Navy Frank Knox saw the chance to avenge Pearl Harbor. He sent an urgent cablegram to the Army Air Force commander on Guadalcanal. The cable outlined the details of Yamamoto's trip. It ended saying every effort should be made to "GET YAMAMOTO". Our guys didn't need to be told twice. They accepted the challenge.

The morning of April 18 found a formation of P-38s that had flown 450 miles overwater, approaching the spot where the Navy said Yamamoto's plane was scheduled to be at 9:30 A.M. Two of the P-38 pilots, Major John W. Mitchell and Captain Thomas G. Lamphier, Jr. had specific orders: "Shoot down the plane carrying Yamamoto at all costs."

Known for his punctuality, Admiral Yamamoto was on time. At almost the exact hour, the P-38 formation spotted two Mitsubishis *"Betty"* bombers escorted by six Zeros. At first, the Japs did not see the attackers. (They were so sure the P-38s would never venture so far from home.) When the Zeros did spot the *"Lightnings,"* the protectors were determined to get between them and the Admiral's plane. The two *"Betty's"* dropped down to tree top level trying to escape.

Lamphier spotted them, flew into a melee of *"Zeros,"* shot one down, and dived after the fleeing bomber-transports which he was sure carried the Admiral's party. Firing a steady stream of .50 caliber and .20mm cannon fire across the escaping plane's flight path, Lamphier saw one of the *"Betty's"* engines catch fire. The next moment a whole wing burst into flames and fell off. The *"Betty"* exploded in a ball of fire as it hit the ground. It marked a fiery grave for Yamamoto. The other bomber was hit, too, by gunfire from another P-38 and crash-landed in the sea.

On board the second *"Betty"* was Japanese Vice Admiral Matome Ugaki, who survived the crash. Later, Ugaki would write in his diary details of the entire episode which confirmed the death of Admiral Yamamoto.

There was great celebration back at Henderson Field on Guadalcanal. A bolt of *"Lightning"* that came out of nowhere had struck the Japs where it hurt the most. The P-38s got Yamamoto!

From that moment on the tide of conquest for Japan turned to defeat. And when the Pacific War was over, it was a formation of P-38s that escorted the planes carrying high-ranking Japanese officials to Ie Shima to sign the surrender papers. Afterwards, *Lightnings"* also stayed in Japan with the Occupation Forces. They remained with the U. S. Air Forces as second-line fighters until 1949 when they were phased out.

Besides the legendary tales it wrote across the skies in its wartime role, the P-38 left another kind of high heritage. The first 400-mph aircraft, it taught designers and engineers a lot about high speed flight. Its wing design and flap arrangements brought into being many innovations that made flying safer in the high-speed range. Its battle with "compressibility" forwarned plane-makers and pilots of unknowns ahead in the attempt to fly faster than sound. As a flying camera platform, it pioneered many new techniques in aerial photography. In the beginning, it was the "flying testbed" for the turbo-supercharger, and later its experimental pressurized cockpit taught us a lot about cabin pressurization and the dangers of decompression, safety measures that later appeared in high-flying airliners. It was also the first fighter to have a tricycle landing gear, pioneering new trends in the development of this type undercarriage.

When they closed down the P-38 production line at Lockheed, they never closed the book on the lessons the revolutionary pursuit brought to light and proved with its performance record.

Lockheed took basic P-38 profile and tried experimental version XP-58 called "Chain Lightning." Plane was powered with 2,000-horsepower engines and designed to carry two-man crew and automatic fire-control system. Nothing ever came of the king-sized P-38.

For one thing, they took the basic P-38 wing and many of its other features, and applied them to an airliner design that would become the new "queen of the skies".

We know it today as the Lockheed *"Constellation."*

First "Constellations" designated C-69s were ear-marked for the Army Air Corps as command ships, personnel transports and cargo planes. This batch with Army insignia (white star in blue circle) on wings and fuselage were awaiting delivery. Picture is historic one because it shows various types of aircraft Lockheed built during war—"Constellation," Model-10 "Electras," Model-12 as military personnel transport and (upper right hand corner) the vaunted P-38 "Lightning." Note size of "Constellation" as compared with the "Super Electras."

CHAPTER SIX

Connie Was A Lady

On June 23, 1938, President Franklin D. Roosevelt signed into law the Civil Aeronautics Act, and all civil aviation—scheduled airlines, business flyers, private flyers—got a new set of rules to live by. Known also as the McCarran—Lea Bill (after Senator Patrick A. McCarran and Representative Clarence Lea, who authored it) the Act took U.S. Aviation out of a state of chaos and confusion, gave it purpose and mission, and in particular, put the growing air transport industry on the runway heading in the right direction. For the first time, there was law and order along the airways. Both the government and the air transport industry had their responsibilities spelled out for them. Aviation was geared for growth, with new safety regulations, and assured government financial support in needed areas such as an improved airways system and better airports.

The proof was almost instantaneous: With the government obliged to help air transportation as it did railroad transportation, the privately-owned airlines were able to get new capital to put into the development for new equipment, new terminals, expanded services, better safety standards and training techniques for pilots and ground personnel. In the first two years, under the new law, the airlines set an unprecedented safety record. From March 26, 1939, when a Braniff Airliner crashed near Oklahoma City, until August 31, 1940, when a Pennsylvania-Central plane went down near Lovettsville, Virginia—the scheduled airlines flew millions of

miles without a single fatality. There was not even a minor accident.

The number of air travelers quadrupled. Overnight, the airliner became a full-fledged member of the nation's transportation family along with passenger ships, trains and the Greyhound bus. The future looked even brighter. Airline operators began looking around for bigger planes to accommodate the potential growth. The effect was like a blood transfusion for the Big Three builders of commercial-type airliners—Douglas, Boeing and Lockheed.

The Douglas Aircraft Company of Santa Monica, fat and rich with its popular DC-3 airliner flying air routes all over the world under the flag of almost every nation which had an air transport system, was first in the skies with a four-engined airliner. The plane, designated the DC-4E was three times the size of the DC-3, a 42-passenger sky giant. Far ahead of its time, the big plane made its first flight two months before the Civil Aeronautics Act became law!

Up in Seattle, Washington, the Boeing Airplane Company also had a new four-engined design about ready to test its wings. They called it the *"Stratoliner"*, Boeing Model-307, capable of carrying 33-passengers in a pressurized cabin, an idea Lockheed had pioneered with the XC-35 Army Substratosphere airplane, the forerunner of all pressurized cabin aircraft.

Both the Douglas DC-4E and the *"Stratoliner"* had been developed by Douglas and Boeing in a joint effort with American

This Douglas DC-4E (1939) was probably the first of the modern sky giants. Only one was built, later sold to Japan before Pearl Harbor. Successors, the DC-4s with single tail and DC-6s during the postwar era were competition for "Constellations."

Boeing 307 "Stratoliner" was also flying before first "Constellation" and could claim to be first in-service (TWA and Pan American) airliner with pressurized cabin which Lockheed had pioneered in the XC-35.

Airlines, Eastern Airlines, Transcontinental & Western Airlines, Inc. (TWA), United Airlines and Pan American "pooling" monies to share in the development cost. Moreover, future orders from these carriers for the bigger airliners were virtually assured.

Where was Lockheed?

The biggest plane Lockheed had flying at this time was the twin-engined *"Lodestar"*, and these were being phased out by their airline operators. The company, too, was bursting at the seams, turning out bombers for Britain, and the first orders for the *"Lightning"*, P-38 pursuit. There wasn't really much time to work on a new transport.

But "Bob Gross & Company" did have a four-engined design on paper. When time permitted, they were going ahead with wind tunnel testing and mock-up of *"Excalibur"*, which if the war in Europe hadn't taken the turn it did, probably would have beaten the DC-4E and the *"Stratoliner"* into the sky. It was to have been the next step beyond the *"Lodestar"* as far back as the summer of 1937.

The "on paper" design looked pretty good. *"Excalibur"* was proposed as a four-engined, low-wing, transport, capable of carrying 32 passengers and a crew of four. She was big, a 95-foot wing span, fuselage length, 73 feet, 2 inches, resting on a tricycle landing gear. Her top speed was about 250-275 mph., capable of flying 2,000 miles non-stop with fuel to spare. There was talk she might have a pressurized cabin.

It was too bad she never got to spread her wings. But the "know-how" Lockheed had gained from her design studies put them in a good position when opportunity knocked.

It happened unexpectedly. And when Bob Gross opened the door, the man standing there was Howard Hughes, multi-millionaire oil man, movie producer, racing plane designer, and the hero of the round-the-world flight in the modified Lockheed Model 14, the exploit which put the *"Electras"* in the public eye and, probably more than anything else, attracted its many airline customers.

Hughes got into the picture because of something that happened inside the airline industry which even the Civil Aeronautics Act couldn't control—stiff, cut-throat competition among the airlines battling for superior equipment. Of the Big Three transcontinental carriers (United, American and TWA) the latter, because of its route structure was taking one helluva beating. Its "mid-continent" route simp-

ly didn't hit the populated areas that United's northern route and American's southern route touched. Understandably, the bigger cities were the most fertile markets for the flying businessman, the airlines' prime customer in the thirties. TWA had to do something or face getting its wings clipped.

And Hughes owned controlling interest in TWA. With the help of Jack Frye, vice-president of operations for TWA, Hughes had managed secretly to buy up the majority of the airline's stock. He promptly made Frye President. Both pilots, they faced the problems from the airman's point of view and for a time, TWA was known as "The Airline Run By Flyers." The slogan was even emblazoned on the fuselage of

Artist's drawing of Lockheed "Excalibur" proposed four-engined 32-passenger airliner. Pan American was very much interested.

The wooden mock-up of "Excalibur" showed fuselage profile not unlike an over-sized "Electra." First version had twin-tail.

Later version of "Excalibur" in mock-up stages had entirely different nose which shows some ressemblance to "Stratoliner."

Connie Was A Lady

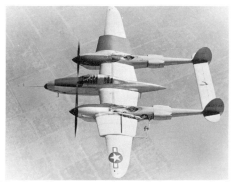

This P-38E was used as flying test bed for "Constellation" wing. "Lightning's" air foil greatly influenced that on "Constellations."

some of its planes.

Hughes' and Frye's viewpoint was to build a better airliner and offer faster coast-to-coast service. According to Jack Frye: "Howard had the idea he could steal a lot of the Hollywood crowd's business away from the other fellows, if we had a super deluxe airliner that could fly non-stop, LA to New York, or even one-stop via Chicago. He was talking eight or nine hours flying time, coast-to-coast; about posh-posh interiors with a "club car" atmosphere in a day-plane, and Pullman-type berths for the night trip. It all sounded far out, but Hughes was dead serious."

When we were working together on a history of TWA just before the outbreak of World War II shelved the idea, Jack Frye told the author: "One time he (Hughes) called me long-distance LA to New York, and talked for eight hours or more about the ideas he wanted in this super airliner. They included a 'blue room' in the tail which was to be for his private use. But they also made a lot of sense, and before he hung up we had drafted a whole list of specifications. I know. I had writer's cramp, and my ear ached from holding it to the receiver."

Frye concluded: "Finally, I told him that TWA would go broke paying the toll charges on the call. Howard retorted—"Hell, they're already broke. You go get somebody to build this damn thing!"

Douglas wasn't interested because of its DC-4 planes. Boeing was "out" because of the Model 307 "Stratoliner" project. Frye talked to Ruben Fleet at Consolidated Aircraft in San Diego, but even Fleet 'turned thumbs down on the idea. With all of this going on the word got back to Bob Gross of Lockheed, who went after the business wing and propeller.

He told Kelly Johnson and Hall Hibbard, his design team, to "come up with something", and they did. In a surprisingly short time, they were meeting with Hughes and Frye and some other TWA people in secret at a house on Romaine Street in Hollywood; pouring over sheafs of sketches, plans, performance data and costs that constituted Lockheed's formal proposal.

The company designation was Model 049, and they had named it the *"Constellation,"* because the design incorporated so many ideas already proven in the Lockheed "winged star" series. Included was the plan form and airfoil of the P-38's wing and its Lockheed-Fowler flap arrangement, providing high-lift, high-speed characteristics and minimum take-off and landing capabilities.

Other features were:

Construction to be an all-metal, low-wing, semi-monocoque land monoplane. *Powerplants*—four Wright *Cyclone*, air-cooled, radial, 2200-horsepower engines. *Propellers*—Hamilton Standard, 3-blade, hydromatic, quick-feathering, 15 ft., 2 inches in diameter. *Weight empty*—51,000 to 52,300 pounds with a payload in excess of 6,000 pounds. *Accomodations*—As an "Air Coach", 64 passengers, crew of six. As a "Sleeper", 34 berths or 48 seats. "Club Cruiser"—48 seats, lounge-bar. "Empire Cruiser", 30 reclining seats, game room (the "blue room"?) They didn't want to forget this to please Mr. Hughes.

The original spec continues: *Dimensions*—Wing span, 123 feet. Fuselage length, 95 feet, one and 3/16th inches. Height, 18 feet, eight and 3/16th inches. Height of Vertical tail, 23 feet, seven and 7/8ths inches. Wing area, 1,650 square feet. *Passenger Comfort Features*—Pressurized cabin, maintaining 8,000-foot atmosphere at 20,000-feet altitude. Complete lavatory, coat room, galley. *Performance*—Top speed (with full load) 340 miles per hour! Top cruising speed (65% power) over 300 miles per hour. Landing speed, 80 miles per hour. Useful load, over 17 tons. Service ceiling on four engines, over 25,000 feet; on any *two* engines, 6,700 feet. *Service potentials*—New York to Chicago, 724 miles, with 64 passengers and cargo. New York to Los Angeles, one stop, 2440 miles, with 48 passengers and cargo, in 8 hours 48 minutes. New York to London, *non-stop,* 3500 miles, with 16 sleeper passengers and baggage, in 17 hours and 20 minutes!

There were many more details, but these were the major points in Lockheed's proposal to meet the Hughes/Frye requirements. To make the

L-1011 TriStar and The Lockheed Story

Lockheed's smiling Bob Gross (left) and Jack Frye, TWA's President at formal signing of "Constellation" contract. Hughes paid bills.

presentation Lockheed had its top people at the secret meeting; Bob Gross, brother Courtlandt, Kelly Johnson and Hall Hibbard. The discussions went on for hours.

Recalling the event, years later, Jack Frye told the author: "I remember Howard came in late. He listened to a quick run down of the presentation, then, started to do a lot of nit-picking. He wanted this. He wanted that. I think, there were fifteen or twenty changes he wanted, and some new ideas added."

"After that, he just sat there a few minutes thinking. Then, he looked at Bob Gross, and asked him how much 40 of the planes would cost."

"Gross quoted him a price—$425,000 apiece!"

"I'll never forget Howard's reaction. He was sitting on the floor, like an Indian at a pow-wow and he rocked back and forth a couple of minutes. Then, he said—*"Hell, TWA can't pay for them, the damn airline's broke. We can't take it to the banks, they'd think we were nuts talking about a 300-mph airliner. Hell, I guess I'll have to pay for them myself!"*

"He looked at Gross and said—*"Go ahead and build them. Send the bills to the Hughes Tool Co."* And he got up and left the room. I saw him later, and he remarked—*"When we get through with 'em we'll have one helluva airplane."*

There are many stories about the role Hughes played in the design and mock-up of the *"Constellation"*. Some say he designed the wing. He didn't. He may have made some suggestions

here and there, but the Connie's wing was essentially an enlarged P-38 wing and flaps. What he did do was contribute a lot to the cockpit configuration, the control boost system, and the interior arrangement in the cabin. A detail like demanding big buttons on the curtains for the berths in the sleeperplane. *"Who the Hell wants to get it caught in a zipper?"*

It is also true that he held many secret meetings in secret places at odd times of the night with Gross and with Frye to discuss changes he wanted. Sometimes, he'd come out to the plant where the mock-up was and request all the workers leave while he got inside and studied the thing. He might stay in there for hours. Then, he'd come up with changes he wanted made. Some very practical; some fuddy-duddyish. The engineering people and production planning people, of course, didn't cotton to these interruptions. But, after all, it was Hughes' money; he owned the Hughes Tool Company, and TWA.

One time Bob Gross told the author—"We had our ups and downs. But as the project moved along, we began to respect some of his ideas and he ours. Howard had more in-born engineering ability and know-how about systems and instruments than anybody gave him credit for, and he had a human-engineering touch that gave the plane a lot of personality. He gave a lot more to the effort than the dollar sign. Of course, there were knock-down and drag out incidents about finances. . ."

It is probably true that Hughes may not have been the "father of the *Constellation*", but he paid all the hospital bills, and he sat up all night with the baby during its growing pains.

The first flight of the *"Constellation"* prototype took place on January 9, 1943. At its controls was test pilot "Eddie" Allen (on loan from Boeing) because Allen, probably more than anybody else, had more experience flying four-engined airplanes. The co-pilot was Milo Burcham, Lockheed's chief test pilot at the time. Also on board were Kelly Johnson, Lockheed's chief design engineer; Rudy Thoren, an engine specialist, and Dick Stanton, chief mechanic. The plane performed so remarkably that it made six more flights the same day.

It was, for a reason that had nothing to do with the splendid performance, a big disappointment to Jack Frye and Howard Hughes. Their "dreamplane" instead of being a silvery queen in the bright red TWA markings, was olive-drab with the white-star in a blue circle insignia of the

First "Constellation" (C-69) in Army Air Corps khaki on first flight. Triple-tail, sharklike fuselage virtually an "airfoil" itself and stilted nose-wheel would make "Connie" recognizable anywhere. Plane No. 1961 would play major role in design and development of future models as research aircraft.

Army Air Corps on its fuselage, and it bore the designation C-69. After Pearl Harbor the order had gone out—"no more commercial airliner production"—and the Army had taken over the *"Constellation"* as a cargo plane. TWA and Pan American which had joined in the effort, would

have to wait. "Connie" was drafted before she was really developed.

Reportedly, Howard Hughes, when he saw the *"Constellation"* for the first time in her Army configuration remarked—"How the hell could they take out all the seats and plush-plush and

YESTERDAY AND TOMORROW. First "Constellation" Army Air Corps' C-69 poses for her picture with Lockheed "Vega" also in uniform as Army personnel transport. The latter, vintage 1933, was ten years old when "Connie" appeared on the scene, but still in use. Note, despite wartime garb the Lockheed Winged Star is proudly displayed on nose.

L-1011 TriStar and The Lockheed Story

All decked-out in TWA colors this "Connie" with Howard Hughes and Jack Frye as pilots made record-breaking flight Burbank to Washington, D.C. a preview of post-war air travel. Flight was made before Allied armies invaded Europe on D-Day and plane was delivered to Army Air Corps for static testing at Wright Field. (Reportedly Hughes insisted on TWA colors to show airline had pioneered "Constellation" development.) The flight got a million dollars worth of publicity, deserved credit for Hughes, Lockheed, TWA and engine manufacturers for advanced design airliner.

still add weight? She looks like a pygmalion!" He and TWA had little more to do with the plane until after the war. It cost TWA a well-deserved lead over its competition, and probably set commercial air transportation back half a decade.

In its war role "Connie" stayed pretty much in the wings. Lockheed was too busy building combat aircraft, and the Douglas C-54 (the single-tailed cargo version of the DC-4E) took over as the "workhorse" with the Air Transport Command. The first *"Constellation"* (XC-69) was delivered to Wright Field for Air Corps acceptance tests in July 1943. And there was an initial order for 50 of the planes to be modified as long-range troop carriers.

In one version, the C-69B, the plane was to carry a crew of six and 94 fully-equipped troops in benches along the side of the cabin. It wound up as the C-69C, a 43-passenger plushed-up command transport. By V-J Day the Air Corps had taken delivery on only 15 planes, and cancellations resulted in virtual abandonment of the design as a troop transport. The Air Corps got five more in 1946, a total military order of 20 delivered, and most of these were declared surplus.

At one time the Army Air Corps had ordered 260 "Connies" but the order was cut back to 73 in 1945 with victory in sight, and the contract terminated at war's end. The production line was shut down for five days, a time for decision that would effect thousands of Lockheed employees.

Vice President Carl B. Squier described it this way—"During that five-day shutdown, we explored two roads we could take with the *"Constellation"*. (1)—We could develop an even more modern airliner which would mean laying off thousands during the design and tooling. (2)—We could buy back government surplus tooling, parts, materials, and five partly completed C-69s and turn them into luxury liners. We chose the second plan."

At this point Hughes got back into the picture. He bought four of the surplus C-69s, took the *Pygmalion* and made her a new "queen of the skies." He also ordered for TWA a substantial number of new planes, the Model 749, which would become one of the most popular planes with airlines all over the world. She became the "brightest of the winged stars" to make a name for itself along the world's air routes for ten years.

The public actually got a glimpse of *"Connie's"* performance capabilities before the end of the war. First of the modified C-69s, all decked-up in TWA's colors, made a record-breaking flight from Los Angeles to Washington, D.C.

With Howard Hughes as pilot on the first half the journey, and Jack Frye taking over for the last half, the sleek *"Constellation"* made the 2400 mile trip in six hours and 58 minutes. The plane took off in the early morning darkness from Burbank (3:56 AM Pacific Time) and landed at Washington Airport at 1:45 PM, (Eastern Time) on Monday, April 17, 1944. The crew in the cockpit also included Edward T. Bolton, navigator; R. L. Proctor, Flight Engineer and Charles L. Glover, radio man. Back in the cabin were 12 passengers, Lockheed

Howard Hughes (left) and Jack Frye, in sports clothes, disembark after piloting "Constellation" on record-breaking cross-country flight.

and TWA officials.

Although this plane bore TWA markings, its interior was no preview of the luxuries aloft the post-war *"Connies"* would offer. There were a few bunks and some canvass seats, for the flight was no real demonstration as an airliner but rather, a routine delivery flight to turn the plane over to the Army. News stories, however, heralded the flight as a "preview of post-war air travel."

COAST-TO-COAST IN LESS THAN SEVEN HOURS, screamed one banner headline. "Passengers slept in comfortable bunks, four miles above the earth," reported another newspaper. "At times, the plane reached speeds over 325 mph. . .Over the highest mountains she rode sturdily, like a battleship biting its way through heavy seas. At 18,500 feet with outside temperatures at 25 below zero, because of the cabin supercharging and environmental system, passengers were in their shirtsleeves, and moved about in living room comfort."

Editorially, the *New York Times* said the flight was an *"outline of the shape of things to come in air transportation."*

Quoting from the *Congressional Record,*

April 18, 1944, we find: "From a long-range point of view the implication of this flight is for a more closely knit world of tomorrow which is of special interest. The performance graphically illustrates the fact that we must learn to measure tomorrow's world in terms of time rather than space units, and that under this yardstick it will be a small world indeed. The Lockheed Corporation, TWA, and the Wright Aeronautical Corporation, builder of the 2200-horsepower engines, jointly, deserve praise for achieving another milestone on the roads to the sky."

It was not until November, 1945, that TWA accepted delivery of its plushed-up, modified-for-commercial use, first *"Constellation"*. Lockheed delivered nine more before the end of the year. By December, the Civil Aeronautics

Air Corps Chief Henry "Hap" Arnold with Howard Hughes in rare photograph together at Washington National Airport after "Connie's" record flight, 1944. The two men rarely agreed on anything, and tempers often flared up. Arnold was "part politician" which Howard despised. Jack Frye was sometime successful "mediator".

"Constellation" at Wright Field, Dayton, Ohio in 1944 had VIP guest up front in cockpit, Orville Wright, co-inventor of the airplane. Author was standing beside photographer who took this photograph of Orville in right-hand seat. It was the famous inventor's last flight before his death in 1948. He was very excited about the "Constellation" and later remarked, "I wish they'd build more of these and not so many bombers."

Board had granted an approved type certificate, as a public conveyance, after the *"Constellation"* had passed rigid flight performance tests in the record time of 27 flying hours. Shortly after that, the planes went into regular scheduled service, proudly flying the colors of TWA and Pan American. For the air traveler, it was the dawn of a new age of flying.

Back at Burbank, for Lockheed, it was a "bonanza out of the blue." The *"Constellations'"* proven performance records, put the advanced Model 049s far ahead of any competition. The pressurized Douglas DC-6s and the Boeing Model 377 "Stratocruisers" were 18 months behind.

Indeed, a few days after V-J Day, Lockheed's Bob Gross announced with pride that the company had orders for 103 *"Constellations"* ($75,-500,000 worth of business) from eight major airlines.

Hurdles lay ahead for the *"Constellations"*. But they established new standards of luxury postwar air travel and set new records on each airline route they flew. In military and civilian

Western Airlines was also one of first of domestic carriers to put "Constellations" into service. Early 049 models like this one all had small round-port-hole windows. In foreground is famous Douglas DC-3 which larger airliners relegated to lesser roles.

Connie Was A Lady

"Connies" joined The Great Silver Fleet of Eastern Airlines and EAL president Captain "Eddie" Ricken-backer praised them as "most advanced airliner." This Model-649 "Gold Plate" had special "pod" slung under belly, a Lockheed invention that permited increased cargo capacity.

versions they were to bring the company nearly *$1.5 billion* in sales income in the first 12 years of the postwar period.

"OF MEN AND STARS", an official Lockheed Company history tells us—"In the five months that followed introduction of the Model 049 to commercial airline service in February, 1946, the majestic triple-tailed transports set new standards of speed, comfort and safety. They made 300-mph schedules a reality, ocean-to-ocean nonstop flights commonplace. . .By July, 1946, *"Constellations"* had flown nearly 200 million passenger miles without injury of any sort to passenger or crew member, an all-time record for any airplane of any type."

There was "rough air" ahead. On July 11, 1946, one of TWA's *"Constellations"* took off on a training flight from Reading, Pa., and minutes later the baggage compartment and flight deck were filled with smoke. Blinded, the crew couldn't see, and the plane crashed killing five of its six occupants. There had been other reports of engine fires. As a result the CAA temporarily grounded all *"Constellations"* in commercial airline service. People back at Lockheed

felt "the end of the world had come." More than $50,000,000 worth of "Connies" were idled. Something had to be done about it. Modifications included redesigned electrical connectors in the bulkheads, new engine exhaust parts, additional automatic fire extinguisher equipment, and fuel injection systems to replace carburetors.

The "Connies" got back into the air again with a green light from the CAA safety people. The airlines' entire fleet was operating six weeks after the grounding order. Encouraging was a survey of the air traveling public after the Reading accident that said 81 per cent would fly in *"Constellations"* if they were available. Also keeping the faith, airlines which had ordered the 049s never mentioned cancelling.

Last of the Model 049s came off the assembly line in July, 1946, but right behind it was a Model 649 "Gold Plate"—a super luxurious *"Constellation"* which incorporated all the latest 049 modifications and many other new interior features. When the 649s joined "The Great Silver Fleet" of Eastern Air Lines, Eddie Rickebacker called it the "world's most advanced airliner." That claim was short-lived; a

General of the Armies, Douglas MacArthur had plushed-up "Connie"—BATAAN—for his personal aircraft.

better "Connie" was on the way.

The improved version was literally forced into being. About the same time that Eastern took delivery of its "Gold Plate Special", in the spring of 1947, airline surveys indicated a 100 per cent increase in trans-ocean travel, especially between the U.S. and Europe. Everybody wanted long-range aircraft, and with a few new additions "Connie" was just what the doctor ordered.

They didn't change her external dimensions, but they put in more powerful engines now available, beefed up the landing gear, and added outer wing tanks to up the maximum take-off gross weight by about 22 per cent. Designated Model 749, the plane had extended ranges for operation on cross-country and intercontinental routes carrying 65 persons. Capable of speeds up to 350-mph it became the most popular of the *"Constellation"* series of aircraft. Passengers loved the Model 749. So did Lockheed sales people.

Ten airlines, including big foreign carriers like KLM, Air France, Qantas and Air India bought 100 of the 749s almost before the first plane flew. By the end of 1949 the number of the planes delivered to, or ordered by 14 airlines, was 219, and the "Connie" line of transport planes began to pay for itself. In the four-engined category, Lockheed had taken over as the leading commercial aircraft manufacturer, a lead that Douglas once held with the famous DC-3 airliner. But the competition was getting tougher.

With the pressurized Douglas DC-6s and Boeing *"Stratocruisers"* penetrating into the market, sales of the Model 749 began to fall off. At one point Lockheed even considered shutting down the line.

An Air Force order saved the day. The newly created U. S. Air Forces, now a separate arm of the U.S. military establishment (by Act of Congress, 1947) bought ten Model 749s in specialized configurations. The planes (C-121s by USAF designation) joined the Military Air Transport Service to carry "VIPs"—high-ranking military, government and diplomatic officials—on long-range missions, sometimes, so critical during that period when Russia and the U.S. were in a very "hot", cold war. Two of the planes became famous, one as General Douglas MacArthur's personal command ship named *"Bataan"*; the other, General Dwight D. Eisenhower's *"Columbine"* which he used when NATO Commander.

The Navy also got into the act to give "Connie" a long-life expectancy. Two of the 749 *Constellations* were to become the first of many "picket planes" designed to carry early-warning radar to alert the continental defense guardians in case any potential enemy might launch an atomic bomber attack. These modified "Connies" took on grotesque shapes with a large radome underneath the fuselage and a big vertical fin on top housing sensitive electronic detection equipment. The planes called PO-1Ws, later designated WV-1s by the Navy, flew long-range missions at extreme high-altitudes; "eyes in the sky" to spot any enemy aircraft or surface ships.

The Air Force C-121s also proved themselves during the famed Berlin Airlift. When the Russians set up their blockade of Berlin in June, 1948, the Lockheed C-121 *"Constellations"* joined the C-54s to establish the "high-supply road" into the isolated city. During "Operation Vittles"—as the great airlift was popularly called—the C-121s flew some 5.9 million passenger miles shuttling personnel and cargo from Westover Air Force Base, Massachusetts, to Berlin's Rhein-Main Airport.

Admittedly, it was the "emergency" Air Force and Navy orders that kept the *"Constellations"* alive when commercial sales were slim pickens. The unexpected business gave the company enough backlog orders to permit a bold venture into the commercial market with a *"Super Constellation"* series.

Model 1049 emerged as a "stretched version" of the original Army Air Corps C-69 cargo

Connie Was A Lady

First Lockheed "Constellation" adapted as "aerial Paul Revere" was this WV-1 modified to carry special radar equipment in plump "fins" above and below fuselage mid-section. The WV-1 extended warning net hundreds of miles to sea from American shores.

Strangest and farthest looking shape in the sky was U.S. Navy's "flying saucer" EC-121L, a modified "Super Constellation." Looking like a flying saucer riding piggy-back the big radome housed antenna and electronic eyes which could do the early warning task of dozens of ground radar stations.

Model-1049 "Super-G Constellation" was actually stretched version of the original Army C-69 "Old 1961" (Note N6201C license number) and when planes went into service they were biggest airliners in the skies.

L-1011 TriStar and The Lockheed Story

Military Air Transport Service (MATS) Super-G "Constellation." Engines are turbo-compounds. Increased power made possible "long stretch" with same wing.

NAVY went one step further with this R-7V-2 powered with Pratt & Whitney T-34 turbo-prop engines. It and others using same powerplants were fastest "Connies"—over 400-mph!

transport. Paradoxically, it was this first "Connie" plane No. 1961—that became the prototype of the *"Super Constellation"*. Still using the same wing, engineers lengthened the fuselage 18 feet by insertion of two nine-foot sections forward and aft of the wing. "Old 1961" also served as the flying testbed for the more powerful (2700-hp) Wright engines which with the added cabin space permitted a 40 per cent increase in payload. In its original form "Connie" was designed to carry 65 passengers; Model 1049 could carry 99 passengers.

The "Super Connies" had other distinguishing features which proved attractive to airline customers. Square windows replaced the round "portholes" to give a new look. Lockheed developed new integrally-stiffened skin panel techniques that improved structural strength without adding weight. Cabin heating and pressurization was also improved. Pilots also got a new windshield configuration that improved cockpit visibility. A new de-icing system and other added features caught the eye of old customers and new ones.

Model 1049C version of the *"Constellation"* because of more modern sound-proofing techniques was acclaimed as the quietest airliner to date. It also introduced something else that pleased passengers—compartmentization and eye appeal. The long fuselage was broken up with cabin dividers and different color schemes to break the monotony of "riding in a tube." Famed industrial designer Henry Dreyfuss, hired to fashion the 1049C's cabin decor added smart, lively colors, wood paneling, diffused lighting and other touches that offered a new mode for luxury aloft.

With the Model 1049s Lockheed held onto its lead in the commercial airliner field despite the challenge of the new Douglas DC-6B and the roomy Boeing "Stratocruisers" this latter, famous for the spiral staircase leading to a lounge below the main cabin. The "Super Connies" could still fly farther and faster.

Both the Air Force and the Navy also ordered versions of the *"Super Constellation"*. They stood ready, with the outbreak of the Korean conflict, to haul troops and cargo over long stretches of the Pacific. One Navy version, R7V-1 went into production as the first exclusive freighter version of the *"Constellation"*. It also made use of the new Turbo-Compound engine developed by Wright Aeronautical and the Navy. The engine carried exhaust gases out through turbine wheels that recovered and returned the energy to the propellers with a 20 per cent increase in power, permitting tremendous cargo loads on the long runs.

Taking advantage of its experience with the Navy and the new turbo compound engine, Lockheed quickly put the powerplants into a commercial airliner version, Model 1049G (called the "Super-G") and nothing in the air could touch it. She remained undisputed "queen of the skies" until Douglas introduced the DC-7C "Seven Seas" which proved a little faster.

Lockheed also came up with a 1049H ("Husky") which could carry 92 passengers as a luxury liner, but could be easily converted into an all-cargo plane capable of carrying 20 tons of freight. Conversion took about two hours, and "Husky" could carry as much as two freight cars at 350 mph!

These "Connies" got a big sister to challenge

Connie Was A Lady

LAST OF THE LINE in the "Constellation" series was this Model-1649 which featured completely new wing, turbo-compound engines and brought a new kind of luxury "compartmentized" interior to the air traveler. Extreme long-range capability made possible first east-to-west non-stop Atlantic crossings and over the North Pole non-stop routes.

the DC-7Cs, Model 1649 *"Super Super Constellation"*. With a wing span of 150 feet (27 feet more than the original *"Constellations"*) and a completely re-vamped, much thinner airfoil, the Model 1649 brought a new dimension to air transportation.

Improved Turbo-Compound engines gave the 1649A—called the "Starliner" by Lockheed and the "Jetstream" by TWA, first to put the plane into service—more payload, range and performance. One of these sky giants, a TWA "Jetstream", in November, 1957, established a record for non-stop commercial flight. The plane flew 6000 miles over the Polar Route from San Francisco to London in 21 hours, 49 minutes. With a fuel capacity of 9,000 gallons, the "Starliners" permitted carriers flying the Atlantic to offer, for the first time, *east to west* non-stop schedules from any European capital to the U.S. The big planes almost seemed to be the ultimate in propeller-driven airliner design.

But there was to be yet another member of the

"Constellation" family. Fastest of all the "Connies" were the Navy R7V-2s and Air Force C-121Fs, "Super Constellations" powered with four Pratt & Whitney T-34 turboprop engines, gas turbines driving wide, 4-bladed propellers. Producing some 21,000-horsepower, the big engines permitted a gross weight of 75 tons, and pushed "Connie" speeds up over 400-mph!

"Connie was a lady," someone remarked, "who simply had to keep up with the latest styles. Nobody was surprised when she made her debut into the Jet Age as a turbo-prop transport."

Her sleek lines, the shark-like profile of her fuselage, her distinctive triple-tail, and the many advanced features she pioneered, left a high heritage in the annals of commercial aviation.

She had class, grace and beauty. And of all the so-called "Sky Queens" her reign will never be forgotten.

Her marriage with the airlines took the air

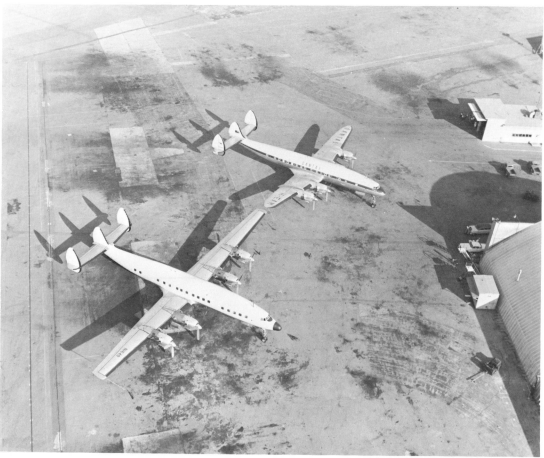

Long-range Model 1649s gave Australia's famous QANTAS airline ideal vehicle for flying great distances across the Pacific. In this photograph one gets a good comparison of the size and new wing configuration between "Super Constellation" and Model 1649.

traveler by the hand and led him pridefully up the stairway to the stars.

It would take a whole new kind of power, jet propulsion, and a whole new generation of jetliners to equal the changes she brought into existence for air transportation.

CHAPTER SEVEN

Another Gal Named Lulu Belle

One hundred years before Christ, Hero, an Egyptian scholar physicist and inventor built the first jet engine. Called the *Aeolipile* (after the Greek God *Aeolus,* ruler of the winds) Hero's invention probably can best be described as a "pressure cooker", the steam rising through pipes into a ball on an axle, with jets of steam shooting out through bent tubes in the ball causing it to spin rapidly.

Ironically, Hero, himself, probably didn't know why it worked. Not until 1687 did Sir Isaac Newton define the principle in his laws of motion—*for every action there is an equal and opposite reaction.* Hero, then, must be credited (perhaps, more accurately) with having invented and built the first *reaction engine.* But the principle of jet propulsion was there all along, as old as the pyramids.

The next breakthrough came in 1791 when an Englishman, John Barber patented a turbine device using the jet principle. The trouble was, Barber's machine took so much energy to turn the turbine wheel, itself, that there wasn't any energy left to do anything else. Later, in 1884 his fellow countryman, Sir Charles Parsons, perfected the first practical steam turbine. Jet propulsion started to move things; steamboats, steam trains and Stanley Steamers.

It was not, however, until 1930 that Dr. Adolph Meyer of the Brown-Boveri Company in Switzerland, developed the first modern gas turbine. He used it for powering motorboats. About the same time, records tell us, that engineers in Britain and in Germany started serious experiments for the development of a gas turbine engine to power aircraft. Whether it was for reasons of military security or because of many failures in early attempts, one will never know, but the experiments in both countries were carried out with great secrecy.

We do know that here in the United States, Dr. Sanford Moss, whom we met earlier (See Chapter Three) ran into great difficulties in the development of the turbo-supercharger (the gas turbine principle) and "many more problems" in his effort to design a propulsion motor for aircraft. General Electric, who had assigned Moss and a group of engineers to the project, kept their work secret, too, because of the slow progress. In Italy, Ing. Secondo Campini was also working on the idea. It was no secret that just about everybody, everywhere, was thinking about the gas turbine as a new means of propulsion for aircraft. Nobody seemed to be getting anywhere.

Surprisingly, the Italians were first to announce publicly they had developed a propellerless aircraft using the jet principle to move the plane through the air. The "principle" in its simplest form is best illustrated, perhaps, by the toy balloon.

Remember, when you were a kid, and blew up the balloon you got on Circus Day? Just for fun, sometimes, when the balloon got BIG, you let go of it, and all the air escaping through the small opening sent the rubber sleeve flying erratically through the air. Maybe you didn't know it, but that's—*jet propulsion!* You build up a lot of pressure inside a chamber (the balloon) and release it through the small opening with the resultant force (jet) pushing the thing forward.

The jet engine operates the same way only it uses a lot of fans, compressors and heat energy to expand the air inside the chamber, and kick it out a tailpipe to produce forward thrust. Campini, who built the jet engine for Italy's pioneer jet aircraft used a large conventional aircraft gasoline piston engine to drive turbine wheels (like wind-mill vanes) that compressed hot exhaust gases, and let them escape through a small opening in the tail. Far from being a pure jet because of the piston-engine used to drive the compressors, it put the age of jet propulsion one step nearer. The Caproni-built airframe they designed around Campini's "powerplant" flew

Elongated nose on ING. Secondo Campini's jetplane housed piston engine driving turbine, compressors, but plane was propellerless.

Campini "jet powerplant" in Caproni-built airframe made many public flights. But Italy's jetplane flew little faster than 200-mph.

successfully, although at very slow speeds, in 1940.

Italy's proud announcement to the world of its "first successful jet-powered aircraft"—if nothing else—spurted development here at home and abroad. There was a lot of "catching up" to be done. Already England, France and Germany were at war.

There were those who said that jet-propelled aircraft, when perfected, would offer speed and other performance potentials which would give air supremacy to the nation that first introduced them into combat. In the last days of World War II, the Germans almost made that prophecy come true.

The author remembers meeting Germany's World War I Ace, famous stunt flyer and one of Hitler's highest-ranking *Luftwaffe* officers, Ernest Udet, at Wright Field in August, 1939, when Udet was a guest at a big Air Show celebrating the 30th Anniversary of the Army Air Corps. (August 2, 1909, was the date the Aviation Section of the Army Signal Corps accepted the first Wright Aeroplane, and heavier-than-air Army aviation was born.) Udet was talking with a group of Wright Field officers after witnessing some high-speed fly-bys of the latest U.S. pursuit planes.

"We've got to have a lot more power to get them to fly much faster," I heard him remark. "What are you doing about jet propulsion motors? That's the future. The propeller is dead."

Was Udet trying to find out if the U. S. were working on a jet-propelled aircraft? Or, was he tipping us off that the Germans were already working on the idea?

Nobody, as I remember, answered Udet's question. And the German ace ventured no further information. But he must have known that the famous German aircraft designer, Dr. Ernest Heinkel was about to fly the first turbojet aircraft. Indeed, much later, captured Nazi documents revealed that the Heinkel (He-178) a small high-wing monoplane, jet-propelled, flew successfully on August 27, 1939—the first true

Lockheed XP-80 "Shooting Star" a product of the Skunk Works shows off her sleek, smooth lines. It became the first U.S. combat jet fighter and remained in production for five full years. Prototypes were flying before end of World War II, but planes didn't see combat until Korean war.

Another Gal Named Lulu Belle

Lockheed engineer Nathan Price, right, shows L-1000 turbo-jet engine to Hall Hibbard. Price was working on engine as far back as 1940.

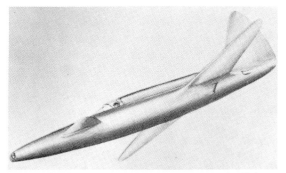

At beginning of World War II this L-133 jet fighter design was offered Air Corps which turned it down. Note forward horizontal stabilizer.

jet-propelled aircraft. The Nazi also had the first jet fighters in combat, tne Me-262s, that raised Hell with our bombers and fighters in the last days of the air war over Germany. One wonders, if our bombers hadn't knocked out the jet plane factories what might have happened.

Fortunately, by that time, there was a U.S. jet fighter in production, designed and built by Lockheed, ready to challenge the Me-262s. The Air Corps called it, the P-80. Lockheed named it—*"The Shooting Star!"*

But, let's go back to the beginning. About the time that the He-178 first flew in Germany (although, admittedly nobody in the U.S. knew about it) Lockheed's men of vision were also thinking about a jet fighter; the next step beyond the P-38. "We all knew that the piston engine had its limitations," Hall Hibbard would recall later. "The problem was to come up with a good jet powerplant."

Early in 1940 Lockheed assigned a young engineer, Nathan Price, to develop a jet engine. Price did just that. Within 24 months he had developed a two spool, high compression jet engine with afterburner, all revolutionary ideas that were ten years ahead of their time.

Called the L-1000 engine, it remained only for the airframe design group to wrap an airplane around it. There emerged a Canard-type design (with the horizontal stabilizer and elevators in front) and built mostly of stainless steel, a revolutionary type structure as well. Designated, Model L-133, Lockheed called it a high-speed interceptor, and Bob Gross took the design data to Wright Field trying to stir up some military orders.

He caused some lifted eye brows in the Fighter Branch of the Engineering Division. But the Production and Procurement people—gearing up for the wartime effort in 1942—gave him the cold shoulder; in fact, a slap on the wrist.

"Forget it," they told him, "and keep the pursuits and bombers coming. Or face stiff penalties."

What they didn't tell him at the time was that Wright Field people were working closely with the British, whose Air Commodore Frank Whittle (later knighted for his achievement) had developed a successful jet powerplant. Secretly, the Whittle engine had powered an RAF *"Gloster"* fighter which flew for the first time on May 15, 1941, and the British thought they had the first successful jet propelled aircraft. Drawings of Sir Frank's engine had been flown to the U.S. and General Electric had been assigned to design, develop and deliver an improved version for a fighter design, XP-59, to be built by Bell Aircraft. The whole project was very top secret, top priority.

Lockheed's L-133 design would have to wait. But not for long would the company be on the outside looking in on the jet business. The Bell XP-59 ("Aircomet") first flew on October 1, 1942, the first U.S.-built jet plane. The Air Corps ordered some YP-59s as service test airplanes, but performance was not much better than the latest P-38s, P-47s and P-51s, piston-engine pursuits. Our Jet effort went *pfft* in its initial stages.

On a visit to Wright Field in June of 1943, Kelly Johnson learned about this. The Fighter Branch people wanted to know if Lockheed would be interested in building an airframe around a new British engine, the DeHavilland *Goblin* which showed a lot of promise. Johnson hopped the next TWA plane back to Burbank.

He talked things over with Bob Gross and Hall Hibbard and met with a lot of enthusiasm. Everybody felt great that Lockheed might get back in the jet picture again. Then, Johnson dropped a bombshell—"Wright Field said they want the thing flying in 180 days." He had

Don Palmer (left) "Kelly" Johnson and Art Viereck, day and night watched over the XP-80 during the 183 days of rapid assembly.

forgotten to mention that at the beginning of the discussion.

"Go ahead, Kelly," Gross told him. "We'll back you."

A week later Johnson was back at Wright Field, bundles of sketches, drawings and specifications under his arm. The Fighter Branch liked his ideas, and kept the wires hot to Washington until they got the approval of General Henry H. Arnold, Chief of the Army Air Corps. "Hap" Arnold liked the "180-day spread."

"I hope the Hell they can do it," he told Brigadier General Frank O. Carroll, Chief of the Wright Field Engineering Division.

Kelly Johnson didn't waste any time. He set up business in a tent-like shelter, away from everybody, near the wind tunnel at Lockheed's Burbank facility, and hand-picked himself a crew of engineers, structures people, mechanics and shop workers. He chose W. P. Ralston and Don Palmer as assistant project engineers, and made Art Viereck supervisor of the shop. They, in turn, picked key personnel to put the thing together. There was a lot of comradeship and pride in the elite group that worked zealously, night and day, to meet the deadline. Their improvised "factory" they called "Kelly's Skunk Works" from the Li'l Abner comic strip. The

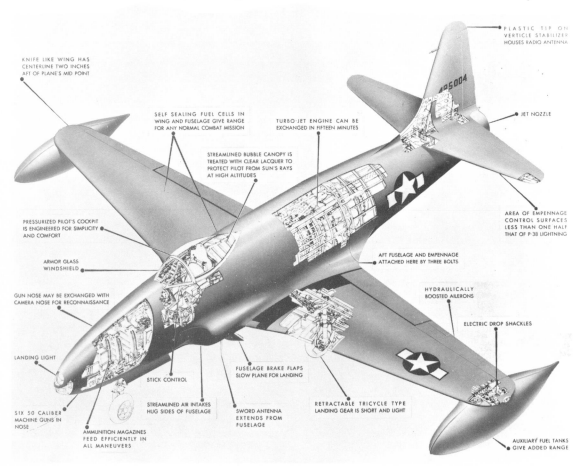

PLASTIC TIP ON VERTICLE STABILIZER HOUSES RADIO ANTENNA

KNIFE LIKE WING HAS CENTERLINE TWO INCHES AFT OF PLANE'S MID POINT

SELF SEALING FUEL CELLS IN WING AND FUSELAGE GIVE RANGE FOR ANY NORMAL COMBAT MISSION

TURBO-JET ENGINE CAN BE EXCHANGED IN FIFTEEN MINUTES

JET NOZZLE

STREAMLINED BUBBLE CANOPY IS TREATED WITH CLEAR LACQUER TO PROTECT PILOT FROM SUN'S RAYS AT HIGH ALTITUDES

AREA OF EMPENNAGE CONTROL SURFACES LESS THAN ONE HALF THAT OF P-38 LIGHTNING

PRESSURIZED PILOT'S COCKPIT IS ENGINEERED FOR SIMPLICITY AND COMFORT

AFT FUSELAGE AND EMPENNAGE ATTACHED HERE BY THREE BOLTS

ARMOR GLASS WINDSHIELD

HYDRAULICALLY BOOSTED AILERONS

GUN NOSE MAY BE EXCHANGED WITH CAMERA NOSE FOR RECONNAISSANCE

ELECTRIC DROP SHACKLES

LANDING LIGHT

FUSELAGE BRAKE FLAPS SLOW PLANE FOR LANDING

STICK CONTROL

SIX 50 CALIBER MACHINE GUNS IN NOSE

STREAMLINED AIR INTAKES HUG SIDES OF FUSELAGE

SWORD ANTENNA EXTENDS FROM FUSELAGE

RETRACTABLE TRICYCLE TYPE LANDING GEAR IS SHORT AND LIGHT

AMMUNITION MAGAZINES FEED EFFICIENTLY IN ALL MANEUVERS

AUXILIARY FUEL TANKS GIVE ADDED RANGE

This cut-a-way drawing shows XP-80s many design features.

plane they were working to build, they called "Lulu Belle" after another Li'l Abner character.

Officially, the "Skunk Works" would become the Advanced Development Projects group (ADP) from which would flow many new designs. The plane, officially called the XP-80, named by Bob Gross, the *"Shooting Star"* and her many successors would fly into immortality. More important, for this story, at least, *"Lulu-Belle"* tied Lockheed to her apron strings and led the company into the Jet Age.

She really wasn't anything too radical in design, just simple and clean; slim and trim, with smooth lines, flush-riveted skin that glistened in the sunlight. She had a wing span of 37 feet and weighed, empty, only 6200 pounds. She could scream like a witch, but she had lady-like manners. The sky was her stage, and she performed like a Barrymore.

As she went together, piece by piece, in her secret shelter, they hauled her at night by truck to the Air Corps' desert test base at Muroc Dry Lake (now Edwards Air Force Base) where she was to try her wings. Remarkably, *"Lulu-Belle"* was ready for that test 143 days after Kelly had turned on the juice in the "Skunk Works."

It was November 15, 1943.

The star was ready but the show didn't go on. During a final run-up, something cracked in the engine housing, and it would be almost two months before another engine arrived from England. Things weren't going too well for the Allies that Fall of '43. There was more concern about happenings in the African desert than out in the Mojave.

On the morning of January 8, 1944, *"Lulu-Belle"* got another chance. Chief engineering test pilot, Milo Burcham, climbed into the cockpit, slammed shut the bubble canopy, and took the XP-80 up for its maiden flight. The flight lasted only a few minutes, when Burcham landed for some minor adjustments. But he was back in the air again shortly, and this time, he put on quite a show.

Observers on the ground described it—"We saw a tiny speck on the horizon. The next ins-

General Electric "centrifugal flow" turbo jet engine which powered XP-80A "Gray Ghost" to many new records.

tant, the speck was a full-scale airplane that swooshed by in a blur, and disappeared."

Kelly Johnson said, excitedly—"A blast of sound surrounded us, and nobody seemed to know where it came from. It was a new sensation!"

Back on the ground Milo Burcham commented—"Boy, what a ride! What an airplane!"

Air Corps officers present liked what they saw, but they wanted just a little bit more. Result: The XP-80A, two feet more wing span, a prototype built around the more powerful General Electric engine. XP-80A came out of the "Skunk Works" in a record-breaking 132 days. Dubbed the *"Gray Ghost"*, she set the sky on fire with a top speed of almost 600-mph, a ceiling of 40,000 feet and a rate of climb of 7,000 feet per minute.

Such performance, virtually, assured U.S. fighter superiority over the German Messerschmitt, Heinkel and other jets making their appearance in Europe's skies. *If we could get them in time?* Lockheed tooled up for mass production of the P-80As, North American Aviation was also geared into the program. They would build the plane in a Kansas City plant. Production goal was *thirty planes a day.*

The P-80s never hit that 30-a-day production mark because the war in Europe and the Pacific ended before things got into high gear. The P-80s (changed to F-80s when the Air Corps dropped the term *pursuit* in favor of *fighter*) never saw combat in World War II. They became, however, the first line aircraft of our postwar expanding all-jet Air Force. For Lockheed they took over where the P-38 left off.

The author remembers back in 1945, walking through the plant one day with Bob Gross and seeing P-38s and P-80s moving along in parallel lines; the old and the new. "You asked me, what about the future?" Bob Gross remarked. "There it is, right before your eyes, the age of jet-propelled aircraft. We're already thinking about jet transports. Ask Hall Hibbard about it."

We'll talk about that a little later, but first, let's take a closer look at the exploits of the *"Shooting Star"* which shattered just about every airplane record in the immediate postwar period. More "piston-pilots" became "jet jockeys" in a modified version (the T-33) than in

Before end of World War II Lockheed had the F80 "Shooting Stars" moving down the assembly line along with its famous P-38 "Lightnings." This was the scene author saw at Burbank in spring of 1945.

Another Gal Named Lulu Belle

With Colonel Albert Boyd, Wright Field Chief of Test pilots at the controls, this P-80 returned World's speed record to U.S. in 1946.

any other type aircraft trainer. And the *"Shooting Star"* was ready for an important role in a "shooting war" when Korea became the hot spot.

Performance-wise the F-80 in peacetime activities made everybody sit up and take notice. Taking off from Long Beach, Wright Field pilot Colonel William H. Councill in January, 1946 landed at LaGuardia Field, 2,470 miles away, 4 hours and 13 minutes later, a new non-stop transcontinental record that would stand for seven years. The next year at the 1947 Cleveland National Air Races, Lt. Col. Bob L. Petit proved the plane's maneuverability, when he made the sharp turns around the pylons of the cramped 22.5 mile closed-course in the Jet Division of the famed Thompson Trophy Race. Petit averaged 500.7-mph to win the event. A hundred thousand people witnessed the new "sound sensation" Kelly Johnson had talked about, as Petit's jet swooshed past the grandstand crowd. That same year, for the first time in almost a quarter of a century the world's airplane speed

record came back to the United States. It was a *"Shooting Star"* that did the job. With Colonel Al Boyd at the controls, the plane averaged 623.8 mph over a measured course at Muroc Dry Lake test base.

Big things were happening in the air and on the ground. On July 26, 1947, the United States Air Force (USAF) became an independent air arm under the Armed Services Unification Act. About the same time President Truman named a five-man Air Policy Committee headed by Thomas K. Finletter, New York attorney, to study the ills of all U.S. aviation, military and civilian, and come up with some recommendations. In gist, the report, released six months later, said the U.S. was allowing itself to become a "second rate" airpower, and it warned of "dangers ahead" from potential enemies that already had or would have their own atomic bomb. The U.S. must *not* for national security let this happen.

The Finletter report urged keeping a healthy aircraft industry, increasing numerically Army

Another Wright Field pilot, Colonel Councill set new coast-to-coast record in this P-80, Long Beach to New York in 4 hours, 13 minutes.

The Lockheed T-33, two-place jet trainer, was developed from the F-80 fighter. These four put on demonstration of close-formation flying over rugged, mountainous terrain.

and Navy air squadrons equipped with the latest advanced technical weapons. Hang the cost; there was no time to lose. Russia wrote the epilogue when we learned she had exploded her first A-bomb!

A wise (or scared Congress) appropriated $2.3 billion for openers in the 1949 budget to build new muscle for America's Air Arm, the Sunday Punch we might need one day. Most of the money would go to build an all-jet Air Force and wings for the Fleet. With the F-80 "Shooting Star" our only operational jet fighter at the time, a lot of eyes were focused on Lockheed to take the lead.

In Burbank they were already one jump ahead. Heads had huddled together; Bob Gross, Kelly Johnson, Hall Hibbard, Carl Squier, Carl Haddon were well pleased with the success of the "Constellations" and the superb "Shooting Stars," their prideful attitude well earned. By the end of 1947 Lockheed was turning out better than 20 per cent of all U.S. airframe industry, military and commercial. Big stuff. "In this business," Bob Gross admonished, "today's laurels are tomorrow's laments. You can't stand still."

The F-80 success had thrust them into the middle of tomorrow. At one of their meetings, Mac Short, vice-president military relations, "a kind of liason officer with the Army and Navy," tossed a new idea into the hopper. His information, Short pointed out, indicated the military was going all-jet, fighters and bombers. To get this jet power off the ground, they needed jet pilots, and to get jet pilots they needed a jet trainer.

"Why don't we take the P-80 and make it into one?" Short proposed.

"What the Hell, Mac," somebody remarked. "It's the best fighter they've got. Why make it a dodo?"

Mac V. F. Short wasn't just "liason-type", he had been vice-president, engineering at Lockheed's Vega plant during the war years, and he kept harping on the idea until he got management approval. The jet trainer was born out of the F-80, and a whole generation of Air Force, Navy and civilian pilots and non-pilots got their jet wings in the *T-Bird*, the popular name given the first jet age trainer.

The famous T-33 "T-Bird" first jet trainer poses for her picture. Remarkably, the two-place trainer performed like single-place fighter. Later it would serve as basic design for Lockheed's first supersonic fighter. Author got first taste of jet flight in "T-Bird" in 1950.

Another Gal Named Lulu Belle

"Shooting Stars" over Korea. It was a P-80 that downed a Russian MIG in history's first jet "dogfight," November 8, 1950.

Lockheed put up $1,000,000 of its own money to go ahead with the modification program. They took an F-80 off the production line, stretched the fuselage some three feet, and put in an extra seat for the student behind the pilot. In March, 1948, Pilot Tony LeVier took the plane up for its maiden flight. Tony couldn't believe it. "It handles better than the F-80," he remarked. "And it's faster!"

The took the *T-Bird* on a tour of military bases. The plane "sold" itself. Generals, veteran piston pilots, enlisted men, newspapermen (including the author) rode in the extra seat, and got their first taste of what jet flying was like. The Air Force, Navy and Marine Corps placed orders. Designated T-33s (Air Force) and TV-2s (Navy/Marine) versions, the versatile *T-Bird* hitched the world to a "shooting star." It has been said probably no other plane played such an important role in helping to build the Free World's air defenses.

It taught pilots to fly jets. It was used as a winged platform for air-to-air and air-to-ground gunnery practice—a new art which, with their

high-speeds, jet-propelled aircraft introduced. It was a "flying classroom" for Jet Age aerial navigation and night flying techniques. Pilots from 26 different nations received their first jet instruction in *T-Birds*. Under license arrangement the planes were built in Canada and in Japan. Lockheed, alone, received orders for more than 5800. As this is written, 1972, many are still performing their original task.

The Captain of our TWA Lockheed L-1011 *"Tri-Star"* enroute non-stop Chicago-San Francisco confided—"I learned to fly in the *T-Bird*. It gave birth to a new breed of four-stripers."

The F80 *"Shooting Star"* as a front line fighter, vastly improved over the original *"Lulu-Belle"* would play another important role. On November 8, 1950 in Korean skies, an F-80 piloted by Lieutenant Russell Brown of Pasadena, California, shot down a Russian MIG. It was history's first all-jet air battle.

During the Korean conflict F-80s flew 40 per cent of all U.S. combat missions. In the initial seven months of the war, they flew 26,000 sorties and held the line until newer, faster F-86s took

93

Navy version of "T-Bird" was called T2V-1 "SeaStar" which introduced "boundary layer control" wing. Last of basic P-80s to go into production.

over. They flew high altitude recon missions. They flew low-level strafing missions against ground troops and equipment.

The F-80s, more specifically the *T-Birds*, back home in their factory nest were making another significant contribution, while their paternal F-80s were fighting over Korea. There, the weather was so stinko, that the Air Force saw the need for an all-weather fighter. Lockheed entered the competition with a modified F-80 design (see Chapter Nine) and a whole new family of jet fighters was started.

Another *"Shooting Star"* that came into being during the Korean War was a Navy jet trainer, the T2V-1 *"SeaStar"*. The design with a roomier cockpit, emerged as a modified T-33 using the new "boundary layer control"

system—forced air over the wing to increase lift and improve control—which gave it a slow landing speed, excellent stability, ideal for a carrier-based trainer. The first plane flew in December 1953.

The Navy already had placed a sizeable order. The *"SeaStar"* still in use, designated T-1A Jet Trainer, was the last of the basic configuration P-80 to go into production.

Pioneering the "boundary layer" principle, the *"SeaStar"* marked another milestone for Lockheed and the Navy as partners in progress. It is pertinent we digress a moment and tell more of that relationship.

As we shall see, the Navy "helped lay the keel" for today's fabulous *TriStar*.

CHAPTER EIGHT

Wings For The Blue And Gold

About the time that Allan Loughead, age 20, made his first solo flight after teaching himself to fly, aviation pioneer Glenn Curtiss, wrote a letter to the Secretary of the Navy offering to train a naval officer to be a pilot. There would be no fee, Curtiss said. But he thought that the aeroplane, especially a seaplane, could be of use to the Navy as "eyes for the Fleet" and that Navy interest would help stimulate public interest in aviation. The whole idea should be beneficial to both parties.

The Secretary never did answer the letter. But about Christmas time, 1910, a young Navy lieutenant turned up at Glenn Curtiss' base in San Diego, California, with orders to learn to fly. His name was Theodore ("Ted") G. Ellyson, and he became Naval Aviator No. 1, first entitled to wear the wings of gold.

It was a strange anachronism: The Navy had a trained pilot before it had an aircraft for him to fly. It also already had an aircraft carrier. The *U.S.S. Birmingham*, a cruiser, had been fitted with a flight deck, and civilian pilot, Eugene Ely on November 14, 1910, had demonstrated successfully how an airplane could take-off from a ship at sea. Then, two months later, with "Ted" Ellyson watching, Ely landed on the specially constructed flight deck aboard the cruiser, *U.S.S. Pennsylvania* in San Francisco

Bay, and took off again an hour later.

From that day forward, Naval Aviation was here to stay.

Lockheed and the Navy got together for the first time in 1918 when Allan Lockheed was making flights with the triple-tailed F-1 seaplane, the second plane the Lockheed Brothers built. As we have pointed out (Chapter One) Navy officers from the San Diego Naval Base were greatly impressed, and the F-1 was subjected to rigid tests at the North Island Navy Air Station. The plane didn't make it, but the Navy did contract with Lockheed as an alternate source to build Curtiss flying boats as part of its World War I expansion program. With the signing of the Armistice, the contract was cancelled. Significantly, however, Lockheed and the Navy had struck up a friendship that would last a lifetime.

It was like the boy and girl who lived a couple of houses from each other, but neither knew the other was around until they met at college. Admiral Jack Towers once remarked—"They were like the sailor and the spinster; they lived in different worlds between wars."

Then it happened. With the outbreak of World War II in Europe, one day the sailor "winked" at the girl next door. They started to date, had a whirlwind wartime courtship, and

Curtiss Model HS21 built by the Loughead Aircraft Manufacturing Company. Contract for 50 planes was cancelled when World War One ended. It marked, however, company's first contact with Navy.

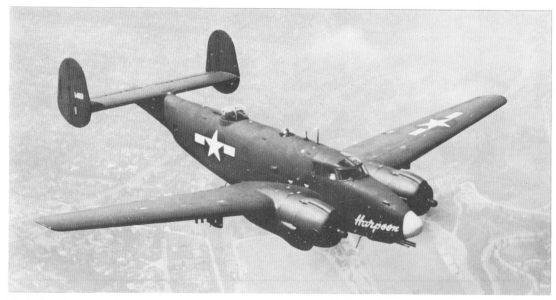

Built by Vega Airplane Company Navy PV-2 called the "Harpoon" flew in Aleutian campaign. Plane came out of basic "Ventura" design.

wound up at the altar, a marriage that has produced many outstanding offspring that proudly wear the Navy insignia.

It all began, really, with the PV-1 and PV-2, Navy versions of the *"Ventura"* bomber, itself a descendant of the Model 14 *"Electra"* and the *"Lodestar"* modified for a variety of military missions. Although the company had received some small orders from the Navy for the basic *"Electra"* models for use as personnel transports and reconnaissance, orders for the PV-1s and PV-2s would total more than 3,000 before they reached the end of the line. For the first time, Lockheed and the Navy were doing "big business" together. In war and peacetime, it would be a fruitful partnership. The name *"Ventura"*—translated to mean "Lucky Star" indeed, spelled good fortune for Lockheed, the Navy, and the Allied war effort.

Originally, the *"Ventura"* was built for the RAF in Lockheed's new Vega subsidary plant. The first plane flew in July, 1940. As rapidly as the planes came off the assembly line they were shipped and flown overseas, and the British put them to work as low-level bombers. They followed the *"Hudsons"* to carry the "offensive" to Axis Europe. The Army Air Corps was so impressed, it ordered 200, designated as B-34 bombers. The U.S. had not yet entered the war as a "shooting" ally.

But the war was coming much closer to our shores with Nazi U-boats raising hell with shipping off the Atlantic coast. The Navy got the job

to put a stop to it. Based on the success of the RAF *"Hudsons"* and *"Venturas"* faced with the same mission off Britain, Navy strategists, for the first time decided to turn to land-based patrol bombers. They looked to Lockheed to come up with something a little better than the *"Ventura"*. Although, outwardly similar, there came into being the PV-1, capable of carrying more bombs and especially more electronic equipment for sub detection.

By 1943, the PV-1s were in action and playing a major role in minimizing the sub menace. Tailored to Navy specifications, the PV-1s could carry depth charges, rockets and torpedoes. They had a 2,000-mile range, speeds of more than 300 mph. With its land-based PV-1s, the Navy had its own air war going. The plane flew combat missions of all types from the Kuriles in the Arctic Circle to the Marianas and the Philippines.

When the Marines landed to secure airstrips, so did the PV-1s. They fought Jap Zeros and knocked them out of the sky. They bombed and strafed and torpedoed Jap shipping and land bases. And they did it so effectively even the Air Corps fliers got jealous. In the early days of the Pacific War they were among the best bombers we had.

The Navy was so pleased, that it barely had taken delivery on the first PV-1 when it told Lockheed (in early 1942) to see if it couldn't "stretch" the basic design once more to get better performance. Result was the PV-2 with a greater wing span, more crew capacity, more payload, and a redesigned tail to give it more stability. After its first flight, late in 1943, the PV-2 went into production immediately, the Navy was so satisfied with its performance. The planes first saw action in the Aleutians where they helped drive the Japs from that Island chain. The Navy dubbed the PV-2 *"Harpoon"*. There were 535 built, and production went on even after the end of the war.

When the line finally was shut down, it marked the end of the famous Model-14 *"Super Electra"* basic design which had appeared in so many versions and in so many roles (commercial and military) with nations all over the world. Both Lockheed and the Navy had other ideas. They were already building a new postwar design, the P2V called *"Neptune"*—after the mythical Sea God. The wings of *"Neptune"* would be responsible for a whole new family of Navy aircraft which Lockheed would build. In turn, the Navy would use the planes in progressive development of new techniques for submarine detection and destruction.

These "sub-hunters" and "sub-killers" would bring into being a whole new Navy concept with regard to a prime Naval mission—anti submarine warfare. In World War I, for example, the destroyer-type surface vessel, fast and maneuverable with its depth charges was con-sidered the greatest defender against submarines. The picture changed in World War II with carrier-based and land-based, short-range Navy patrol bombers relegating the "Tin Cans" (slang for Destroyers) to a major role as escorts for convoys. Then, in the immediate postwar period, the advent of the long-range, land-based, Navy planes, especially designed to carry sophisticated electronic submarine detection devices, their own defensive and destructive weapons (ASW) suddenly came to mean "airborne submarine warfare." Lockheed's P2V *"Neptune"* probably had history's most significant effect in changing the roles of airpower and seapower.

Here's what happened:

The first work order on the P2V was issued December 6, 1941, the day *before* Pearl Harbor. Getting the job done was slow because the pressure was on to build more and more *"Hudsons"*, *"Venturas"* and *"Harpoons"* and as a result, the first *"Neptune"* (XP2V-1) didn't make its maiden flight until May 17, 1945, ten days after Germany surrendered. Japan was out of the war about three months later.

It was a time when the Army and Navy cut-back drastically on all aircraft contracts. The airframe industry, in particular, with billions of dollars in backlog orders had its wings clipped. Lockheed, fortunately, was better off than most

Navy's P2V "Neptune" was first in a series of long-range patrol planes. Above, 3rd production model "The Turtle" set world record.

companies in the field. It had the F-80s, the *"Constellations"* and the Navy P2Vs to keep postwar production lines moving. The Navy business was a welcome cushion.

But even the Navy, as was the case with all the military services, had trouble "selling" Congress on appropriations to keep its Air Arm equipped with the latest planes and auxiliary weapons and advancing electronics. Admirals, wisely admonished, that the *"Neptune"* was needed in this trying period more than ever, pointing to the increasing number of Russian submarines appearing in the Atlantic. Nobody was sure of the Soviet stand. Nobody wanted another "Pearl Harbor" in Brooklyn.

The P2V *"Neptune"* was good insurance. It was "loaded" with electronic gear to facilitate submarine search and detection. It had improved radar to find surfaced submarines and could localize submerged subs by using sonobuoys dropped from the air. P2V crews could even detect enemy radar and get a "fix" on a submarine. The *"Neptune"* also had LORAN, the newest long-range navigational system.

On a spectacular flight (September 29, 1946) with a crew of four and a pet kangaroo aboard, plus 8,467 gallons of gasoline, a P2V called *"The Truculent Turtle"* flew non-stop 11,236 miles from Perth, Australia, to Columbus, Ohio. The Navy had a long arm for its ASW role. It is still there guarding the face of America.

The *"Neptune"* enjoyed 20 years of continuous production, through seven different model configurations, a total of 1,051 aircraft built. These planes also became the first international subhunters, flying in the maritime patrol forces of The Netherlands, Canada, England, Australia, Brazil, Japan, Argentina and France.

The Navy/Lockheed marriage was for keeps. The "couple" had money in the bank, and in lean times it helped Lockheed go ahead with other projects which, otherwise, might not have been possible. Navy orders for modified *"Connies"* and *"Super Connies"* (WV2-Es) radar picket planes, we know, helped write the final chapters of The Constellation Story, and keep the basic design in production into the midfifties.

NATS, the wartime Naval Air Transport Service, aerial lifeline of the Pacific Fleet, was a springboard for an experiment in SIZE which gave Lockheed a head start in the BIG PLANE business that would greatly influence the company's decisions in a field which it dominates

Navy's P2V-4 first production aircraft to use turbo-compound engines. Belly "bubble" houses latest electronic hardware.

Polar Bear Version of P2V was fitted with 16-foot aluminum skis as well as wheels to operate in strategic Arctic and Antarctic areas.

Fitted with JATO (jet assist take-off) rockets P2V demonstrates versatility taking off from flight deck of "U.S.S. Coral Sea."

Crew of Lockheed P2V "Truculent Turtle" which flew non-stop from Perth, Australia to Columbus, Ohio. Left to right are: Commanders Eugene Rankin, Walter Reid and Thomas Davies, and Lt. Commander Roy Tabeling. Aircraft commander Davies is now Rear Admiral.

Up-dated version of the "Neptune" the P-2H had two pod-mounted jet engines under wing to give extra power for high-speed attacks or short-runway operation. Stinger tail houses sub search gear.

Double-decked "Constitution" was one of two prototypes built for Navy. Basic design was considered for airliner. It never materialized.

with the C5A *"Galaxy"*, the world's largest airplane in the 1970s. As a follow-up of its *"Super Constellation"* line, Lockheed, just before World War II, was considering a king-sized airliner that would dwarf even the biggest of the *"Constellations."* The idea was that the plane, which Lockheed called its Model 89, would replace the Pan Am flying boats on the long Pacific routes. Pan American and Lockheed had had long discussions, and there was real interest building when the U.S. got into the war.

The ban imposed by the military on any

Fitted as personnel transport, "Constitution's" upper deck seated 92. Staircase in center, pre-staged famous "spiral stairs" of 747 by more than a quarter of a century.

civilian commercial transport development, naturally, slowed Pan Am enthusiasm. But there was nothing that said the Navy couldn't go ahead. The Navy did, ordering two prototypes and development began as far back as 1942 on the Model 89 called the *"Constitution"*, appropriately named by Bob Gross after "Old Ironsides", the frigate *U.S.S. "Constitution"* which won glory in the War of 1812. For the first time Lockheed had departed from its usual practice of naming its planes after the heavenly bodies. Was the winged star dying out?

Biggest transport type of its day, "Constitution" could carry 180 personnel, including its own flight crew of twelve men.

Wings For The Blue And Gold

Both ship and plane had one thing in common: The frigate *"Constitution"*, launched in 1797 at Boston, was the largest ship in the embryonic U. S. Navy. Lockheed's *"Constitution"* was the largest transport plane of its day. It had a wing span of 189 feet only 15 feet shorter than the length of the frigate. Interestingly, Uncle Sam's "Man-O-War" of 1797 had a top speed of about 15 miles per hour. The winged *"Constitution"* could hit 300-mph. She was 20 times as fast, and still weighed 92 tons, about 1/20th of the tonnage of the frigate!

The ship had two decks. So did the winged *"Constitution"*. Its fuselage in cross-section was shaped like a "figure 8", and it was pressurized for flight at 25,000 feet. The frigate had "sailpower" (43,000 square feet of canvass) and the plane had four 3,500-horsepower engines, later augmented by six JATO (jet assist take-off) rockets. The original *"Constitution"* was built as a warship and carried a 400-man fighting crew. The plane was built as a troop transport and cargo carrier. It carried a crew of 12 and 180 passengers—92 on the top deck, 75 on the lower deck. A stairway connected the upper and lower

sections. "Old Ironsides" got her name because she had wide strips of metal, protective armor, wrapped around her wooden hull. The plane was all-metal, but it had extra strength metal flooring to be able to take heavy equipment as cargo hauler.

When the Navy took delivery of its two Lockheed *"Constitutions"*, it gave them the official designation (R6Vs) and they were immediately put to use flying priority personnel and cargo. They flew some missions during the Korean War. But a payload of only 35 tons for a 92-ton aircraft didn't balance out well economically; the big plane simply was far ahead of its time and the powerplants available when it was laid down. Turboprop engines and jet power had not yet materialized to any practical degree.

The Navy got its money's worth, probably, because the two planes were flown all around the country at air shows and for special occasions. They became major attractions where ever they appeared. The author first saw one of the *"Constitutions"* on the ground at the Cleveland Air Races. He remembers hearing an awestruck

Navy flew "Constitution" around country on tour and wherever the sky giant appeared it attracted long lines of visitors. Here at one Air Show the giant up-stages her sister P-80 "Shooting Star".

Vertical riser, the Navy-Lockheed XFV-1, was pioneer experiment in vertical take-off feature. Engine "bugs" cancelled project.

spectator remark—"My God, can that thing fly? They'll never build anything any bigger and get it off the ground."

That afternoon, the big plane took off in a cloud of smoke from its JATO rockets right behind a DC-3 airliner, and it didn't use much more runway. And a few weeks later down at Forth Worth, Texas, we looked (a little awestruck, too) at the giant Consolidated C-99, the Air Force cargo version of its six-engined B-36 bomber, capable of carrying 400 fully-equipped combat troops. It was almost twice the size and weight of the *"Constitution"*. The day of the sky giants had arrived.

Lockheed got its money's worth out of the *"Constitution"* experiment, too. It learned a lot about big plane structures, design problems and new fabrication techniques. All of this was like "know-how" in the bank, when the company in 1962, twenty years after the Model 89 was started, accepted the challenge to design an entry for the Air Forces' C-5 competition. The spin-off would also help when the *"TriStar"* (L-1011) began, a shimmering glimmer on the future horizon. The present can't escape from the past. No way!

The Navy/Lockheed "team" were also pioneers in another field of flight—vertical take-

off aircraft. Result was the Navy XFV-1 fighter, vintage 1954, the plane "that stood on its tail." According to a press release—"the plane (XFV-1) gave man his first vehicle capable of high-speed, straight-up flight. It was designed to rise vertically, level off for swift, horizontal flight and land on its tail wheels, hanging suspended by contrarotating propellers geared to a single powerful turbo-prop engine. For flight tests the airplane was equipped with conventional landing gear. A "one-of-kind" experiment, the XFV-1 could hover motionless in the air like a hummingbird. The research program was concluded in 1955 after providing much valuable data for military consideration on VTOL (vertical takeoff and landing) aircraft.

The press release did not say the plane never did take-off straight-up from a standing start. Engine difficulties and lack of power hampered the fulfillment of this goal.

More important, the idea has never died, and VTOL aircraft are sure to play an important role in the company's future.

About the same time that it was working with the Navy in the development of the XFV-1, Lockheed was going ahead on its own with a four-engined turbo-prop airliner, the second generation *"Electra"*. (See Chapter Eleven) When the Navy heard about it, evaluation tests were conducted with the turbo-prop *"Electra"* as a potential successor to famous *"Neptune"* series of ASW aircraft.

The need was there. Submarines had become faster, quieter and able to submerge for longer periods. With the development of the snorkeling

First P-3C "Orion" advanced antisubmarine patrol aircraft takes off on its maiden flight. The P-3Cs joined the Navy's ASW patrol forces in 1969 flying from bases around the world.

sub and, later, the nuclear submarine, the Navy saw the need for an aircraft that could go out farther, faster, and stay on ocean patrol for longer periods of time. Out of the basic *"Electra"* design came the Navy P-3 *"Orion"*.

As did the second generation turbo-prop *"Electra"* perpetuate the name of the Model 10 *"Electra"*, first of the company's twin-engined airliners; the name *"Orion"* kept alive the memory of the single-engined, low-winged *"Orion"* last of the wooden planes Lockheed built in the thirties. Today, 40 years later, the Navy's *"Orion"* ASW aircraft are among the brightest stars, stellar sentinentals in the sky.

The YP3V-1 *"Orion"* prototype first flew in November, 1959. The first production model, later designated P-3A, flew in April, two years later and deliveries to the Navy commenced in August, 1962. By mid-1968, Lockheed had delivered 250 of the planes to the Navy. In addition, *"Orions"* had been delivered to New Zealand and Australia, and were being produced for Norway. More than half of the world's ocean area was under the planes' surveillance.

Latest model, the P-3C, which joined the Fleet in 1969, represents, virtually, the ultimate in anti-submarine warfare technique. It has speed in excess of 400-knots, but it can also "loiter" over a search area at slow speed of less than 180 knots. It can remain aloft 24 hours and more, flying to search areas 1500 miles from its base, patrolling there, and returning home.

Carrying a crew of ten in comfortable environmental quarters, including airborne galleys, radar stoves, and other necessities for the long duty tours above the earth, the *"Orion"* is filled with more than 300 pieces of avionics equipment. Its "black boxes" make it possible to *see, sense,* and *hear* any submarine, anywhere. And its weapons system can sink the sub if the need is there.

As one Admiral puts it: "The potential threat proposed by the ever increasing number of Soviet submarines, necessitates our ASW capabilities must keep pace if we as a nation are to maintain the freedom to use the seas in our national interest. Aircraft like the *"Orion"* both land and sea based, are now and will continue to be vital to our ASW posture."

Cut-a-way of P-3C "Orion" shows plane's sophisticated electronic navigation systems, crews' quarters, and environment in which personnel live for hours on end during long-range patrol missions. "Boxes" represent latest electronic sensors and ASW weapons systems.

Adapted from the second generation "Electra" the P-3C "Orion" kept production line going at Burbank into early 70s. Planes were also sold to Royal Australian Air Force, Royal New Zealand Air Force and Royal Norweigian Air Force.

The Lockheed *"Orion"* series, it has been said, is expected to be the mainstay of the ASW program for the Navy during the next decade.

Designing and building "wings for the blue and gold", it can also be said, has been a mainstay of Lockheed airframe production for more than a quarter of a century. The dollar-value in Navy contracts, alone, would run into the billions.

In terms of lessons learned and "experience" in the design, development, fabrication and production of aircraft of many and varied types and structures probably can never be determined. The answer lies too far into the future.

It could show up one day, perhaps, sooner than we think, in a nuclear-powered ASW *"Orion"* which could stay aloft for days at a time, patrolling the seven seas on a single mission.

CHAPTER NINE

New "Stars" On The Horizon

There never was before, and there probably never will be again such an industrial revolution as that which the U. S. aircraft industry experienced during its World War II expansion period. At peak production in mid 1944 the airframe manufacturers, alone, employed more than *two million* workers, and occupied more than 175,000,000 square feet of factory space. That same year they produced a record 96,000 planes of all types. Altogether from 1940 through 1945 a total of 303,000 aircraft came off the assembly lines. Pearl Harbor to VJ-Day, working 24 hours a day, it figures out to be *one plane every five minutes!*

"We won the Air War," one general remarked, "because every time the enemy knocked *one* of our planes out of the sky we put *five* up there to take its place."

Lockheed did more than its share to make that ratio possible. Bob Gross put it this way: "Before the war we were producing planes by the dozens. During the war we produced them by the thousands."

Nobody, of course, expected to keep on turning out planes at the rate of about 12 an hour, and the entire aircraft industry at war's end faced cutbacks, slow-downs and shut-downs. Lockheed Aircraft Corporation (the Vega Aircraft Corporation had been absorbed into its fold in 1943) was better off than most of the other major airframe manufacturers. By the end of 1945, Gross could report to his stockholders, despite huge military cancellations, that the company still had $213-million backlog in commercial and military orders, and more than $32,-000,000 in working capital.

There were *"Constellations"*, *"Shooting Stars"*, *"T-Birds"*, and *"Neptunes"* moving along the production lines. And there were good prospects of more orders for each of these aircraft and/or improved versions in the offing. More important, there were "new stars" on the horizon.

One of these newcomers evolved as the *"Saturn"*, a twin-engine, high-wing monoplane, Lockheed's answer to the Douglas DC-3 in a bid to get into the "short-haul" airliner market. Before we tell what happened to *Saturn* let us digress a moment to take a look at the role of the scheduled airlines during the war.

Lockheed's post-war bid for small feeder-line commercial airliner was this high-wing "Saturn" which brochure described as 'a flying interurban." Wing planform was similar to original Model-10 "Electra." So was fuselage except for huge dorsal fin and single rudder. "Saturn" lost out to bigger "Convairs" and "Martins."

L-1011 TriStar and The Lockheed Story

Early in 1943, President Roosevelt signed an order which empowered the military establishment to take over the entire U. S. air transportation system, just as the government had done with the railroads in the first World War. Fortunately the airlines, through the efforts of their trade organization, the Air Transport Association Of America (organized in 1936) headed by Colonel Edgar S. Gorrell, got the order rescinded before it ever left FDR's desk. Meeting with Roosevelt and Air Corps Chief General Henry H. Arnold, Gorrell, "the Little Colonel" presented the airlines' own mobilization plan. In essence, Gorrell convinced the President and Arnold that the airlines could do better if they *volunteered* instead of being *drafted*. History was on Gorrell's side: Government ownership and operation of the railroads in World War I had stultifying results, causing confusion and chaos. Aware of this near catastrophe, FDR tore up his order commandeering the air transport industry, but with a strong warning—*the airlines had better make their plan work*.

The plan called for the airlines to put all their skills, services and equipment at the disposal of the military, Army, Navy and Marines, but the airlines could *run* things themselves. The result: Top airline executives went on leave, donned rank and uniform of military top brass to head the Air Transport Command and the Naval Air Transport Service. Veteran airline captains and flight crews pioneered new air routes across the oceans, over steaming jungles and sand-swept deserts, the highest mountains and ice-covered Arctic wastes to the four far corners of the earth. The same flight personnel helped set up flight training centers and served as instructors for Army and Navy pilots, while airline ground personnel, mechanics and other operations people helped train crew chiefs and "grease monkeys"

for the growing elements of airpower. In addition, the airlines sold or leased to the government more than half of their fleet of 359 planes—Douglas DC-2s, DC-3s, Boeing 247s and Lockheed *"Electras"* and *"Lodestars"*. Silver wings turned olive drab. All the while, with skeleton personnel, the air transport industry kept its planes flying, overworked and overloaded, along the nation's pre-war airline routes and many new ones, linking together U.S. cities.

For the job they did, airline personnel in uniform and in mufti at far flung bases around the world and on the home front received some of the highest military and civilian decorations. When it was all over, the entire scheduled air transport industry of the U. S. earned a hearty "well done" even from the White House.

Colonel Gorrell had proven his point: A healthy, privately-owned, geared-for-growth Air Transport Industry could adapt itself to wartime emergency conditions and govern its own operations.

If the airlines helped win the war (and they did) it must also be said that the tremendous aeronautical technological advancements and innovations born of war helped the airlines grow stronger. New airports and ground facilities sprang up overnight. Bigger transport planes, better engines, new operational techniques, new electronic navigational aids and automatic flight systems came into being, all of which could benefit air transportation in the post-war period. Not to mention, of course, the coming of the Jet Age for military aircraft which would spin off into civilian airliners in the years just ahead. Then, too, during the war, traveling under a priorities system and a priority need, more and more people, who never before had ridden in an airplane, turned to air travel. The war-born

End of World War II saw DC-3s still making up bulk of airlines' fleets. This "Super DC-3" was Douglas' answer to the "Saturn." Newer post-war design took over and Douglas closed down the line.

Going in another direction Douglas introduced its own high-wing feeder-line transport, the DC-5 twin. Like "Saturn" plane never went into production.

New "Stars" On The Horizon

over-ocean routes with landplanes opened up vast new vistas for post war air travel.

The war, indeed, put air transportation in a show-case. Air transport proved it could fly almost anything, anywhere, anytime, in all kinds of weather, on time, and with a high degree of safety. The day of the airliner and the "air freighter" had arrived; it would challenge all other forms of transportation.

Everybody wanted in on the act. Republic Aviation, builder of the P-47 *"Thunderbolt"* fighters was building a four-engined passenger airliner, *"The Rainbow"*. Consolidated Aircraft Corporation of San Diego, builder of the B-24 four-engined *"Liberator"* bombers was offering the twin-engined *"Convair"* airliner; the Glenn Martin Company, builder of the B-26 *"Marauder"* bombers, also had a twin-engined airliner (the "202") to challenge the market. Boeing Airplane Company of *"Flying Fortress"* fame wanted in, with its Model 377 *"Stratocruiser"*, an airliner version of the military KC-97 "flying tanker." Douglas was coming out with a *"Super DC-3"* and the four-engined, pressurized DC-6 to challenge the *"Constellations."* Other companies had airliner designs on-paper or in the mock-up stages. The big plane builders were desperate to get into the commercial sales columns. The race was on.

In the four-engine class, Lockheed was way out in front with the *"Constellation."* But it didn't have an entry in the twin-engined category until the *"Saturn"* came along.

Back in late 1944, with the war going pretty much in favor of an Allied victory, Vice President Carl Squier with Leon K. Schwartz, a key marketing analyst, conducted a nation-wide survey, talking to hundreds of people from all walks of life, about the future of air travel. Was there fear of flying? Who would fly? Who wouldn't? What kind of air service was needed for what kind of jobs? Was there a real boom coming in air travel? They asked such questions as these. And they got some interesting answers.

The businessman in Kankakee, Illinois, would take the plane and ship by air if there were air service to Kokomo. The school teacher in Madison, Wisconsin, would fly in a *"Constellation"* from Chicago to California for her vacation. But she'd like also to take a plane from Madison to Chicago. Concensus of the survey was that a lot of people from "Main Street, U.S.A." would use air transport if air service was available in the smaller cities and towns. There was, indeed, a need for a small feeder-line airliner. The market hadn't even been tapped yet.

"Saturn" was designed to fill the slot. "DESIGNED TO DO THE BIG BUSINESS FOR THE LITTLE AIRLINE AND THE LITTLE BUSINESS FOR THE BIG AIRLINE," said one of the sales brochures. Another pitched—"BRING AIR TRAVEL TO MAIN STREET. .AND TO THE WORLD'S BYWAYS."

There was good response from the smaller feeder lines. The price was right, $85,000 per unit. And *"Saturn"* for that dollar sign was a lot of airliner: wing span, 74 feet. Fuselage length, 51 feet, 6 inches. Capable of carrying 16 passengers. Able to land and take off from short fields without paved runways. Fast,

Republic "Seabee" (left) And North American's "Navion" two post-war private planes that were competition for Lockheed entry in this field.

107

"Airtrooper" John Thorp's single-place midget plane originally built for Army to give individual infantryman his own wings.

capable of 225-mph cruising speeds; economical for ranges from 60 miles to 600 miles.

Potential sales looked like 500 or more, but there were no firm orders. Lockheed went ahead, anyway, and built two prototypes. Neither ever linked Kankakee with Kokomo or Madison with Milwaukee.

Unfortunately, when the war ended there were labor troubles, a shortage of materials, rising costs of everything. *"Saturn's"* price tag went up—$100,000. The first plane flew in June, 1946, but its performance was far below expectations. It had grown too heavy. It needed more powerful engines. The second prototype flew a year later with the bigger engines and other refinements. Something else happened.

The bottom fell out of the sky. Airports that were supposed to be, never developed in many of the smaller cities. The smaller airlines, with limited capital to begin with, turned to the War Assets Administration, where war surplus transport planes, easily converted to airliners could be purchased by the highest bidder. One could, for instance, buy a surplus Lockheed 16-passenger *"Lodestar"* for one-third the price of the new Lockheed twin-engine *"Saturn"* design.

The two *"Saturn"* prototypes were scrapped. To be turned into pots and pans, who knows?

Management took another look at the post-war civil aviation picture. What about the private plane market? The war had produced tens of thousands of pilots who might want their own plane. There was talk of a plane in every garage; of the skyways jammed with "family flivvers"! The *"Mustang"* people, North American Aviation, builders of the famous P-51 fighter, the plane that challenged the P-38, were building a small single-engined plane, the *"Navion."* The *"Thunderbolt"* people, Republic Aviation, builders of the P-47 fighters, were coming out with an amphibian, *"The Seabee",*

for the private flyer.

Why shouldn't Lockheed take a crack at it? Remember, the S-1, the little sportsplane that the Loughead Aircraft Corporation had designed and built right after World War I? Maybe, now, twenty-five years later, the time was ripe.

John Thorp, a young engineer in Mac Short's Special Projects Group, just before the war ended, was working on a small plane design, a single-seater, that caught the eye of Army visitors to the plant, who envisioned a "flying cavalry." The idea was that every trooper would have his own Pegasus and they could "attack like a swarm of locusts." Nothing ever came of the "aerial horse army," but Lockheed did build a prototype of the little plane. The Army called it the "Airtrooper". Only one was built. The military contract was cancelled with war's end.

As small things do, the little plane fascinated just about everybody, especially with its performance. It could be airborne in 100 feet, climb at a rate of 800 feet a minute, putt-putt along at 40-mph, cruise at 90-mph, hit 100 top speed, and land on a 75-foot strip. A two-cylinder, air-cooled 50-horsepower engine was its powerplant. *"Airtrooper"* had a 25-foot wing span, and weighed only 425 pounds, empty. "You don't sit in this airplane", one pilot said, "you wear it."

The *"Airtrooper"* was "shot down" before it had a chance, but there were those who couldn't get it out of their minds. Bob Gross for one. He confessed that he kept seeing that little airplane as a "plane for everybody"—a "fly-for fun, motorcycle of the air."

In a bid for this market potential, Lockheed built a civilian version of the *"Airtrooper"*.

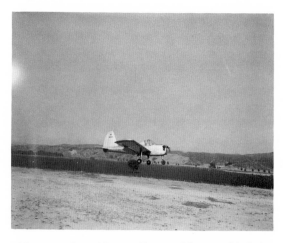

"Airtrooper" could get off ground in one-third the length of a football field. There was talk of it becoming everybody's flivver.

Gross called it the *"Little Dipper"*. There wasn't much interest in the wee one, but sales people thought there might be a chance for a slightly larger version. The result was a revolutionary design, appropriately called, *"Big Dipper"*.

Bob Reedy, then chief project engineer, and John Thorp were chiefly responsible for the "Big Dipper" design which emerged as a research project, trying out several advanced ideas. Among these were: A moveable horizontal stabilizer replacing the conventional elevators; a 100-horsepower engine mounted mid-way *inside* the fuselage with a long drive-shaft connected to a *pusher* propeller in the extreme tail behind the vertical rudder. The plane also had a fixed, tricycle landing gear.

Designated the Model-34, the *"Big Dipper"* was a two-place, low-wing monoplane, capable of cruising at about 120-mph with a top speed of 136-mph, and a ceiling of 16,000 feet. Lockheed had hopes of selling it to the Army as a "flying jeep" and to private flyers as a "flying automobile". Neither idea sparked any real interest.

What market there was with the private flyer,

Mac Short (left), "Big Dipper", designer discusses plane with test pilot Prentice Cleaves.

"Big Dipper" was two-place, pusher which might have made it as a small private plane except for slumping market. Engine inside fuselage near center of gravity, shaft-driven propeller in rear, were experimental features. It also had "flying tail" which would later appear on "TriStar."

First prototype of "JetStar" a twin-engined personnel transport built for USAF competion takes off on maiden flight. Plane in four-engined configuration would be offered to corporate fleets.

the pre-war lightplane manufacturers like Piper, Aeronca, Cessna, Beechcraft and others had pretty much already saturated with their own post-war designs. Even so, the market wasn't anywhere near what the industry had predicted. There was no sudden rush to get back up into the sky again by the returning wartime flyers and others who got their first taste of flying during the war. The "Sunday Driver" behind the wheel of his own plane simply wasn't there.

Any real mass market for the private plane, in the immediate post-war era, was a myth. Certainly, *"Big Dipper"*, as fine a little ship as it was, wasn't the answer. And when the prototype crashed on take off at the Lockheed Air Terminal early in 1946, the company closed the books on the project.

For the time being, at least, Lockheed was out of the personal plane market. It would not build anything but commercial airliners, military cargo planes, Air Force and Navy fighters and patrol planes for more than a decade.

By then, there was a whole new market, wide open and waiting. "Business flying" was the new bonanza in the sky. In 1956, when Lockheed decided to enter the field, there were more than 20,000 executive aircraft, or corporate aircraft flying; a fleet 15 times the size of the scheduled airlines' fleets. And the market was growing,

with many corporations preferring to operate their own "anytime, anywhere, air services" over regular commercial airline operations whose schedules, too often, didn't fit the business needs. It is interesting that Lockheed was the first big airframe manufacturer to come up with a plane designed expressly for the corporate fleet.

The truth is, the company "backed into the business" but they came in the front door with a front runner. The Air Force had announced that it was interested in a small transport, a multi-engine jet as a utility aircraft, a personal plane for high-ranking officers, small cargo carrier or navigation trainer. The specs called for a plane capable of carrying ten passengers and a crew of two; having a range of 2000 miles and capable of 500-mile-an-hour speeds.

As usual, Kelly Johnson and his Advanced Development Projects Staff got the job. Design work on two prototypes, one a two-engine design, the other having four engines, started in January, 1957. The twin flew eight months later on September 4, and Johnson, who was present called it "the finest first flight we've ever made." The 241 days from drawing board to first flight was a record for a plane of this size. But, admittedly, Lockheed had a slight edge when it tackled the problem.

New "Stars" On The Horizon

Back in 1950 when just about everybody was talking about a Jet Age airliner, Lockheed had made numerous design studies. One of these had evolved as the Model L-193 "global jet transport", which had a double-deck fuselage like the *"Constitution"* with four turbo jet engines mounted in pods, two on each side of the fuselage in the tail. Nothing ever came of the proposal. But when Lockheed's utility jet transport entry was submitted to the Air Force, it looked like a smaller version of the L-193. Likely, some of the design data previously accumulated gave Johnson's people a head start. Their work paid off: Lockheed won the competition.

The first prototype was a twin-engined, swept-wing (53-foot span) powered with British *"Orpheus"* jets. But the Air Force wanted a little more, and it got it.

Model 1329, called the *"JetStar,"* emerged in the same configuration only powered with four Pratt & Whitney turbojet engines, each developing 3,300 pounds thrust. The *"JetStar"* could climb out at about 4,000 feet a minute, take off and land at just about any airport that could handle a DC-3. It was capable of carrying ten passengers and a crew of two at 10-mile-a-minute speeds, in a pressurized cabin, at altitudes up to 45,000 feet. The standards it set were ideal for military cargo (5,000 pounds), a

"JetStar" with camoflage dress in Vietnam.

navigational trainer, or VIP transport.

One general remarked—"It's about time we got something like this. Flying in the slow, propeller aircraft, by the time a staff officer caught up with his fast moving forces to make a decision, there was nothing left to decide." The Air Force ordered *"JetStars"*, called C-140s.

Lockheed, which had spent $6,000,000 of its own money on the plane's development, took another look at the civilian market.

To paraphrase the general's remarks—"Top executives and key sales people, flying at 300-mph, often got there too late to close the big deal." The 575-mph *"JetStar"* appealed to some of the big corporations. Soon the planes were proudly flying the colors of corporate giants like

"JetStar" as it finally emerged with four-engines in aft fuselage. It was one of first jets designed expressly as executive aircraft.

111

L-1011 TriStar and The Lockheed Story

One of "JetStars" was fitted as flying office for nation's Number One Executive. President Johnson called it "Air Force ONE-HALF."

United Aircraft Corporation, Continental Can, West Germany's Krupp Works, the Hercules Powder Company of Canada, Superior Oil Company and others. Price tag today—about $1,750,000 per plane, including spare parts, pilot training and indoctrination and service.

The first two prototypes of *"JetStar"* were built at the Lockheed Burbank facility, but the production models became the responsibility of the Lockheed—Georgia Division at Marietta, Georgia, established in 1951 as part of the expansion demands to meet the Korean War crisis. The first production *"JetStar"* rolled out of the huge Marietta plant in the spring of 1960.

Significantly, the *"JetStar"* was Lockheed's first pure jet transport. When first introduced the plane was a pioneer in the executive Jet aircraft field. As this is written (1973) *"JetStars"* with many improvements, of course, still are in production at Marietta, and are still among the most popular corporate aircraft in the skies. Twelve years ago they were ahead of everybody by eighteen months.

Lockheed's entry into the Jet Age with an airliner would come with a turbo-prop airliner, the second generation *"Electra"* (see Chapter Eleven) and it would not have a pure jetliner in airline service until the advent of the wide-bodied L-1011 *"TriStar"* in the spring of 1972. By then, it had had more experience building large, jet-powered transports and cargo planes,

including the world's largest (C-5A *"Galaxy"*) than any other aircraft manufacturer.

Under the same roof with the *"JetStar"* at the Marietta plant, the fabulous C-130 *"Hercules"*, the C-141 *"StarLifters"* and the gigantic C-5A *"Galaxy"* move along assembly lines. They have made this Georgia city the "airlift capital of the world."

Lockheed's move south in 1951-52, it has been said, was the greatest thing for the Southland since Scarlet O'Hara and "Gone With The Wind."

Interior of "JetStar" fitted as a flying office. Vastly improved versions are still very popular with growing corporate fleets.

CHAPTER TEN

Hercules And The Starlifters

It was the spring of 1972, and South Vietnamese forces around An Loc were taking a terrible pasting from Viet Cong artillery; a thousand rounds of mortor fire and rockets a day. Wrote John L. Frisbee, Executive Editor of *Air Force* magazine, who was on the scene—"The performance of the South Vietamese Army, who successfuly defended An Loc can only be described as heroic. The wonder is that any of them—or any civilians in that beleaguered city—survived. . . .It is doubtful that these defenders could have held out had it not been for some fantastic aerial supply work by USAF (*"Hercules"*) C-130s, using techniques that had never before been tested in combat."

The big Lockheed C-130 cargo planes, flying with the 374th Tactical Airlift Wing, U.S. Air Force, based at Tan Son Nhut near Saigon, shuttled back and forth dropping tons of supplies to the defenders. Equipped with airborne radar and computers called AWADS (Adverse Weather Aerial Delivery System) the C-130s were able to pinpoint dropping supplies into a drop zone the size of a soccer field, from altitudes above 10,000 feet, out of reach of VC ground fire. Altogether, they dropped 3700 tons of needed supplies, and the South Vietnamese garrison held.

An Loc became the Bastogne of World War II in the Viet War. The courageous South Vietnamese troops who held out there dulled the

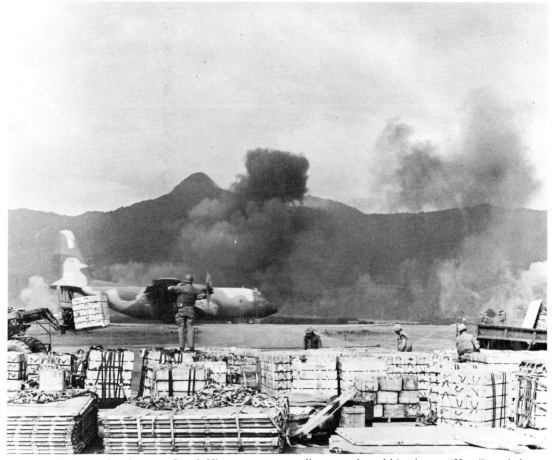

"Hercules" C-130s in Vietnam. South Vietnamese troops line up to board big planes. "Herc" carried tons of supplies and troops to hot spots whenever support was needed. In addition, all during Viet conflict these planes kept aerial lifeline open from U.S.

A glistening "Hercules" one of latest versions operating with USAF shows off plane's sleek lines. After two decades the fabulous planes are still in production at Lockheed-Georgia plant.

vaunted Viet Cong offensive. Undoubtedly their gallant effort, bolstered by the U.S. airlift, contributed its share to the change in attitude of the Viet Cong representatives at the Paris peace talks. Thanks to the C-130s, the United States had a stronger bargaining weapon at the peace table.

With the cease-fire and the freeing of American POWs, the C-130s proudly participated in flying the men home, as they had done in the role of "flying ambulances" since the U.S. entry into the undeclared war.

A remarkable thing about these planes is that the basic design of the C-130 *"Hercules"* in 1972 was twenty years old. Yet, serving with the air forces of many nations and as commercial airliners and airfreighters, the combined *"Hercules"* fleets are still flying 75,000 to 100,000 hours a month; the equivalent of circling the globe almost twice every 60 minutes!

Dan Haughton, chairman of the board of Lockheed Aircraft Corporation in a Corporate Management Memo dated August 28, 1972,

would write—"Hercules today is 20 years young as much superior to aircraft of 20 years ago as a new Cadillac is better than one of 1952 vintage; the result of continual improvements in a superb basic airplane which is as vital a competitor in the world aviation marketplace as when it first entered that arena."

The same memo pointed out—"Some 1200 *'Hercules'* have been built in 45 versions for the U.S. Air Force, Navy, Coast Guard, Marine Corps, U.S. and foreign airlines (as L-100s) and 25 foreign governments. The Air Force is currently requesting funding for up to 30 more *'Hercules'* in fiscal year 1973. The Navy in fiscal 1973 will buy five ski-equipped *'Hercules'* and the Coast Guard two more rescue aircraft. Production is presently at three a month."

Haughton added: "It isn't often that an airplane gets to celebrate the 20th anniversary of its first production go-ahead with its assembly line still going strong."

Let's turn back the clock, and take a look at what happened to give the Lockheed C-130

Hercules And The Starlifters

"Hercules" a life-span unequalled by any other large transport type aircraft in aviation history.

With the splendid example of the value of *airlift* as exemplified by *"Operation Vittles"* (The Berlin Airlift) in mind, the Defense Department late in 1949 put out a call for a fast, mobile, air transport plane that could rush men and materials to emergency areas quickly and inexpensively. Lockheed, Boeing, Douglas, Martin and Consolidated (Convair)—the big builders of transport-type aircraft—went at it hot and heavy to win the competition. In 1950 it was announced that Lockheed was the winner.

The development team led by Kelly Johnson, Willis Hawkins and E. C. Frost came up with a design which Johnson referred to as the "modern combination of the jeep, the truck and the transport plane." The Air Force called it the C-130. Lockheed, keeping alive its symbol of the winged star, called it the *"Hercules"* after a northern constellation between *Lyra* and *Corona*

Borealis.

Kelly's "jeep or truck", more like a couple of winged box cars, was capable of airlifting 20 tons of equipment or supplies, or 90 fully-equipped combat troops. Squat, square and rugged, the *"Hercules"* prototype with a fuselage length of 95 feet, was a far cry from a streamlined, shark-shaped body of the *"Constellation."* It was a high-wing monoplane (132-foot span) powered with four Allison 3750-horsepower turbo-prop engines. The aft section of the fuselage slanted up sharply to a single tail, fixed horizontal stabilizer-elevator configuration. A wide door which dropped down like a ramp in the aft section permitted driving a gasoline tanker truck inside. There was also a side door in the fuselage.

There were two prototype C-130s built at the Lockheed Burbank factory. The first of these flew on August 23, 1954, with test pilot Stanley Beltz at the controls. The plane lifted off the

"Hercules" with Royal Saudi Air Force markings is typical of penetration into foreign market. The big planes still are flying the colors of some 25 different nations performing with both military and civilian air agencies.

115

Civilian freighter (L-100) demonstrates rear loading technique. Like a giant whale the plane swallows an entire transportable Post Office.

During Korean emergency Lockheed-Georgia Company turned out B-47 "Stratojets". Here, first plane rolls out of final assembly hangar.

runway at Lockheed Air Terminal in only 850 feet. Beltz reported—"She's a real flying machine."

During the design and development stage of the two prototypes, Lockheed Aircraft Corporation was going through another expansion program. Another war, the Korean "Police Action" as President Truman called it, was chiefly responsible for the new growth period. United Nations forces in Korea, late in 1950, were being pushed back, almost to the brink of a second Dunkirk. The U.S. had to throw everything it hadinto the action to prevent such a catastrophe. That meant pulling B-29 *"Superfortresses"* out of mothballs, getting into high-gear with production of more *"Shooting Stars"* and newer, faster, harder-hitting fighters, the F-86 North American *"Sabrejets"* and Republic F-84 *"Thunderjets"* to match the Russian-madeMIGs. With no end of the hostilities in sight, the U.S. also wanted mass production of its new B-47, four-engined "Stratojet" A-bombers, just in case, Korea might explode into World War III, God forbid.

As a result, the Air Force, late in 1950, asked Lockheed to re-open the big Marietta, Georgia, plant, a 4,500,000-square factory, all under one roof, where, as part of a "pool" arrangement, Bell Aircraft during World War II had turned out nearly 700 Boeing-designed B-29s. And Lockheed accepted the challenge. The Lockheed-Georgia division (later to become the Lockheed-Georgia Company) was born.

Named general manager of the Lockheed Georgia operation was James V. Carmichael, a native of Marietta, who had directed the Bell Marietta B-29 program. Appointed assistant

general manager was another southerner, Alabama-born Daniel J. Haughton, who had been with Lockheed since 1939 and was being "groomed by Gross" for bigger things.

The two didn't waste any time. With a handful of key Lockheed-Burbank employees they moved to Marietta. By February 5, 1951, they had re-activated the "Bell bomber works". The gargantuan Air Force Plant No. 6, largest aircraft factory under one roof in the world until Boeing built its 747 plant at Everett, Washington, in 1966, grew from 150 employees to more than 10,000 in a year's time. Under Lockheed management, ever since, it has never stopped turning out giant airplanes. To list a few—the C-130 turbo-prop *"Hercules"*, the bigger, C-141, turbo-jet *"StarLifter"*, and the C-5A *"Galaxy"*, largest landplane in the world·

But that's getting ahead of our story. In the beginning, Lockheed-Georgia began operations with a modification program—"de-cocooning" 120 World War II Boeing B-29s. The big *"Superfortresses"* had been stored in the blazing desert sun at Pyote, Texas. They were "cranked up" and flown to Marietta for modernization, and then flown to Korea. For some of these big birds which were built at Marietta in World War II it was like coming home to roost.

The task force that re-opened the Marietta facility found a facility made up of 19 major buildings with the main assembly building (where later, *"Hercules"* would go into mass production) a quarter of a mile wide and half a mile long. It was B I G!

So was the second major phase assigned to the new Lockheed-Georgia organization—help build the Boeing-designed B-47 *"Stratojet"*

One of first production C-130s flies over in salute to Boeing B-47 "Stratojet" also built at the Lockheed-Georgia Company.

which would become the Strategic Air Command's new strike force. Boeing-Douglas-Lockheed, the same as the trio had done in World War II building B-17s, started turning out the first of SAC's jet bomber. About the time that a B-47 participated in secret tests at Eniwetok in 1952 when the H-bomb (the "first thermonuclear device in history) was exploded, the first Marietta-built B-47 rolled out of the huge plant in Marietta, Georgia.

When the B-47 program was near finished in 1954, Dan Haughton, promoted to a corporate vice-president, influenced the decision to produce the *"Hercules"* at the Lockheed Marietta plant. The first flight of a production C-130 took place at Marietta on April 7, 1955.

"We did our first production delivery on December 9, 1956," Haughton recalled. "The Air Force activated its first operational C-130 squadron, January 3, 1957. But none of us at that time who were involved in the start of the 'Hercules' program fully grasped the great future this aircraft had ahead of it."

"The C-130 aircraft possesses a unique versatility that has enabled it to perform a wide variety of difficult missions," Dan Haughton, 20 years later as Lockheed Board Chairman would write. "This is the key to why we are still building them in 1972, and the demand is continuing."

Haughton pointed out, pridefully, that *"Hercules"* has served as cargo-troop carrier, flying hospital, inflight refueling tanker for helicopters and fighter planes, stable gunship for close air support (in Vietnam), as a surveillance ship carrying classified sensor equipment, aerial photo-mapper, search and rescue aircraft, airborne command post and air-mobile communications center, iceberg hunter, weather observer and cloud seeder. These planes have

"Hercules" C-130s on production line at Lockheed-Georgia plant in Marietta. The line never stopped for more than twenty years.

Mercy Missions: In 1962 "Hercs" airlifted Tibetan children out of mountain hide-away when Red Chinese took-over. Planes operated from 11,000-foot high primitive airstrip in treacherous Himalayas.

taken part in search missions flying above the scorching Sahara. With ski-and-wheel combination undercarriage *"Hercules"* has served as a support aircraft for explorations in the Arctic and Antarctic.

"Hercules" pioneered a new cargo airdrop technique, the container delivery system. In a two year period in Vietnam, these aircraft airlifted more than 780,000 tons (one billion, 560 million pounds) an unprecedented feat.

The C-130s played other roles than in the combat areas: Flying Red Cross relief cargos to earthquake victims in Italy, Morocco, Iran and Peru; airlifting doctors, medicines and foodstuff to cholera and famine victims in Africa; To victims of tidal waves in the Bay of Bengal, typhoons in Japan and Guam. They have been called "Angels of Mercy" swooping down out of the sky.

In a commercial version (the L-100 series) *"Hercules"* has airlifted massive oil drilling equipment and heavy road building machinery over the Andes into jungles of Peru. Using a Lockheed Seat-Pak, a cabin pod arrangement, the *"Hercs"* are used as airliners flying between Lima and Cuzco, Peru. In Columbia, S.A., *"Hercules"* flies purebred cattle to better pasturelands. Chile gets meat from Argentina by

Historic moment: LC-130F "Hercules" kicks up a miniature snowstorm as it slides to a halt at the South Pole. Ski-equipped C-130Ds supported U.S. Navy's Operation Deep Freeze enabling scientists to accelerate South Pole studies.

Out of "Hercules" turbo-prop experience came Lockheed second generation "Electra", first U.S.-built Jet Age commercial airliner.

"Hercules" airlift.

The stretched version L-100-20, serving eight commercial air carriers, has demonstrated that airfreight can be a paying proposition, and helped open new vistas for civilian air cargo operations. An even larger version, the *"Super Hercules"* portends a bright future for air freight "planeloadings."

The big plane can even carry the huge jet engines, eight feet in diameter, that power the L-1011 *"TriStar"* latest to join the fleet of famous Lockheed transport planes. *"Super Hercules"* can haul as many as three of the turbo-fan engines inside its cavernous cargo hull. The plane can carry up to 52,500 pounds of cargo. It can operate from unpaved surfaces, sand, bare dirt, gravel or metal landing mats.

Beyond its splendid performance record, the basic C-130 design and the many versions that followed had great impact on the future of Lockheed Aircraft Corporation. "Of corporate significance," Dan Haughton declared, "orders for this aircraft have brought us nearly a quarter of a billion dollars in operating profit, a real hedge against the ups and downs of our industry. Moreover, sales to foreign countries have totaled more than $1-billion of its $2.8 billion overall sales to date (mid-year 1972) a significant contribution to the U.S. net balance of payments."

It can also be said that *"Hercules"* helped give the company a head start in the commercial Jet Age. One must remember that the initial pair of C-130s built at Burbank—the start of the *"Hercules"* program—were also the first American-built transport planes designed around the revolutionary turbo-prop powerplant. This "know-how", plus the production and fabrication experience gleaned from the *"Hercules"* program at the Lockheed-Georgia Company, both with regard to the airframe and the powerplants, was like money in the bank. In late 1954, American Airlines announced a design competition for a turbine engine, short-to-medium range airliner.

Boeing, Douglas, Convair and the British, whose turbo-prop *"Viscount"* was already flying in the U.S., were all in on the competition. The Lockheed entry won hands down. It was a low-wing design powered with four Allison 3750-horsepower engines, the same as those on the C-130. Capable of carrying 66 to 91 passengers, the plane was designed for a cruising speed of over 400 miles per hour, faster than any of the piston-engined airliners then flying. Slung low to the ground, it rested on a tricycle undercarriage and could operate from airports in more than 100 U.S. cities and as many more abroad.

Bob Gross named it the *"Electra"* feeling, perhaps, that as the first turbo-jet transport built in this country, it would penetrate the airline market just as did the original Model 10 *"Electra"* of two decades before. American Airlines was first with an order for 35 and Eastern Airlines followed with 40 more. Other airlines at home and abroad soon hitched their future to the new star.

Unfortunate accidents which befell the British DeHavilland *"Comet"*, world's first passenger jet airliner, had led U.S. carriers to believe that the turbo-prop airliner was a more cautious approach into the Jet Era. C. R. Smith, President of American Airlines would say—"The *'Electra'* is a logical airplane for an important era in air transportation."

The second generation *"Electra"* went into production at Burbank in December, 1955, using many of the same tools and dies that were used in the prototype *"Hercules"* program. *"Electra"*

No. II flew on December 6, 1957, two weeks ahead of the Boeing turbojet prototype *"Dash-Eighty"* Model 707 and months ahead of the Douglas DC-8 and Convair 880 jetliners.

By the end of 1957 Lockheed reported $300 million worth of *"Electra"* orders, the largest in dollar value for any commercial model the company had ever built. As we have pointed out, (in Chapter Eight) modified versions for the Navy *"Electras"* are still in production 15 years later. But even that can't equal the 20 year record—and still going strong—of the fabulous *"Hercules"* which one might call *"Electra's"* kissing cousin.

The success story of *"Hercules"* also launched the company into another venture. On December 17, 1963—sixty years to the day after Orville Wright first flew in a power-driven machine at Kitty Hawk, N. C.—the C-141 *"StarLifter"*, a four-engined turbojet airfreighter made its maiden flight. The

Sixty years after Wright Brothers' at Kitty Hawk, Lockheed's C-141 "Starlifter" spread its wings. The C-141 was bigger and faster than turbo-prop "Hercules." It was short-lived because of demand for larger cargo planes resulting in C-5A Sky Galaxy.

Hercules And The Starlifters

"*StarLifter*" was another Lockheed-Georgia Company project, larger and faster than the C-130s.

The "*StarLifter*" was the first pure jet (turbojet) aircraft developed from the start as a cargo plane. With a maximum gross weight of 330,000-pounds, wing span of 160 feet and fuselage length of 145 feet, it was by far the largest jet transport type aircraft flying. It had a speed of 550-mph (150-190-mph faster than the "*Hercules*") and a range, with 60,000-pound payload, of 4,600 miles.

Delivered to the Military Airlift Command (MAC) in 1965, the "*StarLifters*" immediately began flying men and supplies to Vietnam. Equipped as "flying hospitals" they brought back many of the wounded and returnees on the return trip.

With 185 of the C-141s on order for the military services, it looked as though Lockheed

"Starlifters" capable of carrying 20-tons of cargo at Tan Son Nhut Air Base in South Vietnam. At jet speeds, planes delivered tons of supplies daily across vast expanse of Pacific. At war's end they brought first returning POWs back to the United States.

had another "*Hercules*" going for it. But the "*StarLifter's*" production life was cut short, when in 1965, Lockheed won a competition for a

Turbojet "Starlifters" gave Military Airlift Command 600-mph delivery capability. These seven could airlift more than 280,000 pounds of cargo in single movement. Planes gave Lockheed lead in production of large transport airframe and turbo-fan engine application. C-5A "Galaxy" and "TriStar" were logical next step.

super-sized cargo plane which would become the C-5A. With this sky giant coming, the *"StarLifter"* was relegated to an intermediate role.

Its size, configuration and fabrication techniques, however, would play an important part in the design and development of the C-5A. Certainly, its power units, four Pratt & Whitney, 21,000-thrust power turbo-fan engines, gave the airframe people, designers and engineers, and production experts an opportunity to learn the great potential of the turbo-fan powerplants. Indeed, it was not until the advent of and the availability of these turbo-fan engines, with great thrustpower growth potential, that the big

planemakers—Boeing, Douglas, Convair and Lockheed—began seriously thinking about the king-sized, wide-bodied jetliners. Certainly, the Lockheed *"TriStar"*, Boeing 747 and Douglas DC-10, wouldn't have come along as quickly as they did.

Lockheed was "turbofan conscious" with its design and development of the *"StarLifter"*.

It was a leader with the turbo-prop *"Electra"* in introducing the Jet Age to the air traveler.

With the *"Hercules"* second generation *"Electra"* and the *"StarLifter"* programs, it could claim more experience building big jet-powered transport aircraft than any other company.

CHAPTER ELEVEN

Second Generation Electra

Author's Note: This story about the second generation "Electra" was obtained in exclusive interview with veteran American Airlines' Captain Arthur Weidman in the summer of 1961. It is written in the first person as told to the author. The story appeared originally in AIR PROGRESS *Magazine.*

There she was—the new Lockheed *"Electra"* airliner—sitting on the ramp at Amon-Carter Field, Forth Worth, Texas. And there I was, walking toward the ship, about to climb aboard for my first "check ride" in the plane I had been hearing about for months.

The company had sent me down there in the Texas sun to take a short transition course for pilots who had been flying the conventional, piston-powered jobs and were moving up to the turboprop transports which American Airlines was integrating into its Flagship Fleet as rapidly as possible. I was to become a pilot supervisor and instructor for the Electra program.

That was more than 18 months ago and, I remember, during the indoctrination period, they told us this aircraft had everything. Unexcelled crew comfort in a "front office" that was air-conditioned, roomy and equipped with the very latest instrumentation and automatic devices as helpmates. They said she had fingertip control, power-steering, power-brakes and built-in "fail safe" features that would let her de-

Lockheed's second generation "Electra" was first U.S.-built jetliner to enter commercial service. Plane had entirely new high-lift wing which seemed "almost no wing at all" because of huge nacelle configuration and extremely wide-blades of four-bladed propellers. Note DC-3s and "Constellations" at top of picture. "Electra" was designed to replace them.

fend herself capably against any known emergency. She was designed and built, specifically and scientifically to meet the peculiar requirements of airline operations, many of which were recommended by pilots, like myself, who day-in and day-out fly the commercial airplanes. No airplane ever before had been subjected to such a rigid and rugged ground and flight test shake-down period. She had come through with flying colors.

It all sounded like an airborne Utopia. But pilots are a skeptical lot and, admittedly, I was one of them. Then, I flew the *"Electra"* and when we came down, I was a complete convert. There was no doubt about it in my opinion—she was everything they said she was and more.

Today, after almost a thousand hours at her controls, flying in all kinds of weather under all kinds of conditions over almost every segment of American's vast route system, I'm convinced that she is the best all-round airplane I've ever flown. And for almost half my lifetime, since early 1944 when I started chauffering DC-3's for the airline, I've spent thousands of hours "up front" in the Convairs, DC-6's and DC-7's. The *"Electra"* is in a class all by herself.

That's not just my opinion, alone. Every pilot I know who has been assigned to the aircraft feels the same way about it. The best proof, perhaps, is that old-timers use their seniority at every opportunity to get on the waiting list to fly the *"Electras"* over any other prop driven transport. In this business nobody does that, unless the plum is a juicy one. The reason is, *"Electra"* is every inch a pilot's airplane.

This is true despite the fact that the airplane, since it was introduced into service in early 1959, has had more than her share of bad accidents. And pilots seldom court a "hard luck" airplane with much enthusiasm.

Before the plane really had a chance, five crashes smacked her down and smashed her pride. As a result, perhaps, no other airplane in the history of air transportation has been subjected to so much public criticism or stirred up so much controversy. Unfortunately, too much attention has been focused on her faults and failures without equal emphasis on her advanced design and advantageous assets which have made notable contributions to the Jet Age. The time has come, I believe, to set the record straight.

First, let's briefly review those crashes. There's nothing to hide, and in cases where the trouble was definitely pin-pointed, remedial ac-tions were taken so that it can't happen again.

Accident No. 1 occurred shortly after the new airliner went into service, when an *"Electra"*, during an instrument approach, plunged into New York's East River only seven hundred yards from the runway at LaGuardia Field. Then, on September 29, 1959, another ship crashed at Buffalo, Texas followed six months later (March 17, 1960) by a third disaster at Cannelton, Indiana. Both of these crashes occurred under very mysterious circumstances and their pattern was very similar—the two planes apparently disintegrated in the air. No. 4 involved an *"Electra"* that struck a new dike obstruction during a landing at LaGuardia. All passengers and crew walked away. The fifth accident, a freakish one in which thousands of starlings were sucked into the turbine engines, occurred seconds after a take-off at Boston.

What happened?

Investigators classed the East River, LaGuardia dike and the Boston accidents as disasters which could conceivably befall any aircraft. They blamed the weather, inadequate navigational aids, instrument malfunction, pilot error and the bird menace. There was nothing wrong structurally, mechanically or design-wise with the *"Electra."* But, for a long time, nobody was sure what happened in the Texas or Indiana skies, and it touched off the most extensive crash investigation program ever conducted. Within a comparatively short time, they tracked down the culprit.

It was a build-up of a unique combination of forces and reactions unknown, unheard-of and unprecedented in aviation technology. This phenomena occurred when three basic elements, by coincidence, joined forces. This combination, it was the conclusion of the investigators, could and did tear the airplane apart.

Naturally, pilots were briefed by engineers about this phenomena. The technical people had a new name for it—"Whirl mode." Here's how they explained it to us: A weakening in an outboard engine mount caused the propeller to get out of its normal plane of rotation. Normally, this condition would be dampened out by designed flexibility in the engine mounting. In a perfectly healthy airplane, the problem is not hazardous. Unquestionably, it has occurred millions of times with all propeller-driven aircraft, but nothing happened because the mount is designed to correct the situation. But, as the "whirl mode" progressed in a damaged installation, the frequency of the mode could have ap-

Second Generation Electra

Beefed-up engine mounts and nacelle structure cured "Electra's" early ills. Engines were Allison (General Motors) Model 501-D13 turbine engines geared to 13 1/4-foot Aeroproducts propellers. Slung low to ground "Electra" had single point fuel loading system, shown here. She could take on 350 gallons a minute!

proached the natural frequency of the wing which in turn would tend to perpetuate the "whirl mode." The result—induced flutter which could produce a catastrophic failure through oscillatory divergence. Finally, as each oscillation of the wing itself became greater, the wing structure failed and broke-up. It never happened before, most probably, because propeller-driven planes of this size had not previously approached the advantageous speeds of which the *"Electra"* is capable.

"Identification of the whirl mode phenomenon," says an official Federal Aviation Agency report, "became the key to the mystery which had baffled the aviation industry for months. The correction of the various wing, powerplant and nacelle deficiencies was, in retrospect, relatively simple once the problem was identified."

There was no grounding of the *"Electras"*. The multi-million dollar investigation had proved conclusively that within certain speed ranges

the airplane was safe. Consequently, the FAA "red-tagged" the airplane and pilots were instructed not to fly it at speeds in excess of 259 mph indicated, until modifications were accomplished.

These modifications included: Additional mounts to stabilize the propeller should any mount fail, or should breakage occur between the gearbox and the power section. A strengthened nacelle structure. Increasing of the thickness of three lower surface "planks" and one upper surface "plank" in the wing. Reinforcing of the front spar and lower wing surface. Strengthening of 18 ribs in each wing by additional diagonal braces and reinforcements.

When the changes were made, dramatic flight tests were conducted by Lockheed, the FAA and the airlines. In one test, the torque shaft and the torque shaft housing were removed prior to flight. In this weakened condition, the airplane was dived at speeds up to 418 miles per hour. Severe flight loads were imposed by the pilot to record strains on the critical parts of the structure. Instruments revealed complete absence of the whirl phenomenon or any other adverse condition. The tests also included a rigorous 100-hour program of run-ups, take-offs and landings and numerous abnormal emergencies not likely to occur in normal operation.

As this is written, the Lockheed Company at its Burbank, California plant, is modifying the entire *"Electra"* fleet at a rate which will permit all the planes to be back in the air again by the middle of 1961. As each airplane is completed, its speed restrictions are automatically removed. By the time you read this, the airlines will undoubtedly be flying the *"Electra"* once more at their designed-for operational speeds and the faster schedules will be in effect. The plane's future is bright.

Incidentally, I've flown the modified *"Electra"* and I still feel the same way I did the first time I sat in the left-hand seat for that "check ride." She's all airplane. But, let's take a closer look at some of her features that explain the reasons why she leaves one with such definite feelings about her capabilities.

As far back as 1947, the Lockheed Aircraft Corporation, builders of America's first combat jet aircraft (the P-80, later F-80 fighters) and the famous Constellation series airliners, decided to hang a propeller on the jet engine and enter the Jet Age transport competition with a turboprop airliner. The company was convinced that while propellerless jets were excellent on long-range flights, the airlines would be better served by having an effective vehicle for short and medium route segments.

There followed an extensive survey of the entire air transport industry to learn exactly what the airlines' people needed in the "ideal" short and medium-range transport. What the lines wanted was a big order: (1) An airplane smaller than the then current four-engined airliners but faster, much quieter, and more economical to buy, operate and maintain; (2) An airplane large enough to carry up to 99 passengers, yet show profits with only a 50 per cent payload; (3) An airplane capable of taking off fully-loaded with fuel and passengers and making multiple-stop flights most of the way across the United States without pause for re-fueling; (4) An airplane with new concepts of comfort for passengers and crew, superior handling characteristics, excellent controllability and power response, and 24-hour-a-day, day-in-and-day-out reliability.

Around these requirements, Lockheed started research and design studies to achieve those difficult-to-reach goals. Although it was generally known that the company was secretly "considering" a new transport design, the first disclosure of the *"Electra"* by name didn't come until June 8, 1955 when American Airlines announced it was buying 35 of Lockheed's "on-paper" airliner. The first of the planes didn't roll off the assembly line until November, two years later. The *"Electra"* made its maiden flight on December 6, 1957. Certification by the CAA as a common carrier came on August 22, 1958. By that time more than 161 of the new transports had been ordered by the airlines and others. They came. They saw. They liked what they saw and they bought it.

I'll never forget the first time I saw the *"Elec-*

Pilots praised "front office" of the "Electra" because of large windows, roominess and arrangement of controls and throttles.

Passengers liked "Electra's" wide seats and king-sized square windows. Cabin featured wide aisles and extremely quiet accoustics.

Second Generation Electra

Luxurious interior, like this lounge in extreme tail made turboprop "Electra" very popular. Depending upon airline requirement, cabin could accommodate from 66 to 99 passengers.

tra". During a lay-over on the West Coast, when I was flying DC-6's and DC-7's on the Fort Worth-Los Angeles run, a group of us went out to Burbank to see one of the new ships bearing American Airlines' markings when it was rolled out in the open. There's only one way to describe my first impression—she had "functional beauty."

The same day, we saw a Lockheed test pilot, "Fish" Salmon, take another *"Electra"* up for a test hop. It was quite a show.

For one thing, after listening to the whistles and screams of other smaller turboprop planes during the taxiing and take-off, I had expected this big baby would setup a real howl. To the contrary, the noise level was below that of the piston planes I had been flying.

The plane also got off in a hurry and climbed very rapidly. Obviously, there was a lot of power packed into her streamlined nacelles; thrust to spare in the noticeably wide, flat blades of the propellers. I couldn't help thinking—"Boy, I'd like to have that kind of reserve power when the chips were down."

We got a good demonstration of what it means a few minutes later when "Fish" did

something I'd never seen accomplished before with any aircraft. If I hadn't seen it with my own eyes I wouldn't have believed that it was possible.

The *"Electra"* came in for a landing, flaps partially extended, wheels down and locked, approaching the runway dead center, everything committed for touchdown. It's a critical moment, as every pilot feels, because there's nothing else you can do at this stage but let her settle, crunch down on the tires and then hit the brakes, kick the props in reverse and bring her to a rolling stop. That's standard operational procedure with the conventional airliner.

Not so with the *"Electra."* I saw the plane's wheels actually brush the runway at the half-way mark and thought for sure the flight was over. But suddenly, without any burst of power audible to my ears, the plane gracefully swooped up into the sky again. Circling the field once, she came around again, this time negotiating a smooth landing and coming to a complete stop in an unbelievably short distance.

Our Lockheed host grinned: "That's what we call the wave-off characteristic. You'll find this airplane is never really committed. You can make as many passes as needed to get down."

To a pilot who has "sweat out" many a landing, coming down through thick, blinding fog, feeling his way every foot during an instrument approach, and with no alternative but to land-this characteristic, alone, is enough to endear heart and soul to the *"Electra"* for life. I know that's how I felt about it when I saw the technique demonstrated. From that moment on, I couldn't wait until it would be my turn to take over command of such an airliner.

In outward appearance, the *"Electra"* has distinctive identifying features all her own. She has a purposeful and powerful profile. The nose slopes downward sharply to provide good forward visibility on the ground and in the air. Then, her lines go straight back along a perfectly cylinderical fuselage to give her a wider cross-section than the DC-7, making possible a cabin more easily adaptable to high-density seating and minimizing pressurization problems. Star-

ting back of the service door, there is a graceful upsweep to dorsal fin and rudder, effecting a sleek, trim, streamline look. Slender nacelles jut forward like giant probes, offering a minimum of frontal resistance. It is hard to believe that each houses a package of power capable of producing 3750-horsepower, take-off, sea-level rating.

Perhaps, her most striking first impression, however, is the location and size of the wing. My first thought was—"My God, where is it?" The *"Electra"* wing appears extremely short. (Actually it is but five-and-a-half feet shorter than the fuselage.) In this respect, she has a "sonic penetration look", like you'd expect to find in a military aircraft. From the front, the wing has an unusual amount of dihedral, its squared-off tips angling upward in a wide-open "V" configuration.

Lockheed is quick to point to the wing as being a completely new airfoil with an extremely

In flight "Electra" shows off her clean lines, picture windows, narrow, thin wing, dorsal fin and towering rudder. PSA (Pacific Southwest Airlines) bought "Electras" from other carriers when turbojet 707s began to replace turbo-prop airliners, and some of planes are still in daily operation on short-haul West Coast runs.

low aspect-ratio, low-drag characteristics and built for speed and strength. The illusion that there isn't enough wing comes from the fact that the four big General Motors, Allison, Model 501 prop-jet engines with their large exhaust nozzles extending to the trailing edge, literally "hide" the wing itself. Moreover, the 13½-foot diameter Hamilton-Standard four-bladed propellers sweep across two-thirds of each wing. She was built to manufacture her own lift in great quantities.

With this ability to generate great masses of air flowing over the wing, the ship has inherent "flyability." The "wave-off" capability is born right here. So is the airplane's exceptionally good control response. The control surfaces, themselves, have strong forces working for them at all times.

I noticed this in particular the first time that I flew the airplane. She responds to control actions more like a fighter than a sixty-ton airliner.

Good control sensitivity is something a pilot likes to feel because you want your charge to obey directions instantaneously, at least, the sooner the better. *"Electra"* has the quick response of a trained kitten. A "booster" control system similar to the principle of power-steering on an automobile, makes this possible. But the real effectiveness comes from the tremendous power available and the design itself, which accepts this power and puts it to the best possible use.

The powerplant system in the *"Electra"* is, indeed, revolutionary to the uninitiated. I remember sitting there in the cockpit before I started the take-off run on my "check ride" and, somehow, things didn't feel right. I kept thinking I had forgotten something.

I started to say—"No warm up?"—then, I remember, the jet engines are always hot! I felt stupid. But what a relief it is and a time-saver, too, not to have to run-up the engines all the time—a bothersome standard operation with piston-powered aircraft.

The *"Electra"* can do it because the Model 501 jet engine is a "constant speed" engine; it stabilizes at 10,000 rpm after initial fire-up. This is the speed at which turbine and compressor are turning, but a reduction gear mechanism reduces propeller speed to 738 rpm. During this stage which they call "ground idle" regime, you can advance the throttle, admitting more fuel to the engine, and have all the power necessary to taxi or maneuver, but the engine speed still remains constant.

The propeller responds automatically to the demand for more power by a change in blade angle for a bigger "bite" of air. In effect, it acts as a governor on the engine which produces a steady, subdued sound—not the accustomed-to roar and shimmy. For take-off, you merely advance the power lever to the next stage, called "flight regime", increasing the engine speed to 13,820 rpm. At this point the turbine inlet temperature gauge shows the maximum temperature allowed and the engine is delivering full take-off horsepower but the turbine speed is still constant. After that, things happen almost too fast. The plane becomes "flyable" quicker than any aircraft I've ever handled including a Piper Cub. Before you know it, the ship has reached a velocity where lift is there, and you have the feel of positive control which builds confidence.

The low sound and vibration level makes the take-off seem effortless and the airplane lifts off a very few seconds after start of the roll. The thumping vibration of piston engines and the long, slow climb-out are things of the past. The *"Electra's"* rate of climb is about twice that of the piston-powered airliner.

Further along in my transition program they threw the book at me with this emergency problem: During in-flight maneuvers my instructor purposely caused a "flame-out" in both port engines; *two engines gone, both on the same side*—a condition that would make a pilot fight like a panther in any conventional-powered four-engined airliner. I know. I've had it happen!

The *"Electra"* seemed to defend herself against the situation. Propellers on the dead engines feathered almost instantaneously. Light pressure on the yoke and rudder pedals corrected the yawing tendency. With a little more power on the remaining engines the ship climbed almost normally.

The engines were started again and we climbed to about 10,000 feet where we put her through another test. *One...two...three* of the engines were purposely shut down! But still we were able to maintain level flight. I don't know of any other propeller airplane that can equal that kind of performance.

Naturally, such things give a pilot a good feeling of security. They are shining examples of the airplane's "fail safe" design philosophy paying big dividends.

Another outstanding feature about the aircraft which pilots like is the way they designed the "front office". Lockheed must have called in the world's greatest ecologists for the cockpit in the *"Electra"* represents just about the last word in "human engineering." I learned from one Lockheed engineer that the company spent more than 50,000 man-hours and tried out more than 100 basic configurations to perfect the airplane's Flight Deck. For my money they did a superb job.

There's plenty of room up front. Pilot, co-pilot and flight engineer—the normal crew complement—don't get in each other's way. The seats are comfortable and adjust to the individual. Grouping of the controls on the pedestal in easy reach is a particularly efficient arrangement. You don't have to be an octopus to go through routine procedures. Things are arranged in a logical order. An extra-wide instrument panel is easy on the eyes. Cockpit windows provide an optimum in visibility. Compared with some aircraft I've flown, the *"Electra"* in this respect, has picture windows, not just peep holes!

QUIET, MEN AT WORK is a sign that might appropriately apply to the cockpit in flight. In some planes it is so noisy that you have to raise your voice to communicate with each other. You can almost talk in a whisper and it comes through clear and audible in the *"Electra"*. It makes a lot of difference, too, when listening to the "voices" over the radio.

Automaticity abounds. About the size of the average apartment's kitchen, the cockpit has many of these push-button gadgets meant to make life easier. In case of abnormal fire in an engine, for example, you can pull a single fire control lever and a lot of things happen: It automatically feathers the propeller, turns off the fuel and oil feed, arms the chemical fire extinguisher in the nacelle, then sets it off, smothering the fire.

It's the same way in combating adverse icing conditions. And ice long has been one of the airman's worst enemies. The *"Electra,"* however, has "hot-air" de-icing and anti-icing system. The plane, in effect, "borrows" hot air from the last compressor stage in the turbine engines. The air is then piped to wing and stabilizer leading edges through stainless steel manifolds and ducts to guard against formation of ice deposits while in flight. The wing gets so hot you can fry an egg on it. You set the whole system in motion by pushing a button.

Is it any wonder we call her a pilot's airplane?

Mechanics also sing her praises. I've talked with ground crews and ground handlers about the *"Electra"* and they point up many of her advantageous characteristics which have simplified things to the nth degree. The plane really hugs the ground, for one thing, providing exceptional "reachability."

One mechanic told me: "It's the first airplane that you can get at without lugging a step-ladder around with you every time you want to open a fuselage inspection plate."

One of "Electra's" features was built-in loading stairs to speed up ground times on short-haul routes. Passengers could board through two doors as shown here. American Airlines, incidentally, introduced "Electra" into service.

Second Generation Electra

Out of basic "Electra" design came the Navy's anti-submarine-warfare P-3C "Orion" shown here flying over Russian ships leaving Cuban waters during the famous "missile crisis". The sophisticated patrol planes are still in production at Lockheed, an assembly line that has been going continuously for more than 15 years!

Small things count too. There's a very important light fixture in all airplanes, the anti-collision rotating beacon. This bright bulb is normally located on the vertical tail; replacement requires use of a crane or portable frame—almost the equivalent of a hook-and-ladder unit.

On the *"Electra"*, the beacons are located on the top and bottom of the fuselage. A maintenance crew member simply enters the cabin to replace the top bulb and replaces the bottom one from the ground. He doesn't even need a nail keg to stand on.

The *"Electra"* is also the first four-engined commercial transport with swift, single-point built-in fueling. When you park the big plane and say, "fill 'er up", fuel is taken on at the rate of 300 gallons a minute, flowing evenly to all four tanks at the same time—or diverted to individual tanks. Total capacity: 5,506 gallons.

You scarcely have time to grab a sandwich, anymore.

They've cut corners at every turn. Watching a propeller and engine over-haul at American's maintenance base in Oklahoma City, I had a shop foreman explain: "They've cut twenty hours off the time required for this job by using self-locking nuts and self-threaded inserts instead of safety wire and cotter-pins."

I also saw them handle a quick engine change. They took out one complete "power egg" and put in another; the whole job took less than two hours.

Inside the same airplane, they can rework the whole cabin decor in about the same length of time. The *"Electra's"* interior consists of pre-trimmed panels that quickly snap into place, changing the trim scheme. Imagine, having a home in which a marred, scratched or soiled wall could be unsnapped and replaced. It's all part of the *"Electra's"* maintenance-minded design.

It's also important, for the city-to-city passenger, to point out that the airplane can be serviced in 12 minutes during enroute stops. Complete turn-around servicing takes as little as 30 minutes. All servicing is from the right-hand side of the plane while passengers enter and depart from the left side. The result? Minimum ramp congestion.

She also has a lot of "P.A."—passenger appeal. I can honestly say that I have had more passengers take time out to offer compliments about this airplane than at any other time in all my years of flying for the airline.

Here are some features that passengers have told me they like about the *"Electra:"* The wide aisle that permits getting up and walking around without bumping into seats. Place for the luggage inside the cabin permitting them to take their baggage aboard, eliminating long waits and confusion at the end of a trip. The special hydraulically actuated airborne stairs, with sturdy hand-rails, that drop down from behind the forward entry door. The two doors in the fuselage that speed up passenger loading and unloading.

There is more. They like the seats of foam plastics and rubber contoured with plenty of space between armrests. Lanky passengers have more leg-room because of the way in which the seatbacks are engineered. Radiant heating and no-draft ventilation system provides the ultimate in cabin comfort. The airplane also has a cooling system that works when it's on the ground. There is also a lot of favorable comment about the large windows which afford passengers a better view.

She can climb up to 30,000 feet—well above most bad weather and turbulent air masses. Her cabin remains pressurized to about 8,000 feet which is normal environment. She climbs quickly and smoothly which makes most of your trip a level flight and not an uphill struggle.

Because of her speed, over-all trip times are short. She can get into small airports with runways as short as 4,700 feet, even under conditions of reduced visibility and extreme low ceilings. No wonder it has been said that she's the DC-3 of the Jet Age.

She can do almost anything the DC-3 can do plus a lot more. The *"Electra"* is a BIG airplane by comparison, and a money-maker for the lines that fly her.

That's probably why they call her the airplane that's got everything.

CHAPTER TWELVE

"Missile With A Man In It"

While Allan Loughead was taking people up for sight-seeing flights over San Francisco with the Model-G in the Fall of 1915 during the Panama-Pacific Exposition, citizens of London, England, were getting a much different impression of an aircraft over their city. The British had been at war with Germany for more than a year when, suddenly, the Kaiser unleashed a new "terror from the skies." Long, grey, cigar-shaped Zeppelins flying from their sheds in Friedrichshafen across the North Sea slipped through the night sky over London, and dropped bombs wantonly on the civilian populace.

Altogether, records show, there were 53 bombing raids against England by the Zeppelins and 63 raids by the German *"Gothas,"* huge biplane bombers. London was bombed twelve times by airship and thirteen times by airplane. The Ger-

mans dropped 275 tons of bombs on England, but before the war was over the British had dropped 5,000 tons of explosives on German targets.

The day of "strategic aviation" had arrived. World War One which introduced air warfare set the pattern—the airplane as an observation platform and spyplane, pursuit aviation and "dogfights" in a new battlefield high above the earth, the aerial bombardment of cities, even the advent of the radio-controlled flying bomb, forerunner of today's guided missile weaponry. And from that day to this, man has looked skyward with fear in his eyes.

The state of the art of strategic aerial warfare, as we know, reached a high-point in World War II with 2,000-plane raids on Berlin and other German cities. The lethal potential of the long-

Agreements between Lockheed and foreign countries led to a consortium which put the "Starfighters" in the air forces of the Free World nations. In this photo "Starfighters" proudly dominate ring of defense posing with USAF "Starfire" and French and British delta wings.

L-1011 TriStar and The Lockheed Story

One of two F-90s which gave birth to a whole new family of fighters with test pilot Tony LeVier at the controls. A close look at aft fuselage shows resemblance to P-80 except for high tail.

range bomber was further exemplified by the performance of B-29 *"Superfortresses"* in raids on Japanese cities, climaxed with the dropping of history's first atomic bombs on Hiroshima and Nagasaki.

All of this is pertinent here, because the long-range bomber and the threat of new rocket bombs (the V-1s and V-2s) which the Nazi introduced in the final days of World War II, forced a radical change in the thinking of those planning our post-war Air Force. Indeed, their strategy would have a decided effect on the future of Lockheed, at home and abroad. The result would be a whole new family of radically different aircraft designs whose technological, aerodynamic and scientific breakthroughs would help give us the L-1011 *"TriStar"*, and the know-how to build the next generation airliner, the supersonic transport. Let's see what happened.

It may be the "Pentagon Planners" read somewhere the words Sir Winston Churchill wrote as far back as 1914, when he was First Sea Lord, and the Admiralty was charged with defending England against the threat of aerial bombings by the Zeppelins which everybody knew were coming. Declared Churchill—*"There can be no question of defending London by artillery against aerial attack. It is quite impossi-*

ble to cover so vast an area; and if London, why not every other city? . . .The great defense against aerial menace is to attack the enemy's aircraft as near as possible to their point of departure!"

Certainly, it seems, that the Air Force specifications for a new fighter which went out to the airframe industry for bids late in 1945, took heed of Churchill's warning of thirty years before. The "specs" called for a *long-range, penetration fighter*. Translated that meant a plane that could *penetrate* the enemy's defenses, and hit any attackers "as near as possible to their point of departure."

Lockheed accepted the challenge. After trying out more than 65 different major designs on the drawing board and with models in the wind tunnel, the Winged Star entry emerged as a needle-nosed, swept-wing configuration designated the XF-90. The plane followed the F-80 *"Shooting Star"* and the T-33 *"T-Bird"* in the company's family of jet fighters.

The XF-90 was twice as heavy as the F-80, powered with a pair of Westinghouse J-34 jet engines each developing 4,000 pounds thrust-power and mounted side-by-side in the fuselage behind the single-place cockpit. It also got a good boost in power from a new device called the afterburner, which the plane introduced ex-

Greater fuel capacity (tip tanks) radar operator and nose full of firepower turned "T-Bird" into deadly F-94 "Starfire" interceptor.

Drag chute in tail reduced F-94C landing distance nearly 50 per cent enabling operation from short field. Lockheed pioneered idea.

"Starfire" F-94C was first fighter without guns. Ring of rockets in nose gave plane a deadly "Sunday punch."

perimentally. The thing injected extra fuel into the tailpipe and ignited it, expanding the already hot gases at the last minute (hence the term "afterburn") before spewing powerful forward thrust into the airstream. Pilots described the feeling when they turned on the afterburner—"like a good swift kick in the pants."

Afterburners would appear on virtually every succeeding jet fighter, but Lockheed with the XF-90 led the way when Test Pilot Tony LeVier flew the plane on its first flight in May, 1949. LeVier called it "a going machine, one of the strongest airplanes ever built."

The plane hit 668-mph in level flight, and pilots dived it many times at speeds faster than sound, but the plane lost in the competition to the McDonnell XF-88 *"Voodoo",* and only two XF-90s were built. Moreover, the Air Force lost interest in the "penetration" fighter because of intelligence that the Soviets had successfully flown new intercontinental bombers with A-bomb capability.

The "new look" for a defensive weapon was for a fast-climbing interceptor that could operate in all kinds of weather. When half a dozen proposals from other airframe companies didn't measure up to the AF requirements, Lockheed got a call from the Fighter Projects Branch at Wright Field. "We need an interim interceptor, and we need it now," was the plea. "Could Lockheed come up with such a plane?"

Lockheed could, and did in a hurry. Advanced Projects Group (The "Skunk Works" gang) took another look at their T-33 *"T-Bird"* adaptation from the F-80 which was the only two-seater jet fighter flying with service squadrons. Could they stretch it a little bit to make room for airborne weather radar? Why not? With a little longer nose the radar hardware would fit, and the cockpit for the student in the trainer could accommodate the radar operator. A little more tail, and they could pack in the afterburner. And there it was!

Since they could work within the framework of the basic F-80 design, by the time the Air Force decided *against* the F-90, the Air Force decided *for* Lockheed's all-weather interceptor. Once more, they had polished the fine points of the *"Shooting Star"* which became the F-94A *"Starfire"* that would fill the need for the "interim interceptor", delivered ahead of time. The Air Force was well satisfied, bought, altogether, 466 of the F-94As and F-94Bs, the latter an improved version, but basically the same aircraft.

Lockheed, however, wasn't satisfied. Project Engineer J. R. Daniel and the design team of Hibbard and Johnson took a closer look at their F-94 creation and did a little doodling on the drawing boards. If they could get a more powerful engine, and rework the wing, they were pretty sure the *"Starfire"* could make the first team, not just an interim aircraft, but a front-runner in the race to build an all-weather interceptor.

Unfortunately, the Air Force didn't share this opinion. There wasn't any support for the idea, but Lockheed went ahead, anyway, and developed the F-94C with company monies. The prototype—only one was built—proved so successful that it made everybody sit up and take notice. Lockheed got a production order for 110 aircraft, and the plane, itself, initiated a whole new set of "firsts" for fighters.

For one thing, it was the first fighter plane *without guns!* Normal firepower of .50-caliber machine guns or rapid-fire .20-mm cannon was replaced with a cluster of 24 "Mighty Mouse" rockets ringed around the nose. The F-94C was also the first fighter to be equipped with the Hughes automatic fire-control system. Complemented by latest radar, the two-man crew in the nearly-automatic *"Starfire"* could electronically stalk, zero-in and blast from the skies a target seen only as a dot on the radar scope.

Designed around the powerful Pratt & Whitney J-48 jet engine and an entirely new wing, super thin with super strength, the F-94C was the first production fighter without a swept-back wing to fly faster than sound. It also introduced the drag chute as a braking device to halve landing distances. Indeed, the *"Starfire"* was a harbinger of wings to come.

The prototype of the F-94C flew for the first time in January, 1950, and the Air Force was so impressed with its performance that Lockheed got an order for 110 of the improved "Starfires." By the time the first production model rolled off the line, USAF pilots found themselves in a new air war in the skies over Korea. And before it was over, "Starfires", in limited numbers, joined their sister ships—the *"Shooting Stars"* (F-80s) and the newer North American swept-wing F-86 *Sabrejets* up against the vaunted Russian MIG-15s which for a while, at least turned famed "MIG-Alley" into a one-way street for the Russians.

"Starfire" F-94As and F-94Bs at far north bases were "sentinals" during Korean peace talks and following months of "cold war."

"Missile With A Man In It"

One of first F-104 "Starfighters" to join Continental Air Defence Command takes off on practice intercept mission. Plane was first truly supersonic fighter capable of supersonic speeds in level flight and in climb.

The superiority of American pilots, not their planes, probably saved the day. Too often, the MIGs demonstrated superior performance. The advanced *"Sabrejets"* and F-94Cs didn't "overcome" until shortly before the truce.

It was an F-94A *"Starfire"* however, that gave the Reds something to think about, introducing a new technique in aerial warfare. The plane, under full radar control flying in pitch darkness, shot down an enemy aircraft without having seen the opposing plane until it burst into flames!

The *"Starfires"* also were among the first planes to be fitted with the experimental Lear F-5 autopilot which, coupled to the ILS (Instrument Landing System) made possible true all-weather operations. Fully automatic landings became almost routine.

It was during the Korean war in 1953 that another F-94C *"Starfire"* made history of a different kind. The plane was the 25,000th aircraft that Lockheed Aircraft Corporation had built since it was organized in 1932. There were many more to come in the next twenty years—fighters, patrol bombers, spyplanes, cargo planes, helicopters and spacecraft. And, of course, *"TriStar,"* the L-1011, which inspired this book.

About the time that plane No. 25,000 rolled off the assembly line Lockheed was in the midst of a top secret program that would have tremendous impact on the company's future. "LOOK TO LOCKHEED FOR LEADERSHIP," the

proud slogan which the famous *"Vegas"* wrote and which still appears on company stationery, was never put to greater test. And, perhaps, never again will the proof be so dramatic. The world would bear witness.

The secret project had its beginning, really, in Korea during the early days of the air war when the MIGs had the upper-hand. The Russian-built planes flown by Chinese pilots made it all too clear there was a need for a much lighter and faster combat plane, capable of performing a variety of missions—an interceptor, fighter, bomber, all rolled into one. Even the latest *"Starfires"* (F-94Cs) with all their advanced technology and automaticity were, really, just one step in the right direction.

Kelly Johnson, invited by the Air Force to go to Korea and see his magnificent F-80 *"Shooting Stars"* in action, proudly accepted, and when he came home, there were a lot of strange goings-on at The Skunk Works. Inside, under tightest security measures, there was being fashioned a metallic bolt of lightning—the XF-104—a plane so radically new in concept that it would be acclaimed as "the most advanced plane of its type ever developed." It was an accolade which for the next ten years, the F-104's stellar performance would prove well deserved.

Design work on the XF-104 was started in November, 1952. On February 8, 1954—fifteen months later—with veteran Test Pilot Tony LeVier at its controls the plane made its first flight. LeVier, now a Lockheed executive,

L-1011 TriStar and The Lockheed Story

Slim needle nose profile of "Starfighter" and short, ultra thin wing were plane's aerodynamic "secrets." Pilots had to wear pressure suits to offset "G" forces during supersonic flight times.

recalls—"It was more like a rocket-plane than a jet." Performance-wise, the design would prove itself in the same class with many short and intermediate range missiles. Newsmen dubbed it *"the missile with a man in it."*

Lockheed called it the *"Starfighter,"* and its performance was so startling that nobody said anything about it during the tests of early models. Then, in April, 1956, the Air Force and Lockheed put on a Hollywood-type premiere. The stage was set at the company's Palmdale Jet Center, about 50 miles northeast of Burbank in a corner of the Mojave Desert. Today the site is better known as the birthplace of the *"TriStar"*—a gigantic star factory in the desert. But back then, the F-104 *"Starfighter"* was the center attraction.

News media, TV, radio and magazine representatives from all over the world were invited to see the latest Winged Star make her public debut. What they saw was a long, stinger-nosed, pencil-like fuselage (54 feet, 9 inches in length) with a T-shaped tail. The wings, the leading edges razor-blade sharp, stuck straight out only seven-and-a-half feet from root to tip, and were located two-thirds of the way back on the fuselage. Gaping at the radically new "profile of progress' observers also saw powerful General Electric J79 jet engine, capable of delivering more thrustpower (15,000-pounds) than any powerplant previously developed. Later, during flight demonstrations they heard its mighty roar, and the clap of thunder when the afterburner kicked in, sending the *"Starfighter"* across the heavens at ultrasonic speeds.

By this time the secret was out. The F-104 had attained speeds heretofore achieved only by experimental rocket-powered aircraft. It was the first aircraft to exceed Mach 2, twice the speed of sound, in level flight. It was the first aircraft that could fly faster than sound while climbing. And it could climb up to altitudes that bordered on the fringe of space.

On December 14, 1959, an F-104C took off from Edwards Air Force Base Flight Test Center, and climbed into the stratosphere establishing a new altitude record of 103,395.5 feet. Before it started the climb, the plane flashed above the desert at Mach 2.36, more than 1500-mph ground speed!

The man who supervised the F-104 design, C. L. "Kelly" Johnson (who else?), summed it up thusly—"Everytime this baby flies it breaks the so-called world's speed mark." Johnson and Lockheed, for the design and development of the *"Starfighter"*, won the 1958 Collier Trophy, America's top award for aeronautical achievement.

What made *"Starfighter"* so great?

"A combination of high thrust and low drag, the *highest* and *lowest*, respectively, for any single-engine aircraft in the world," according to R. R. (Dick) Heppe, an aerodynamicist who helped design the F-104.

To achieve this ratio of *drag* versus *thrust* the design itself introduced several innovative features that contributed to the high performance characteristics. (1) The missile-shaped fuselage snugly housed the F-104's GE engine

Famed aviatrix "Jackie" Cochrane flew this "Super Starfighter" to become first woman ever to fly faster than sound. She had expert instructor, Charles E. "Chuck" Yeager who was first to break sound barrier in Bell XS-1 a decade before first F-104 flew.

ITALIAN F-104 "Starfighter" prototype on ramp at Lockheed Palmdale facility. Italian aircraft industry headed by Fiat later manufactured some 165 of improved version. Italy through NATO was first country to operate 1500-mile-an-hour "Super Starfighters."

(only 3 feet, 4 inches in diameter) offering less "flat plate" area, and thus presenting less resistance to the airstream (the difference between swinging a baseball bat as against swinging the flat surface of a paddle) than any other aircraft up to that period. (2) The same benefit (less resistance) was derived from the thin leading edge of the wing which cut through the air like a hot knife through butter. (3) The T-shaped empennage, permitted the whole horizontal stabilizer to move as an elevator "a flying tail," providing better controllability (although "tricky") at ultra sonic speeds.

These design features, of course, weren't entirely new or revolutionary ideas. They had been tried before. (Paradoxically, Allan Loughead's Model-G had a "flying tail.") The *"Starfire"* had demonstrated the advantages of a thin wing. But *"Starfighter"* put them all together and made them work advantageously. And the GE-engine, coming along when it did, produced the right combination at the right time, reminiscent of the Wright Brothers at Kitty Hawk, when they made the first successful controlled power flight in a heavier-than-air-machine.

The right combination turned out to be more than a "triple threat" member of the USAF team, a plane that could be easily adapted for ground attack, as an interceptor and tactical support fighter and later, as a fighter-bomber. It could carry rockets and cannon and if need be, atomic weapons!

Lockheed got a $100,000,000 contract from the Air Force for F-104As in 1955, followed by another $166,000,000 order a year later which also included some two-seater versions. By February, 1958, the AF had its first operational squadrons flying. The F-104 became the guardian angel of the Air Continental Air Defense Command, responsible for the nation's security against enemy attack.

But this was only part of the story. Agreements between Lockheed and Belgium, Canada, Italy, the Netherlands, West Germany and Japan, resulted in one of the greatest international cooperative ventures in the history of the aerospace business. *"Starfighters"* were manufactured in these countries, a worldwide investment that totaled more than $3,000,000,000 (billion) and which saved millions of dollars through common logistics planning.

The unprecedented consortium concept brought the Winged Star to a new magnitude of brilliancy with *"Starfighters"* moving along production lines in each of these countries providing the Free World with the best available air defense weapon. How strong that defense, is best illustrated, perhaps, by the fact that despite many threats and taunts during the decade of the *"Starfighter"*—the shaky sixties—nobody took a poke at us.

Beyond this, there was a great peace time spin-off of which Lockheed and America can be overly proud. As a result, those nations which took part in the program, gained for themselves a solid industrial capability to produce aircraft, including those of their own design. In addition, numerous companies in allied fields among the *"Starfighter* nations" have emerged as capable and competitive suppliers.

The impact spread the spirit of the American competitive, free-enterprise system from Berlin to Bangkok.

In the light of history, one wonders—as this is written and we read and listen to the plans for rebuilding North Vietnam and all of southeast Asia—why that same spirit cannot stretch itself from Palmdale to Peking?

The Winged Star, what happened in the case of the F-104 program, at least, may have illuminated the way.

Still, there was something wrong with all of this, relative to the future of Lockheed. It was true that the *"Starfighter"* brought a great triumph in technology, and world-wide recognition in shaping the destinies of nations. But in the process, while going ahead at ultra-sonic speed in one direction, Lockheed was going backwards in another.

"Starfighter" fitted with experimental rocket motor in tail takes off straight up for the wild blue yonder. Because of its superior design F-104 was used for many different test missions.

"Missile With A Man In It"

PLACE OF HONOR. A USAF Lockheed F-104 "Starfighter" stands on permanent display in front of the Cadet Chapel at the USAF Academy, Colorado Springs, Colo. Nearly 2500 "Starfighters" have been produced in seven countries. Many still are first line defenders.

Building the fastest and most deadly fighter in the world wasn't exactly the image Bob Gross envisioned when he made the decision that day, twenty years before, to go ahead with the Model-10 *"Electra"* and get the company a chunk of the commercial airliner business. Nor was it what Johnson and Hibbard, Jack Frye and Howard Hughes had in mind when they came up with the *"Constellation"* which, when the first XF-104 was put down on paper, was the fastest and most luxurious airliner flying air routes around the world.

Where was Lockheed leadership in the development of a commercial airliner for the Jet Age?

By the time the first *"Starfighters"* joined the Air Defense Command, Boeing, Douglas and Convair had jet liners, the 707, 727, the DC-8 and the 880 respectively, joining the fleets of scheduled airlines around the world. Lockheed's *"Connies," "Super Connies,"* even the turbo-prop *"Electras"* couldn't match the performance of the new generation of turbo-jet airliners.

Another critical "hour of decision" had arrived. What direction to point the Star?

There was *"Hercules"* and the *"Starlifter"*. Could these cargo planes be converted into passenger jetliners? It was possible.

But, rather, let's go back to that day in 1945 when the author was talking with Bob Gross, and he told us to go and see Hall Hibbard and listen to what he had to say about the future. Perhaps, therein, was a key to Lockheed's future as 1970 approached.

Hibbard was Vice President and chief engineer of Lockheed at the time. *The future transport will be of the pure jet type,"* he prophecied. *"It can be as large as is necessary to meet the demands of the traveling public, for there will be plenty of power available to fly this ship. The cabin will be pressurized for flight above 50,000 feet. The luxurious comfort of this*

141

airplane will surpass anything you have known in the field of transportation."

The author's notes continue:

"In this jet transport traveling above the speed of sound, 10 miles above the earth," Hibbard explained, *"there will be no noise, no vibration, no sense of speed. Weather will make no difference at all, since you will fly over the storms. Radio navigational aids will permit you to land with perfect confidence on an airport that is zeroed in by fog, snow or what have you. . ."*

"This airplane will not be built immediately," he concluded. *"The industry needs a few years to get acquainted with jet propulsion. But within 10 to 15 years it will be yours."*

Hall Hibbard wrote this in 1945.

Was he thinking, perhaps, of a supersonic transport? Or of the *"TriStar?"*

CHAPTER THIRTEEN

Secrets Of The Skunk Works

Clarence L. (Kelly) Johnson was born in Ishpeming, Michigan on February 27, 1910, when the infant Aviation Section of the Army Signal Corps, less than a year old, (Organized August 2, 1909) consisted of one officer, nine enlisted men, one Wright Brothers aeroplane, one Balwin Airship and three captive observation balloons. Today there probably is no individual who has contributed so much toward the design and development of a whole family of military aircraft to help build the USAF into the foremost airpower in the world.

The *"Electras,"* the *"Hudsons,"* the XP-38 *"Lightnings"*, the *"Constellations"*, the XP-80 *"Shooting Star"*, the *"Hercules"* and *"StarLifter"*, the *"Starfire"* and *"Starfighter"*, we have seen his guiding hand in the emergence of each of these designs from drawing board to assembly line—the wings of war and the wings of commerce. He did not do it alone, nor has he

ever hinted at such a thing, but when we think of Lockheed "leadership" the name Kelly Johnson stands out as a great leader.

Certainly, this is borne out in the long list of awards and honors, including two Collier Trophies, (there is no other two-time winner) which he has received for his contributions to the furtherance of the aeronautical sciences. But more important, "Kelly" is a leader of men, demonstrated many times in his ability to inspire the incentive to achieve the impossible among his close associates—engineers, pilots, scientists, management, the man on the assembly line, and the "grease monkey" on the flight line.

The reader may remember meeting him first (Chapter Four) during the birth of the Model-10 *"Electra"*, the man who gave the plane its twin-tail configuration. "Kelly" was 23 then, fresh out of the University of Michigan with a master of science degree in aeronautical engineering.

Clarence L. "Kelly" Johnson, vice president Advanced Development Projects for Lockheed Aircraft Corporation poses beside famed U-2 spyplane which he designed. "Kelly's" military and commercial aircraft designs have brought him more honors than any other living aeronautical engineer.

"The Angel" U-2 spyplane could fly so high that defense against it was almost useless. Note the expansive wing area. Plane had potential of gliding great distances. Some called it a "metallic glider." It was subsonic aircraft.

He joined Lockheed in 1933 as a tool designer. After assignments as flight test engineer, stress analyst, aerodynamicist, weight engineer, and wind tunnel engineer, he became chief research engineer in 1938. We meet him again (Chapter Seven) in 1943 as Head Man of the "Skunk Works" and the Advanced Projects Group which gave us the *"Shooting Star"*, America's first combat jet fighter. It is a "title", he has remarked to friends, that he would rather have than that which he holds today in the Lockheed Aircraft Corporation as *Senior Vice President.*

The SKUNK WORKS is something special. It is, of course, no longer located in a "circus tent" where it was housed back in 1943. It is situated amid modernistic surroundings in an isolated and highly-classified area of the Lockheed-California Company engineering building in Burbank. It has a new name—*Advanced Development Projects,* but its purpose and mission are the same.

"ADP is the sort of place where the government can push an idea under the door and management does the rest", says *Quality Management & Engineering Magazine* in its June, 1971, issue. "Then, in an unreasonably short period of time, effective hardware will be produced, at moderate price, with minimal problems, and it will do the job specified."

"Kelly" Johnson, himself, spells out its mission in these words: *"To set goals never before attained, assign the best talent available to increments of the problem, combine the solutions, and refine the over-all efforts on a tight but practical schedule. Be quick. Be quiet. Be on time."*

This is "Kelly's" technique. It is what he had in mind when he founded the SKUNK WORKS thirty years ago. The formula is mirrored nowhere else in the aerospace industry. It has produced spectacular results.

The development of the U-2 spyplane is a typical example.

The story begins back in 1954. There was a touchy truce in Korea. General of the Armies, Dwight D. Eisenhower, had become President of the United States, and had kept his promise to "stop the fighting in Korea." But Ike had other problems. The Soviet Union in August, 1953, had exploded its own hydrogen bomb.

The Russian bear went into hibernation. There was a period of ultra secrecy behind the Iron Curtain; nobody knew what was going on. Eisenhower, his military mind of a suspicious nature, believed the Bear to be sharpening his claws, not just licking them. For its own security, the U.S. had to make sure.

President Eisenhower knew what was

needed—*air reconnaissance over Russia.* The U.S. should have "eyes in the skies" that would photograph the Bear's every move. The risk was great. What if a U.S. spyplane were shot down on its mission? It could provoke World War III.

The Truman Administration had considered aerial spying, but decided against it. Ike, who gave the word at D-Day, decided to give the "go ahead" and take Russia's picture. The risk could be greater not to know a potential enemy's strength and plans, than to have another Pearl Harbor.

Thus, we find on a December day, 1954, thirteen years after that Day of Infamy, a small group of Air Force people and agents from the CIA (Central Intelligence Agency) huddled together with "Kelly" Johnson and Bob Gross in the latter's Burbank office. The Government people wanted to know: *Could Lockheed build a plane that could fly so high over Soviet territory that no known anti-aircraft defense or interceptor aircraft could shoot it down?*

Everything else was all set. The AF photographic experts had the assurance that specially designed high-altitude cameras and related equipment would be available. The CIA had already recruited pilots who would fly the missions. There was only one thing missing, the plane itself to put a camera platform in the sky.

The meeting lasted for hours. It was so secret that even General Curtiss LeMay, commander of the Strategic Air Command which would be assigned the aircraft, didn't even know the session was in progress. When it was over, the SKUNK WORKS had a new assignment—build such an aircraft in secret, in a hurry!

According to Johnson, he "got together 23 fellows and we went to work." Among themselves they called their creation, "The Angel", and by mid-summer, 1955, "The Angel" spread its wings.

For Air Force records the plane was given a designation—U-2, described as a very-high-altitude weather and photo-reconnaissance aircraft. With a wing span of 80 feet and a fuselage length of 49 feet, 7 inches, in profile, it ressembled more a large streamlined, metallic glider than a 17,000-pound, gross take-off weight jetplane. There was a reason—To give it a bonus in range, (more than 3,000 miles) the pilot could shut off the engine (a Pratt & Whitney J57 turbojet) and the craft could glide for extra distance. Why not? The U-2 could climb to altitudes above 70,000 feet; out of sight and out of sound.

Francis Gary Powers holds model of Lockheed U-2, March 6, 1962 as he begins testimony before Senate Armed Services Committee about his reconnaissance missions over Russia and subsequent imprisonment by Soviets.

It was no speedster; a top speed of about 500-mph, that was all, but it had design-built-in stability to make it an ideal camera platform. There was room for only one crewman, the pilot, who could operate, automatically, a battery of cameras of different types buried in its fuselage and wings.

The cameras started to roll as soon as the planes rolled off the line and completed their preliminary flight test at Edwards Air Force base in the Mojave Desert. "The Angel" flew at will over Russia. The Soviets knew it was there. Fighters with Red Stars on their wings came up to try and shoot it down. Their machines ran out of breath. Even ground-to-air missiles fell short.

Then, one day in May, 1960, spy pilot Gary Francis Powers in a U-2 was shot down near Sverdlovsk, about 100 miles southeast of Moscow. Nobody knows for certain what

In another role, U-2s are used by NASA (National Aeronautics and Space Administration) for "upper air region exploration." (Aerospace Daily)

Lockheed A-11 (prototype of YF-1A interceptor) was first aircraft capable of sustained flight at 2,000-mph, twelve miles above earth.

happened, not even Powers, who was taken prisoner, tried, convicted and released two years later in an exchange for a Soviet spy in the U.S. Best reports are that a SAM (surface-to-air missile) scored a near burst damaging the U-2's engine. Then, trying to glide to a friendly base, Powers' U-2 was hit at lower altitudes by Russian MIGs, a wing shot off, and the plane crashed.

When Powers was shot down, the U.S. cancelled its spy flights over Russia. But for more than three years the U-2s had filmed Russia's defenses, secret bases, missile sites, mountains, lakes, rivers and geographical terrain. Russia wasn't so secret, anymore.

Other U-2s were operating in other parts of the world on recon missions over North Vietnam, Cuba and flown by Nationalist China pilots, over Red China. The planes were also used for "upper air region exploration", providing vital information about winds aloft, storms and other high-altitude phenomena.

Meanwhile, back at the SKUNK WORKS they were secretly busy building a successor to the U-2. They called it "The Thing", and until President Lyndon B. Johnson, on February 29,

1964, broke the news of its existence, it was one of the best kept secrets in the history of the aviation industry. At his news conference, Johnson identified the plane as the A-11, capable of sustained flight at 2,000 miles per hour, twelve miles or more above the earth. "The performance of the A-11 far exceeds that of any other aircraft in the world today," the President said.

"This advanced experimental aircraft—capable of high speed and high altitude and long-range performance of thousands of miles," President Johnson added, "constitutes a technical accomplishment that will facilitate the achievement of a number of important military and commercial requirements."

Concept of the A-11, designation later changed to YF-12A because it was to be used as an interceptor fighter as well as a reconnaissance plane, was first thought of in 1958. Intelligence learned the Soviet Air Force had a "crash" program for a missile that would drive the U-2s from their domain. Nobody doubted the Russians wouldn't come up with a weapon which could shoot down the slow-flying U-2 spyplanes. The challenge was to build a plane that would fly higher and faster.

Top U.S. planemakers were called to a secret meeting in Washington and briefed on the situation. Attending, of course, was "Kelly" Johnson. He listened to questions like these: Could a plane be built that could fly 2500-mph and faster for long periods of time? Could present airframe structures stand friction heat and the shock forces generated at such speeds? Could such a plane and its pilot "live" at altitudes of 100,000 feet or higher? Was such performance possible and still have a minimum range of 4,000 miles?

Here was the toughest set of requirements ever thrown at the aircraft industry. By their own admission the "best brains" weren't sure it could be done.

Flying back to Burbank, "Kelly" made a mental list of some pluses. (1) The U.S. had an experimental rocket-powered plane, the North American X-15 which had flown above 300,000 feet and had hit speeds of 4,000-mph! But the X-15 could fly at ultra sonic speed for only very short periods of time, seconds, not hours. For sustained flight at 2500-mph or faster its skin would burn up. *But design-wise, shape and size, it was on the right track, and there was a lot of "know-how" available.* (2) Another project, the XB-70 supersonic bomber, had brought into being the Pratt & Whitney J58 turbojet engine, 40,000-pounds of thrust or more. *With this kind of thrustpower available in an X-15 profile, or something like it, 2500-mph was not too far out of reach.* (3). The Titanium Metals Corporation was promising a new alloy, lightweight with the strength of steel, and heat resistant to temperatures exceeding anything the X-15 had encountered. *Such a metal could be used for the airframe, wings and fuselage.*

The impossible didn't look so impossible, after all. "Kelly" Johnson was pretty sure Lockheed could deliver.

Out of the "Skunk Works" came a winged wonder, a plane so radically new in shape, structure and performance capabilities that it was acclaimed by aeronautical experts as a "quan-

North American X-15 rocket-powered supersonic "probe" plane with Lockheed F-104 chase plane. X-15 could fly at ultra sonic speeds for only short periods of time, but it gave valuable "know-how" which led to SR-71 configuration.

"Blackbird" shows off her "double delta" wing configuration in this spectacular flight picture.

tum jump in technology." Johnson, himself, has written— "I believe I can truly say that everything on the aircraft from rivets and fluids, up through materials and power plants had to be invented from scratch!" Oddly, the Y-12A emerged as a *biplane,* two wings, but instead of being mounted one above the other (like Allen Lockheed's Model-G) the wings, shaped like arrow heads, were in tandem, one forward, one rearward on a long thin fuselage, virtually a flying fuel tank. The design is called a "double delta".

The forward wing, which didn't look like a wing at all, was a narrow fairing with airfoil characteristics on each side of the fuselage like the eaves of a roof. The rear wing, a wide triangle in the tail, provided the main lift forces in subsonic and transonic flight.

A pair of the high-thrust engines in long tube-like nacelles were mounted on this big "delta", faired to the airfoil like part of the wing, one on each side of the fuselage. Atop each nacelle was a large vertical fin and rudder. "Kelly" was right back where he started—putting a twin tail ("Electra" Model-10) on a Lockheed.

The "double delta" was a major innovation, and proved to be the answer to several problems. As the speed of the plane increased, particularly in the ultrasonic range, the forward "delta" generated an extra bonus in lift and provided desirable control stability, better than previous designs. At the same time, the big "delta" in the rear permitted excellent take-off and landing characteristics. The design would help Lockheed in its thinking about other supersonic aircraft in the future.

The YF-12A had other unusual features, each

a major breakthrough in its particular area. Perhaps, the greatest of the plane's advanced technology was its structural material. Most of the YF-12A was made of **titanium,** an alloy call-Beta B-120, which came along just in time. By trial and error, guesswork and prayer, they had learned to make   behave, and how to work with it to fabricate complex and grotesque-shaped aircraft structures. Lockheed had worked with titanium on a research basis since 1949 according to "Kelly" Johnson. "We attempted to attain high strength-weight ratios, good ductility, and relatively cheap structures, which did not develop very rapidly," he explains.

One reason was that the metal was very brittle, difficult to shape and machine. Fortunately, the new alloy overcame this drawback. But even so, to build the miracle aircraft, it was necessary to invent new drills, cutting machinery, powerheads for profilers, and cutting lubricants. In the process, a whole new welding technique was discovered. Later, it would help in fabricating certain titanium parts for the *"TriStar".*

Performance-wise, the plane passed every test. The U.S. had a superior replacement for the U-2s—a plane which it was unlikely any potential enemy could shoot down with known weapons.

There was only a limited number built, but out of the A-11 and YF-12A programs came an even more advanced design, the SR-71, Strategic

Head-on view of "Blackbird" has some of "Star-fighter" look with elongated needle nose. Note narrow forward delta wing.

Lockheed SR-71 "Blackbird" takes on fuel from KC-35 flying tanker. Ability to accept in-flight refuelling gives plane unlimited range. It can fly at triple sonic speeds for as long as crew can take it.

Reconnaissance aircraft. Even today, almost ten years after the first SR-71 flew at Palmdale (December, 1964) these planes are regarded as vital to the nation's security. In service with the Strategic Air Command's 4200th Strategic Wing, Beale Air Force Base, California, they are daily flying a variety of missions.

Called the *"Blackbird"* (the plane is painted black to reflect off heat waves) the SR-71 is about the same size as the YF-12A but with refined design and improved performance.

Imagine, a plane that can fly in excess of three times the speed of sound for long periods of time, twenty miles or more above the earth, and whose sophisticated advanced observation equipment can survey 60,000 square miles of land or ocean per hour. A plane, equipped to accept refueling from flying tankers, giving it unlimited range to roam the world's skies up so high it has been classified as "suborbital". For an enemy, there is no longer anywhere to hide.

Moreover, the *"Blackbird"* as an interceptor, armed with air-to-air rocket missiles and automatic radar fire-control system, can intercept any known manned-bomber type aircraft that might be heading our way, *before* it reaches the Canadian border. With speed capability, in excess of released figures, it can also chase missiles and shoot them down. The SR-71 could also carry and deliver an H-bomb with perfected guidance aids. The "Blackbird"—indeed—is a scare crow to warn off unwelcome intruders.

One wonders what next will come out of "Kelly's Skunk Works".

President Johnson at that 1964 press conference announcing the existence of the A-11 gave us a hint. Pridefully, the President declared—*"The development of a supersonic commercial transport aircraft will also be greatly assisted by the lessons learned from this A-11 program."*

Lockheed already was working on plans for an SST.

Powered by two highly-advanced Pratt & Whitney J-58 engines that look like "missiles" faired into rear delta wing this YF-12A version of "blackbird" flies at triple-sonic speed with altitude capability exceeding 80,000 feet.

CHAPTER FOURTEEN

Fallen Star And A Super Star

She was an odd-looking little aircraft; no propeller, no jet intakes, only a cluster of rockets in the tail. Her fuselage was round and fat with its needle nose probe presenting a profile like a swordfish. Her thin, tapered wings looked more like a fish's fins. She didn't set normally on her tricycle landing gear; she squatted. And you didn't climb into her tiny cockpit; you crawled in through a square door in her side.

She was built rugged and strong of special metal alloys to withstand high ambient temperatures, friction heat of the rushing air over her sleek skin surface. She was built for speed, to fly like a bullet. They said she could withstand aerodynamic forces up to eighteen times her own weight. They hoped that was true.

She wasn't shiny and silvery like most new planes; she was painted a brilliant orange like a fireball. Maybe, she was. When they fired up her rockets, testing on the ground, she made her presence known like a clap of thunder.

This was the Bell Aircraft Corporation XS-1, the plane the Air Force was betting on to penetrate the invisible, sonic wall, the so-called "sound barrier". There were those skeptics, who said it couldn't be done; that when an aircraft approached the speed of sound there was a danger sign in the sky. Some even said it was a STOP sign that put a limit on how fast man and machine could fly.

Famed British aircraft designer, Geoffrey de Havilland, had tried to crash the mysterious "sound barrier" on September 27, 1946. His plane flashed across the sky like a meteor. But the next instant it blew up, a ball of fire in the sky.

Indeed, strange things happened in the unknown sonic regions. Shock waves—exploding shells of compressed air—hammered at a plane's skin and frame; trip hammers trying to tear it apart. The rudder, ailerons and elevators developed severe buffeting, violent vibrations and flutter. An old enemy—"compressibility". Sometimes, the controls froze; a pilot was helpless. It was believed, for a long time, that when a plane hit the sonic speed range, the craft would disintegrate.

We know better today. The *"Starfire"*, the *"Starfighter"*, the *"Blackbird"* with their ad-

Capt. Charles E. "Chuck" Yeager (now a one-star general) who was first man to fly faster than sound more than quarter of a century ago.

vanced design and technology and new structural materials, have all flown faster than sound, many times faster. But the XS-1 was the first plane to accomplish the feat. And a young Wright Field Air Force test pilot, Captain Charles E. Yeager (now a Brigadier General) became the fastest man

The date was October 14, 1947.

The XS-1, fueled and ready, was carried to an altitude of 21,000 feet by a modified B-29, the small plane snuggled beneath the *"Superfort's"* belly like a baby whale suckling its mother. High in the sky, over California's Mojave Desert (Muroc Dry Lake, today's Edwards Air Force Base), the B-29 circled, while Yeager was lowered into the XS-1 cockpit through the mother plane's bomb bay.

When all was set, they started the count down. . *ten. . nine. . eight. . .ZERO!* And the XS-1 dropped free.

With 5,000 pounds of fuel on board—liquid oxygen and alcohol—fed into the rocket motor by nitrogen pressure, dangerously explosive, she dropped like a big bomb. According to Yeager—*"We dropped several hundred feet to be sure of clearing the B-29. Then, I hit the*

Bell XS-1, rocket-powered supersonic probe was first plane to crash the so-called "sound barrier."

switch igniting one of the rockets. BOOM! It sounded like I had fired a cannon. The XS-1 shot forward. . ."

". . . there was some vibration. It took muscle to hang onto the stick. There were strange noises; Banshees screaming. But the real sensation was I had control; positive control. And we were climbing at a normal angle. I had a comet by the tail and couldn't let go.

"Suddenly the buffeting stopped. Flight was smooth. And silent; only the hissing sound of rushing air over the plane's sleek surfaces."

"I looked at the Mach Meter. The indicator read Mach 1.05. We were flying faster than sound (Mach 1) climbing at better than 700-mph!"

Many lessons were learned from that first penetration into the supersonic region. Perhaps, the most important was the fact that for all his scientific knowledge, man knew so little about this new frontier. So many theories had disintegrated; *the airplane did not!*

Subsequent flights in the XS-1 and newer experimental supersonic designs on up through the remarkable SR-71 and others penetrated deeper and deeper into the unknowns. These winged machines put us on the way to the stars.

Except for the purely experimental and research aircraft, sometimes called our "space probes" the only planes flying at supersonic speeds until the late Sixties were military fighters and bombers. But even as far back as 1945, witness Hall Hibbard's remarks to the author (Chapter 12) Lockheed people were thinking about a commercial airliner that could fly faster than sound. With the coming of the Jet Age and 600-mile-an-hour passenger jetliners which started scheduled service (Innaugurated by National Airlines with Boeing 707 equipment, December 10, 1958 between New York and Miami) the next logical step seemed to be the supersonic passenger transport.

The fact is Lockheed began conducting research and development on supersonic transport configurations two years before. From that time, until submittal of the Phase I bid proposal to the FAA (Federal Aviation Administration) in January, 1964, more than 100 different designs were investigated. Arrow wings, multiple wings, fixed wings, and many

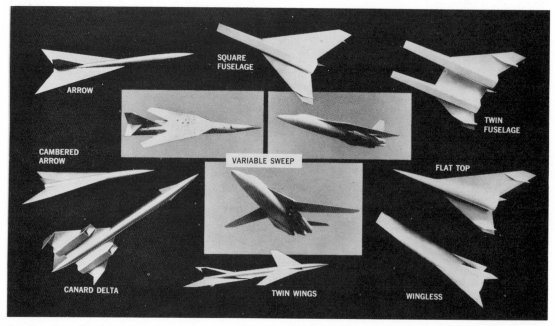

SQUARE FUSELAGE

ARROW

TWIN FUSELAGE

CAMBERED ARROW

VARIABLE SWEEP

FLAT TOP

CANARD DELTA

TWIN WINGS

WINGLESS

Lockheed studies for supersonic transport design involved many tests with various wing designs including even variable sweep.

Fallen Star And A Super Star

British-French entry in the SST race was this prototype "Concorde." Production models are scheduled to go into airline service sometime in 1974-75. First plane flew on March 2, 1969.

others were thoroughly investigated to determine their ability to meet the basic requirements of a long-range commercial transport with high-altitude cruise speeds of about 2,000-mph, and with landing and take-off capabilities equivalent to those of the then current large subsonic jets.

Briefly, here's what happened between the years 1956 and 1964 to put Lockheed a front-runner in what has become known as The Great SST Race. So spectacular was the performance and public acceptance of the subsonic jets (707s, 727s, DC-8s, 880s) that overnight Boeing, Douglas and Consolidated virtually captured the world market in jet liners. The British with their DeHavilland *"Comet"* and the French with their *"Caravelle"* were out of the picture. As a result, to keep alive their aircraft industry, Britain and France announced in 1962 a joint venture to build supersonic airliner, the *"Concorde."* About the same time Russia also announced it was building an SST, the TU-144. Fat and rich with its billion dollar subsonic jet bonanza, the U.S. paid little attention.

Then, suddenly, as *"Concorde"* began to take

shape despite skyrocketing costs upwards of a billion dollars, some U.S. Airlines began placing orders for the plane for future delivery. A warning sign was flashing: With the *"Concorde"* flying twice the speed of sound, cutting flight times over long transcontinental and intercontinental routes in half or better, the whole U.S. scheduled airline industry could easily find itself "horse-and-buggied" with obsolete equipment. At the same time U.S. airframe manufacturers could easily lose the world leadership they had held for three decades, and find themselves "frozen" out of the SST picture. America's prestige in the air was threatened. As well as the prospective loss of billions of dollars in balance of payments with more and more orders building up for the British/French supersonic.

Facing up this challenge, the U.S. Government in 1963 announced it was going to get into the race; taxpayers dollars backing the billion dollar design and development cost, the money to be paid back by airlines upon delivery of the planes. For the first time in history, a government agency, the FAA, was charged as "over-

L-1011 TriStar and The Lockheed Story

Russians were first in the sky with SST, the Tupelov TU-144 which probably will be first in service over trans-Siberian routes. The prototype is shown here. (TASS photo.)

seer" in the selection of a commercial airliner design to be built by private industry. A design competition was announced—similar to the military procedure—with any interested company invited to submit detailed proposals.

Three companies entered the race: Lockheed, The Boeing Airplane Company and North American Aviation. On May 20, 1964—ironically, 37 years to the day since Lindbergh started on his famous New York to Paris flight—the Lockheed and Boeing designs were awarded contracts for further study, called the Phase II competition. The Government wanted improved performance.

Interestingly, both companies, both giants in their field, had two entirely different backgrounds in experience and "know-how." Boeing since the Jet Age began had built more commercial subsonic jetliners than any other company in the world, a master of the art. Lockheed on the otherhand, had more experience than any other company in the western world building supersonic and ultra-sonic fighters.

In a similar divergence, the two companies went their separate ways in their approach to supersonic flight. Boeing chose a "swing wing" or "variable sweep" wing design, which meant the wings changed their planform in flight. At slow speeds, for instance, the wings stick out straight from the fuselage as in conventional jetliners. For supersonic speeds, however, the wings fold back at an angle (not unlike the "delta") to cut down on resistance or drag. Lockheed's approach was basically the "double delta" wing which it had proven so successful in wind tunnels and flight testing of its YF-12A fighter design.

For its final entry (The detailed specifications filled many volumes each, as thick as a Los Angeles telephone directory, a stack five feet high.) Lockheed offered three general arrangements each of which was designed to utilize either the Pratt & Whitney or General Electric high-thrust engines. Designated Model Nos. L-2000-1, L-2000-2 and L-2000-3, the three designs had fuselages of different lengths (214-feet, 225-feet, 7 in. and 245-feet, 5 inches, respectively) but used the same wing (116-foot span, 9,026 square foot area) same powerplants, systems, landing gear, flight station and vertical tail.

Performance-wise the L-2000 was designed to fly at Mach 3.0, about 2,000-mph, triple sonic speeds at altitudes up to 76,000 feet!

With a fuselage diameter of 132-inches, five abreast seating the Model L-2000's passenger capacity varied from 170 in the *small international* (Dash-2) to 250 passengers in the (Dash 3) called the *domestic* airplane. Maximum gross weight was 500,000 pounds with a desired 4,000 mile range, to meet FAA requirements.

Translated into more meaningful terms, Lockheed's proposal pointed out, all of this added up to an SST that could whisk passengers from New York to Los Angeles in *two* hours not *five;* from Washington to Paris in *three* hours not seven; only *eight* hours from Los Angeles to Sydney, *not* 15 1/2 hours at subsonic speeds. The plane would fly high above the weather in the stratosphere its passengers riding in living room comfort inside its pressurized cabin.

Such was the gist of Lockheed's SST presentation the FAA and the President's specially appointed team of professionals who would evaluate the two entries. Who would get the plum Boeing or Lockheed?

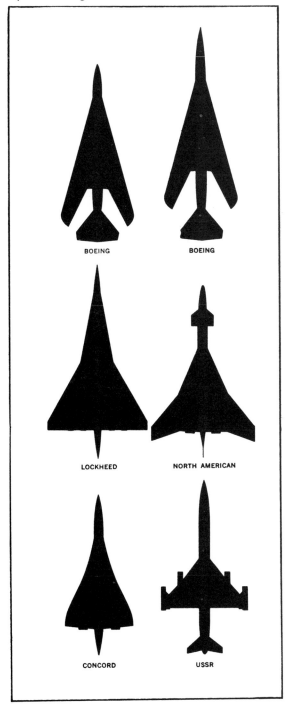

Silhouettes show various SST design shapes presented by three U.S. companies, Boeing, Lockheed, North American, the British-French "Concorde" and USSR's TU-144.

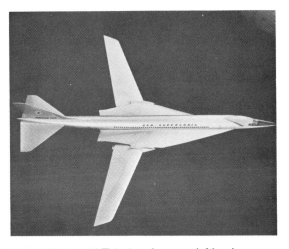

Initial Boeing SST design shows variable wing configuration with wing extended (span 173 feet) for landing and take-off subsonic speeds.

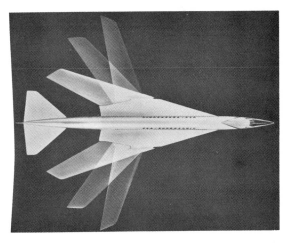

Boeing "swing wing" SST design showing how wing in flight moves back to form arrow shape configuration for Mach 2.7 speeds. In this position wing span is only 86 feet. Variable wing idea was abandoned in Boeing final design proposal which won contract.

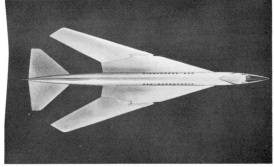

Boeing "swing wing" in folded position for high speed performance.

LOCKHEED SUPERSONIC TRANSPORT

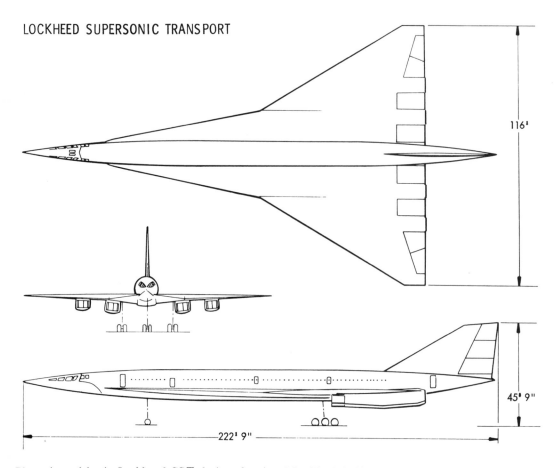

116'

45' 9"

222' 9"

Plan view of basic Lockheed SST design showing "double-delta" wing which Lockheed had already tested on A-11 triple sonic prototype.

The stakes were high, about $4.5 Billion in orders from U.S. airlines, alone.

During the long wait for the winner to be announced Lockheed went ahead building "test structures"—wing sections, fuselage sections and other parts—exploring fabrication techniques with titanium alloys which would be the prime metal used in the airframe because of its lightweight, strength and high heat resistance properties. Nobody had worked with titanium to build such huge structures before. Lockheed was tooling up to accept the challenge.

At the same time millions were spent, not only monies from the Government preliminary design contract but also company money to build fuselage mock-ups, engine mock-ups, and

Artist's concept of Lockheed SST in flight.

Fallen Star And A Super Star

Multi-million miler, Bob Hope gets briefing on supersonic flight in cockpit mock-up of Lockheed SST Model L-2000.

systems mock-ups. Everywhere throughout the entire Lockheed organization there was an "air of confidence."

"We knew the SST was technically feasible," declared Robert A. Bailey, Vice President and SST General Manager Lockheed-California Company, "based upon our wealth of high altitude (U-2) and supersonic (F-104 and YF-12A) design experience. And we had had more experience with titanium aircraft structures than anybody else."

Late in December, 1966 the verdict was handed down; President Johnson announced Boeing the winner in the government's SST competition.

It was three years later, however, before President Nixon gave the final stamp of approval to the U.S. supersonic transport development program, and funds were made available to Boeing for the start of construction of two prototypes. Ironically, in between because of difficulties with the "swing wing" design the finally approved version was a "delta" similar to the original Lockheed entry.

At Lockheed one wag quipped—"You can design'em right, but you don't always get paid for it."

The Lockheed SST was a fallen star.

There was, however, a "super star" on the horizon. And about the time that the "bad news" came on the SST competition loss, Lockheed-Georgia Company was tooling up to build the world's largest airplane—the C-5A *"Galaxy."* Paralleling the SST effort Lockheed had been in another race with Boeing and Douglas in the design and development of a king-sized heavy logistics cargo plane for the Military Airlift Command. In September, 1965—right in the middle of the SST program—Lockheed was awarded the Air Force contract along with General Electric to build the engines. The airframe and engine contracts totaled more than $2 Billion.

"Super Star" Lockheed C-5A, world's largest aircraft (landplane) now serving with U.S. Air Force Military Airlift Command. Note multi-wheeled, truck-type undercarriage which permits plane to land and take-off from short fields, rough terrain.

Scene at Lockheed-Georgia Company's Marietta plant where world's biggest cargo plane, C-5A is moving along assembly line. Last of 53 planes will fly sometime in late 1973. Commercial cargo version L-500 is under consideration.

When Lockheed accepted the challenge to build the sky giant, to be twice the size of any previous aircraft, one engineer described it as—"a quantum jump in size and capability, in systems and manufacturing sophistication."

H. L. Poore, Lockheed vice president in charge of the C-5 program, talking about some of the manufacturing problems was quoted in *Air Force Magazine* as saying—"We had to combine the dimensions and brute strength of a shipyard with the precision of a laser beam. Our tooling and assembly jigs look like shipways. Forward and mid-fuselage sections are too large and heavy for overhead cranes. We fitted them with tooling wheels and rolled them over floors smoothed with epoxy. The vertical fin support is so high above the factory floor that we equip workmen with safety ropes like mountain climbers, in case they lose their footing."

Work began at the Marietta Georgia plant (birthplace of the *"Hercules"* and the *"Starlifter"*) in the fall of 1965. The first C-5 (named *"Galaxy"*) rolled out of the plant on March 2, 1968 with President Lyndon B. Johnson heading a host of dignitaries present for the ceremonies.

On June 30, 1968 the first *"Galaxy"* made its maiden flight. By the spring of 1973 the last of the initial Air Force order for 58 was moving down the assembly lines.

The C-5 is a high wing, subsonic, cargo airplane with a normal flight gross weight of 728,-000 pounds and a maximum design gross of 769,000 pounds. Maximum fuel loading carried in 12 tanks across the 222-foot wing span is 318,000 pounds, and the plane's maximum payload is 265,000 pounds. It is 248 feet from nose to tail, and the rudder and horizontal tail is

65 feet above the ground. The plane is powered by four General Electric TF-39 turbo-fan engines rated at 41,000 pounds of thrust each.

Resting on a unique undercarriage, 24 main wheel tires and four nose-wheel tires to spread its weight, the big ship can land on soft-fields or conventional runways. It can take-off with maximum load in 8000 feet and land in 4,000 feet.

Designed to carry all items organic to Army combat divisions the large cargo compartment is 144 feet long, 19 feet wide, and 13 1/2 feet high with huge cargo doors in the nose and tail. This "drive-through" capability makes it easier to load than ships or railroad cars. The plane's interior has been described as big enough for several bowling alleys. It is longer than a basketball court.

The C-5's top speed is 582-mph at cruise altitude and it is capable of a long range mission of 6,000 miles with a payload of 100,000 pounds. On a maximum payload mission it can carry 265,000 pounds from New York to London, non-stop. As one expert summed it up —"The C-5 because of port charges, damage and other factors can carry cargo long distances cheaper than sea transport."

Quoting John Mecklin in *Fortune* magazine: "During the first month after U.S. intervention in Korea in 1950, 120,000 tons of troops, supplies and weapons were delivered from Japan mostly by sea. A fleet of 200 C-5s could deliver the same tonnage from the continental United States to any point in the world in only twenty days. During the Berlin Airlift, 308 planes were able to carry an average 5700 tons a day. The same job could have been done by twelve C-5s!"

The airplane also featured initial application of the most advance navigational aids and

Poised for take-off this C-5A shows unique high tail design, more than six stories above ground. Called the "Galaxy" plane represents design and manufacturing "know-how" gleaned from five decades of the Winged Star.

USAF "Galaxy" opens wide to take aboard an Army mobile scissors bridge launcher. Big plane can haul two launchers totaling more than 245,000 pounds. Military Air Lift Command says C-5A can give nation "remote presence" permitting rapid delivery of outsized equipment to far-away crises without maintaining large numbers of overseas bases.

automatic flight controls. It can make automatic landings when the ceiling is down to 500 feet with 700-foot runway visual range.

"What we learned from the advanced technology of the C-5 program," declared Robert A. Fuhrman, President of Lockheed-Georgia Company during peak production, "gave us a head start in the design and development of the L-1011 advanced technology trimotor."

At the L-1011 TriStar dedication ceremony, Governor Ronald Reagan of California was principle speaker.

Rollout of the first TriStar was September 15, 1970.

L-1011 TriStar's first flight took place on November 16, 1970. It surpassed all expectations for performance, lack of smoke and quietness.

Flying majestically in the skies of California, the first TriStar displays her distinctive three-engine design.

Cabin interior of the TriStar includes roomier seats, higher ceilings, wider aisles, added storage space, wide screen entertainment, spacious lounges and elegant decor throughout.

Trans World Airlines

Eastern Airlines

First L-1011 TriStar

All Nippon Airways

LTU (Lufttransport Unternehmen)

Air Canada

Pacific Southwest Airlines

Court Line Aviation Ltd.

Delta Airlines

*British European Airways, division of British
Airways*

Six TriStars in final assembly and ten others, at various assembly positions are housed in the giant final assembly building at the desert "Star Factory".

The partially completed, nine building "Star Factory" complex includes one of the largest final assembly buildings in the world.

The flight line is in operation around the clock to conduct final checkout, flight operations and delivery preparations of the L-1011.

A TriStar about to touch down during a test of the automatic landing capability.

A PSA stewardess demonstrates the large size of the air inlet for the Rolls-Royce turbofan engines.

Propulsion system for the TriStar consists of three Rolls-Royce RB.211B high by-pass ratio turbofan engines manufactured at Derby, England. Each engine delivers as much as 42,000 pounds of thrustpower.

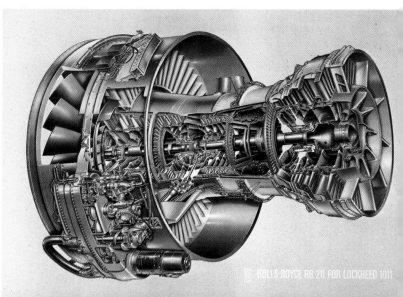

The colorful, majestic TriStar blends into the beauty of a desert scene.

The snowy Sierra Nevada mountains form a backdrop for the L-1011 during a test flight.

CHAPTER FIFTEEN

The "Magic Number" Game

It was the summer of 1965, and the future of the Lockheed Winged Star never appeared to be brighter. Lockheed and Boeing had been awarded contracts to go ahead with major studies in the government's competition for a supersonic transport. A special design group was set up to concentrate on the SST project at Lockheed. Winning the final design competition, the decision to be announced within a few months, would mean a lot of prestige and a multi-billion dollar business bonanza.

At the same time, Lockheed was deep into its C-5 proposal in the race with Boeing and Douglas to get the prime contract to build the Air Force's proposed long-range, king-sized logistics transport. The Navy, also, was doing everything it could to push development of an advanced design, long-range patrol plane.

Any one of these programs that bore fruit would put Lockheed in an enviable position. If it got all three, it would be like winning Horse Racing's Triple Crown—the Kentucky Derby, the Preakness and the Belmont.

We know what happened from previous chapters: Boeing got the SST program and, perhaps, it was just as well, in light of the political headaches and paralyzing heartbreak when the whole project was murdered on Capitol Hill. Lockheed won the C-5 competition, and although the end product, the C-5A *"Galaxy"* was and is a masterful achievement in design and performance, resultant contractual troubles turned some of the sweets of technological victory into sour grapes.

In all of this, there was one underlying and very discouraging factor. Lockheed, after losing the SST, had nothing going for it in the commercial airliner category. There was some ray of hope in the possibility of turning the *"Starlifter"* and the *"Galaxy"* into commercial cargo liners. But there was no new, purely commercial jetliner design on the boards.

Then, during the design studies for the P-3C, in the very early stages, something happened to change the picture. Before it was all over, the first glimmer of the *"TriStar"*, a wide-bodied

William M. "Bill" Hannan, holds model of proposed new Lockheed twin-engine "TriStar" and points to futuristic "stretch" version of world's most advanced technology trimotor.

L-1011 TriStar and The Lockheed Story

Jumbo Jet to compete with the 747 that Boeing was known to be building, appeared on the horizon.

William M. "Bill" Hannan, who became Chief Engineer on the L-1011 *"TriStar"* project in its early phases, and later Deputy Director of L-1011 Engineering described what happened: "We had done a lot of study work and a lot of preliminary design work on proposals for the new Navy patrol bomber. We had studied two engine airplanes and three engine airplanes and four engine airplanes, all of which were typical Navy-type with long skinny fuselages and big wings and lots of "range".

During this stage, Hannan recalled that one of the twin-engined designs suggested, generated a lot of enthusiasm. The Navy, however, didn't like the idea of only two engines for its long, over-water missions, so the "twin" was, momentarily, ruled out, for the Navy, anyway. "But a lot of us couldn't get the thing out of our minds," Hannan confessed. "It just had the appearance of being a pretty reasonable airplane."

"The next time we got together," Hannan explained, "someone asked the question if any of the fellows didn't think that twin engine airplane we had looked at might not make an interesting commercial design. That is, if we put a big enough fuselage on it to get a lot of people inside."

The idea caught fire, and despite the heavy work load on the Navy P3-C, the same guys did a little extra homework on the airliner. What came out of it was a high-wing aircraft with two big fan engines like those that were being considered for the military C-5 program. The fuselage was oval-shaped, wider than it was high, with two aisles, and a seating capacity for about 250 persons. The engines were hung out on the wing, one on each side of the fat fuselage, and in profile the plane looked not unlike Lockheed's last twin venture, the *"Saturn"*, only much larger.

According to Hannan they even went so far as to check the weight and performance of the design in the wind tunnel. But that was the end of it. The Navy job had top priority. Drawings and data for the "little big twin" were rolled up and forgotten.

Something else happened. About six months later, in the Spring of 1966, Lockheed's Chief Engineer Rudy Thoren got a call from Frank W. Kolk, his counterpart with American Airlines. Kolk said he wanted to come out and talk to Lockheed about, maybe, building a plane which American could operate as a kind of "shuttle bus" over its heavy-traffic, New York to Chicago segment.

Thoren set up a date. Kolk came out, and over a long lunch they sounded each other out. "Bill" Hannan, who was present at the meeting remembers—"Frank had with him a little five-page typed document that he called a requirement. It was a very brief description of what he had in mind, a little bit on the performance and so forth. He wanted a 'box' (fuselage) that could carry a maximum number of people at a minimum cost per seat mile. To him this meant two engines, not three or four. He didn't want the plane to be too big, not like the 747 project which Boeing had talked to American about. He had heard about the big new fan engines, too, and he thought they might do the trick.

"There was one thing, though, that he insisted on. American had a decided advantage over other carriers because of their close-in LaGuardia Airport terminus where the airline had millions invested in facilities. But LaGuardia had certain geometric constraints. The terminal was already fixed, the finger satallites were fixed, the turning areas were fixed. And there was a pier under one of its runways which, at that time, was only *approved to carry 270,000 pounds gross weight either taxiing or take-off.* Frank was determined that the airplane he wanted had to be designed right up to those limits, no more. Even the over all length of the airplane was a firm constraint."

Did Lockheed have any ideas to meet such a requirement? Could they stay within the fence of the 270,000-pound gross weight limitation—the "magic number?"

According to Hannan, "All of this rang a bell". After lunch the group went back to Hannan's office, where he had kept the sketches of the forgotten twin, high-wing design.

"I remember," Bill Hannan said, "we got out the drawings and pasted them on the wall in Rudy Thoren's office. Frank Kolk showed a lot of excitement. He confessed this was something close to what he had in mind. And he told us he thought that it was a good opportunity for Lockheed if we'd seriously like to start some work on the design."

Before he left, Frank said he was going down to Long Beach and talk with Douglas to see if they weren't also interested. Nobody took it seriously right at that moment, but the race to build the so-called "Air Bus" was starting.

The "Magic Number" Game

Admittedly, few in the aviation community liked the name "Air Bus". It sounded too slow and groundbound for the airlines whose luxurious jetliners with their 10-mile-a-minute speed had run the once speedy "Greyhound" virtually out of the picture for journeys of 500 miles or more.

Still, in 1966 when all of this was taking place, it was no secret that in Europe there were those who already were making plans to build an "Air Bus" ideal for the continent's short distances between its big cities, and capable of carrying 200, 300 or more passengers. The French, English and Germans had formed a consortium to build such a plane, taking advantage of big new engines that Rolls Royce was promising. Some of the European airlines definitely had shown interest. And some of the U.S. carriers with similar short-haul routes had said the "door was open". They, too, would like to see a product.

Like it or not, the "Air Bus" idea was keeping a lot of U.S. airline, aircraft and engine manufacturing people very busy doing a lot of conjecturing. A lot of "dreamers" sharpened their pencils and went back to the design boards. The whole U.S. aviation industry had to make a decision—*to catch the bus, or miss it.*

Lockheed's decision came a few months after Frank Kolk's visit. Kolk had returned to New York and talked with American's management people. They, in turn contacted Lockheed management and said that American was ready to talk serious business.

"We were given some budget money and some direction to go do something with the airplane," Bill Hannan explained. "We set up a primary design group and from the middle of 1966 for the next six months, we really started to explore seriously the twin engine airplane."

By this time, Hannan pointed out, Lockheed, had been awarded the C-5 contract. He and his group, however, were convinced that there was a good opportunity for a smaller airplane—somewhere in between the huge 747 and the 707 or Douglas DC-8 jetliners—only in the wide-bodied category. There was growing evidence the air traveler was looking forward to the so-called "Spacious Age" aloft.

Between Christmas and New Years 1966, the "Air Bus" concept got a shot in the arm, but not without Lockheed feeling the shock.

"We didn't win the SST program, Boeing did," Hannan recalled "and suddenly we had

about 1200 surplus engineers. I remember, we came in all during Christmas vacation, and spent about 15 hours a day trying to decide what we were going to do with all of those talented guys. We had to have a temporary layoff, while we figured out their assignments. What we did was, we transferred most of the top people we had right over onto the 'Air Bus' project, and jacked it up to full steam ahead."

While Engineering people were making known their views, Management and Sales people had some ideas of their own. Although, the project had started out, sparked by American Airlines' interest, it was just good business to find out what the other carriers wanted in order to broaden the market potential. Consequently, Lockheed "teams" canvassed all of the major trunk lines and some foreign carriers. They learned a lot of things that would affect the basic design consideration.

Eastern Airlines' people, for instance, were deeply concerned about the twin-engined concept. EAL's longest non-stop leg on its route at that time was from New York to San Juan, about 1800 miles, and most of it over water. There was a leaning toward a trijet, not two engines. Moreover, they wanted more than a 900-mile-range airplane. They wanted double that in range. They did, however, like the wide-bodied concept, high-density seating potential. Something big, but not as big as the 747 for economy operation.

Trans World Airlines (TWA) was also very interested, even though it was an early 747

Artist's drawing of European A-300 "Air Bus" built around Rolls Royce RB. 211 engines. Twin engine design was under consideration about same time as L-1011 concept was born. A-300 is now in production in Toulouse, France. It is powered with GE engines, the same powerplants as DC-10.

LOCKHEED 1011 TRISTAR

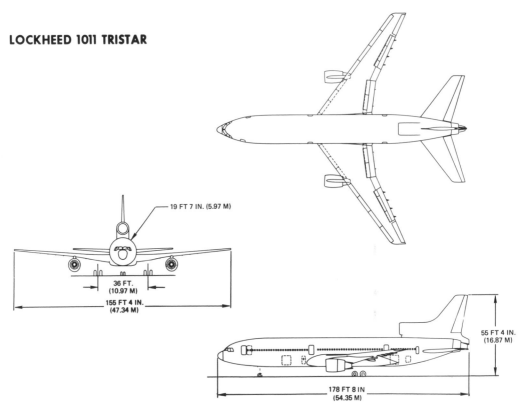

19 FT 7 IN. (5.97 M)

36 FT.
(10.97 M)

155 FT 4 IN.
(47.34 M)

55 FT 4 IN.
(16.87 M)

178 FT 8 IN
(54.35 M)

Plan drawings of basic L-1011 "dash 385" design.

buyer, committed for huge dollar outlays. But for its domestic routes, especially the Chicago-to-Los Angeles, and its Kansas City or St. Louis to the West Coast segments, the 747 was really too large and uneconomical. The idea of a 250-300 passenger "in-between" might be just the ticket. But *two engines?* Some TWA people shook their heads. *What if you had 250 people in the box and you lost an engine over the Rockies? Drift-down procedures to emergency fields, within FAA safety limits, would mean an engine of 55,000 pound thrust, to make it. There was no such an engine at that time.*

Bill Hannan, who was in on most of these airline meetings summed it up this way: "Frank Kolk's original idea to have a little short-range 'shuttle bus' started to stretch a bit. The other airlines had quite a tug of war going, and the up shot of it was, we decided that to satisfy a market big enough for a multi-million dollar investment, we would have to change our early thinking somewhat. We weren't sure the engines available, or soon to be available, would be powerful enough to meet some of the common requirements of the major carriers. There were a lot of ghost stories and claims from the engine

people. But even they admitted, they weren't positive they had the answers. The obvious thing was to lean more toward a trijet."

During the spring months of 1967 numerous studies were made of both two-engine and three-engine proposals. The trimotor won out. During the same period both Lockheed and the airlines evaluated the new engines coming on, which we will discuss further in the next chapter.

Meanwhile, by the end of June, 1967, the "Air Bus" had a more formal designation—L-1011-365.

Still, everybody wasn't thoroughly satisfied. There were further evaluations. The *"Dash 365"* became the "Dash-385" which meant the gross weight had been increased to 385,000 pounds. "We arrived at this figure," Bill Hannan explained, "because if you flew the airplane at that weight it could satisfy the Chicago-West Coast leg (for TWA and United) or the Eastern New York-to-San Juan requirement. Or, with a partial payload, it could be used as a 747 back-up on non-stop transcontinental runs. At the same time, if the plane flew at the proper fuel load for the short-range New York-to-Chicago trip (American's requisite) it would still not exceed

172

the LaGuardia Airport pier restriction."

"Dash 385" had an official designation, L-1011-385-1, and it was also given a popular name. In keeping with tradition Lockheed called the "magic number" airplane—the *"TriStar"*.

"The Lockheed 1011 is designed to meet the critical air transport requirements of the 1970's in terms of capacity, operating characteristics, economics and environmental compatibility," a company brochure described the airplane. *"This new wide-body jet offers spacious accommodations for 272 passengers in a 10 percent first-class, 90 percent coach class mix, and up to 400 passengers in a high density all-tourist configuaration, tailored to the requirements of charter and inclusive tour operators. The design flexibility of the L-1011 interior permits inclusion of special features such as extra lavatories, additional cargo space, alternate galley locations and customized lounges."*

"Thousands of hours of design and test were directed to achieve the correct balance of high speed and low speed performance with good handling characteristics over the whole speed spectrum," the brochure continues. *"A high speed, 35-degree swept wing permits efficient cruise ranging from .82 Mach for long-range operation to .85 Mach for minimum direct operating cost. Full span leading edge slats and large chord double slotted trailing edge flaps provide high lift for takeoff and landing at speeds comparable to today's short-range transports. Direct lift control through use of modulated spoilers provides precise flight path control for landing.*

"The L-1011 can operate economically over distances from 200 to 4000 miles. Direct operating seat mile costs 20 to 25 percent lower than current narrow-body jets, coupled with the passenger appeal of its advanced interior design, will permit increased profits for the airlines.

"The L-1011 will meet the most stringent airport and community noise and smoke emission requirements. Takeoff, sideline, and approach noise levels are significantly below the maximums allowed by Federal Air Regulations, and

In wind tunnels, Lockheed engineers ran hundreds of tests to determine engine nacelle positions on wing and third engine in the tail.

173

In sales' presentation to airlines Lockheed included sumptuous "lounge" arrangement in L-1011 under-floor space.

Experimental model of "TriStar" shows one engine nacelle configuration and wing flap arrangement. Thousands of hours went into wind tunnel testing to arrive at finalized design.

Numerous studies were made with models to fit "TriStar" into conventional patterns for ground equipment, loading techniques at existing airports.

visible smoke is virtually non-existent."

In capsule form, the above (in italics) was the "sales pitch" Lockheed used in talking about its new "TriStar".

By September, 1967, Lockheed was ready to

Full-scale engineering mock-up, of wooden construction, was built of "TriStar." Here engineer studies landing gear.

make its formal proposal to the airline customers based on the L-1011-385-1 specifications and wind tunnel tested performance data.

The "spec" called for a low-wing monoplane with three engines, two engines mounted *port* and *starboard* on wings, and a third engine in the tail. Round, like the Second Generation *"Electra"* the fuselage measured 178 feet, 7 1/2 inches from nose to tail with a passenger cabin 134 feet, 4 inches in length and having a width of 19 feet. Wing span was 155 feet, 4 inches with an area of 3,456 square feet. The tip of its vertical fin and rudder towered 55 feet, 4 inches off the ground, and the plane rested on a tricycle undercarriage, eight main wheels and two-wheeled nose strut arrangement.

This first presentation to the airlines also included price, a selection of two engines (the new Rolls-Royce creation, the RB .211, showing great promise in early tests, or the General Electric CF-6 derived from the engines powering the C-5A which Lockheed was building) computerized performance data and a programmed

L-1011 was still in its formative stages when McDonnell/Douglas announced it was entering the "Air Bus" competition with its DC-10. Original DC-10 concept (above) and larger version (below) show resemblence to "TriStar". Main distinguishing feature is position of engine in the tail.

delivery schedule. The latter set a target date for FAA certification by December, 1971, with airline deliveries in early 1972.

All of this depended, of course, upon whether or not they could *sell* the airplane. Bill Hannan summed it up this way: "When 'Dash-385' became the 'magic number' American Airlines reluctantly agreed that if all the other airlines insisted on that being the airplane, then they would go along with it. We honestly felt we had American in the fold. By this time, TWA was getting pretty interested and Eastern was getting very interested. We'd been playing with the design for two full years and we thought we had a good airplane to sell."

The trouble was Lockheed was not alone in the market. "Up until this time," Hannan pointed out, "we were pretty sure we were far

ahead of everybody, coming up almost on the 10,000-hour mark of wind tunnel testing, with our own ideas pretty firm and going so far even as to begin the facility where we would build the aircraft. But suddenly, we had competition, real competition. Douglas had accelerated their efforts and they had caught up with us real fast."

The Douglas entry, the DC-10, was also a tri-jet with similar profile and planform as the L-1011, about the same size with almost identical programmed performance characteristics. As Bill Hannan described it—"They had decided to make this a real horse race!"

About the same time that Lockheed presented its formal proposal to the airlines, Douglas was doing the same thing. Douglas and Lockheed salesmen bumped into each other all over the world as they visited the home offices of potential airline customers. On top of this, there was a strong rumor that Boeing had plans for "shrinking" its 747 Superjet and coming out with a shorter-range aircraft in the same weight and performance category as the DC-10 and the "TriStar".

Airline executives, pilots and flight crews, technical and sales people and maintenance personnel were also on the move, visiting Lockheed and Douglas to participate in detailed conferences and discussions and view mock-ups of the respective designs. In April, 1967, for instance, Lockheed had engaged the firm of Sundberg-Ferar to make preliminary studies of the interior cabin arrangement for "Dash-385" concentrating on an eight-abreast seating configuration with a unique aisle treatment. A quarter-scale mock-up was shipped to Burbank. Many changes were made, and it was not until September, 1967, that the Lockheed Board of Directors reviewed the full-scale mock-up.

There were also cockpit mock-ups, and system mock-ups which all summer long were shown to various airline representatives. The first airline specification standardization meeting was held October 16-20, 1967, and, as a result, some 250 change requests were processed. A second specification standardization meeting

Stewardesses wheel carts along both aisles to serve passengers in wide-bodied L-1011 mock-up. Airline representatives and Lockheed personnel gave mock-up thorough inspection and evaluation.

Full-scale metal mock-up at Burbank plant was used to check miles of hydraulic lines, wiring and other systems.

conference was held in mid-December, and dealt with the "hard points" which rose from the first meeting of five major airlines. Things were getting down to the "nitty-gritty", and the air transport community was rife with rumors about who was going to get the big plum, Douglas or Lockheed? A billion dollar rainbow hung over the "magic numbers game!" There was no Santa Claus until after Christmas.

Then, in mid-February, American Airlines announced it was ordering twenty-five McDonnell Douglas DC-10 "airbuses"—a $400 million dollar order, and options for twenty-five more!

"That was a real traumatic experience for us," Bill Hannan recalled. "I can remember our Board Chairman, Dan Haughton, coming in that Sunday after we got the news on Friday night, and Dan first thought he had been hoodwinked a bit. But when all the facts began to leak out as to what really had happened, he realized that we had just been honestly skunked in the commercial set."

It has been said that this was the most critical moment in the life (or death) of the L-1011 program before it really ever got off the ground.

Bill Hannan explains: 'Dan Haughton called a meeting and he told us—*"Well, we're really*

going to get in this commercial business or we're going to get out, and I guess, if we're going to get in, the way to do it is to get in all the way. The first thing is, I've got the price too high and we're going to cut the price since we haven't sold any yet." He cut the price down to where we were substantially lower than the price that Douglas had just signed up for with American. .

"Then, we went to TWA and Eastern and we said—Look, now you got American out of the way, we'll change the design of our airplane to fit your needs right where you want it, and all of Frank Kolk's constraints don't count, anymore.

"The L-1011-385-1 became the L-1011-410. We didn't call it that, we still called it the 'Dash-385', but we raised the gross weight because TWA wanted the range and we raised the thrust requirement to 40,600 pounds. Eastern didn't object, particularly because they have some Mexico City requirements and they needed the thrust. Moreover, they had a seasonal interchange agreement brewing with TWA so they would like to have an identical airplane, anyway. Consequently, these two airlines began working very closely with us. It paid off handsomely."

On March 29, 1968, Dan Haughton announced that Lockheed had signed an agreement with Trans World Airlines and Eastern Airlines to build 144 Lockheed L-1011s—fifty to Eastern and forty-four to TWA, and fifty to Air Holdings, Ltd., a British firm which would market them world-wide. The dollar-value of this unprecedented order was $2.16 BILLION. And a few days later Delta Airlines and Northeast announced orders for twenty-eight more *"TriStars"*.

The total of $2.58 BILLION in orders and operations was enough for Lockheed to go into production of the *"TriStar"*.

Lockheed's announcement of the spectacular "coup" also revealed that the planes would be powered with the Rolls-Royce RB.211 engines, part of the deal involving Air Holdings, Ltd., to facilitate a better balance of trade.

The "magic numbers game" was not yet over, however, for there was still one more juicy plum on the airline tree. United Air Lines, biggest U.S. air carrier, hadn't yet made up its mind between the L-1011 or the DC-10 "airbus" designs.

McDonnell Douglas and Lockheed went after United "hammer and tong". What happened would make an interesting book in itself. According to Bill Hannan—"United had a very difficult choice to make. They liked both airplanes,

Artist's concept of "TriStar" minus markings was part of presentation to airlines during critical negotiations. At same time work was started on new plant at Palmdale where L-1011 would be built.

and they had to tell Douglas the American Airlines plane was too small for them because they had the same kind of requirements that TWA had. They liked the Lockheed plane because it was bigger. . ."

"If you'll convince American to change the DC-10 airplane and bring it up to L-1011 size and performance," United told Douglas, "then we'll evaluate you on an even basis."

Douglas convinced American and the DC-10 grew larger. Lockheed was still convinced it would get the United order. But it wasn't in the books.

Reportedly, when the decision was made, United's President George Keck called Dan Haughton and said—"Dan, I'm going to buy the Douglas airplane. I want you to understand, I'm not a statesman or anything like that, but it's a good airplane. It's equal to yours in performance. We've done a lot of business with Douglas through the years. We know the company, and even more important than that, is the fact that if we don't buy that airplane, they will probably drop the DC-10 altogether. And I don't think that's good for Douglas, and I don't

think it's good for the country. Douglas might not stay in the commercial business and and I want them in it!"

The United order was for thirty DC-10s at $465,000,000 with options for thirty more. The "magic numbers game" was over. But the battle of technology was about to begin. Which would pilots, flight crews, maintenance people, and the traveling public choose in the long run—the McDonnell Douglas DC-10 or the Lockheed L-1011 *"TriStar?"*

A disappointed Dan Haughton went back to Burbank, determined that his Lockheed-California Company and all the resources of Lockheed Aircraft Corporation would produce the most advanced technology jetliner in the world.

Work had already started building the factory site where the *"TriStar"* would be built at Palmdale in the Antelope Valley about an hour's drive from Burbank.

And almost 7,000 miles from Burbank, the sound of the quietest jet engine designed to date was emitting from the test stands at Rolls-Royce in Derby, England.

CHAPTER SIXTEEN

Rolls-Royce Choice

Rolls-Royce powered Vickers-Vimy bomber takes off on historic flight, non-stop across the Atlantic, Newfoundland to Ireland.

Heroes Captain John Alcock and Lieutenant Arthur Whitten Brown, first to fly Atlantic, ride in Rolls-Royce car at official welcome.

Most people when they hear the name Rolls-Royce, think of a shining gold or silver trimmed, custom-made limousine built to last forever and priced for presidents and kings, millionaires and movie stars. Certainly, in the automotive world Rolls-Royce is the trademark of a prestige car. What few people outside the aviation community know is that Rolls-Royce since the dawn of the Jet Age has produced more jet propulsion powerplants, both *turboprop* and *turbojet* for commercial jetliners than any other engine manufacturer in the world.

Rolls-Royce began design and development work and the manufacture of engines for aircraft shortly after the beginning of World War I in 1914. Previously, the company had made a name for itself as builder of the precision-engineered Rolls-Royce automobile in the pioneering days of the motor car. It was no surprise to see this "know-how" and technology with automobile engines applied to aero engines when the "mother country" was building her first airplane squadrons to fight the threat of Zeppelin raids and the Hun menace.

During the first World War Rolls-Royce engines powered the famous Bristol fighters, blimp airships and the Handley-Page and Vickers Vimy bombers which carried the air war to German cities. In the immediate post war period, it was two 360-horsepower Rolls-Royce "Eagle" engines that powered the Vickers-Vimy bomber in which Captain John Alcock and Lieutenant Arthur Whitten Brown made the first nonstop transatlantic flight—16 hours and

27 minutes from Newfoundland to Ireland in June, 1919. Indeed, during the 1920s, the aero engines made by RR gained world-wide reputation equal to that of the fabulous motor car that wears the famous *"Spirit of Ecstacy"* emblem as a radiator ornament.

During World War II it was a similar story, the Rolls-Royce *"Merlin"* engine which eventually achieved 2,000-horsepower ratings powered the *"Hurricane"* and *"Spitfire"* fighters which won the "Battle of Britain" history's greatest air victory. The *"Merlin"* also went into some North American P-51 *"Mustangs"* which marked the first tie with American airframe industry and the British engine manufacturer. In all probability Lockheed watched this British/American relationship very closely and continued to watch the progressive evolution of the British powerplant industry.

In the early days of World War II, as we have pointed out in an earlier chapter, the British were credited with the development of the first turbojet engine, Sir Frank Whittle's engine produced by Power Jets, Ltd. It was from this prototype, that Rolls-Royce developed its first production gas turbine engine, the *"Welland"* which powered the early models of the Gloster *"Meteor"* fighter the only Allied jet aircraft to see action before the end of the war in Europe's skies.

Since then, Rolls-Royce and its various divisions have designed, developed and manufactured jet propulsion systems for more than

Rolls-Royce Choice

At Rolls-Royce Engine Division, Derby, England TriStar's RB.211 engines move along assembly line. Engines started in production about same time as L-1011s started on line in Palmdale, California.

eighty different aircraft, fighters, bombers, flying boats, commercial airliners, helicopters, a whole family of research aircraft, and the much talked about *"Concorde"* supersonic transport. More than 130 million hours of operating experience have been accumulated with civil and military gas turbines which have been chosen by over 200 airlines and 80 armed forces around the world. Latest and biggest effort is the manufacture of the turbofan, by-pass RB.211 for the Lockheed L-1011 *"TriStar."*

Today more than 35,000 people at Rolls-Royce Engine Division in Derby, England and at sub-assembly plants in Ireland and Scotland are engaged in turning out first and second generation jet powerplants for the first and second generation L-1011 *"TriStars"* which even the FAA (Federal Aviation Administration) has certified as the quietest jetliner flying.

Lockheed and Rolls-Royce got together for the first time back in 1966 when "Kelly" John-

RB.211 engines at Derby plant in various stages of assembly. Much of engine is built up in vertical position.

Pods and mounting for RB.211 engine, built by Short Brothers & Harland Ltd. of Belfast, Ireland being installed and made ready for shipment to Palmdale.

son had his personal *"JetStar"* modified to accept Rolls Bristol engines. At that time, as we know, the L-1011 was in its conceptual stage.

"Bill" Hannan, whom we met in the last chapter as Chief Engineer on the L-1011 Project tells us why the *Rolls-Royce Choice*. According to Hannan: "Any one of the Big Three engine companies (Pratt & Whitney, General Electric or Rolls-Royce) could have given us a satisfactory engine."

But Hannan points out that in 1967, when the engine choice was pertinent, Pratt & Whitney's JT-9 engines were "frozen" for Boeing's 747 program. Boeing had picked the thrust size they wanted, the diameter they wanted, even the nacelle configuration which had a big effect on the fan cowling and accessory arrangement.

When Lockheed seriously went to P & W in 1967 the engine people were understandably reluctant to change their engine very much because of tooling already started for the 747 program. And Lockheed wanted certain desired changes. For one thing, it wanted a slightly lower thrust class because of the smaller size of the *"TriStar."* Secondly, they wanted all the engine accessories mounted out on the fan and so arranged for better accessability. Thirdly, Lockheed wanted the engine to meet an acoustic level that was substantially lower than the 747 was shooting for, because the L-1011 "Air Bus" concept was going to serve smaller airports and smaller cities.

"You could just see the noise problem coming," Bill Hannan recalled. "I remember having meeting after meeting in the corporate conference room with Dan Haughton, Carl Kotchian, 'Kelly' Johnson, Willis Hawkins and Carl Hadden. We had big round house debates over whether we should invest any money at all in making the airplane quiet, or whether we should go all out and make it *super quiet*, or just where should we draw the target line. I kept pushing for what I called a 100DB (decibel) airplane.

Rolls-Royce Choice

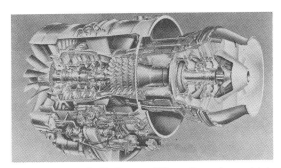

Cut-away of Rolls-Royce "Trent" engine which was first of the three-shaft concept, a revolutionary idea for jet engines.

"We knew the turbo-prop *"Electra"* had a noise signature of about 100DB, and it was a pretty acceptable airplane. Nobody had squawked about it too much. And we figured if we could get a big trijet that quiet it would be acceptable.

"But if we put any more money into it to make it *super quiet* than we were pretty sure the airline buyers would squawk, loud and clear. First, it would mean they would have to pay more. Second, they would be carrying around a lot of extra weight. We finally settled for the 100DB airplane for openers."

All of these factors were included in the "specs" that Lockheed sent to the three engine companies. P&W bowed out gracefully although they left the door open. General Electric which had a similar problem because they were already set with their TF39 engine tooling, however, did a smart thing. They just clipped the fan down in diameter, reduced the by-pass ratio and the thrust down to just about what was wanted for the L-1011 basic design. The result was a fine engine which later went into the DC-10, *"TriStar's"* competitor.

Rolls-Royce in the early design stages of the L-1011 really didn't have an engine. They had a prototype they had built to satisfy themselves which introduced a new three-shafted technology, something nobody else ever had done. In fact, it showed promise of a big breakthrough in jet engine design. At the time Rolls was aiming their production of this engine which they called *"The Trent"* for use in the Fairchild/Fokker F-228 a twin-jet. But beyond this, Rolls had no committments.

"When the F-228 program stopped," Bill Hannan explained, "Rolls, of course, was looking around, and they saw an opportunity to size

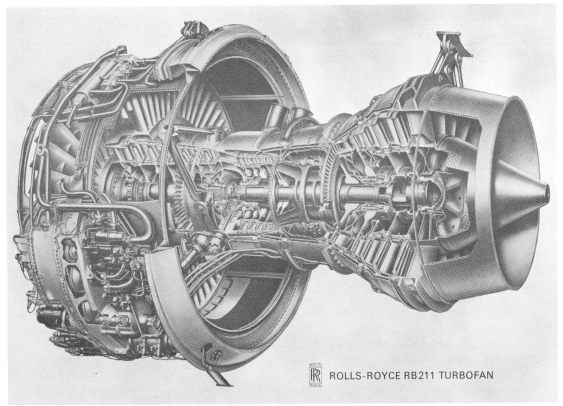

ROLLS-ROYCE RB211 TURBOFAN

Cut-away drawing of Rolls-Royce RB.211 turbo-fan. Huge diameter fan and three-shaft design make possible shorter over-all length.

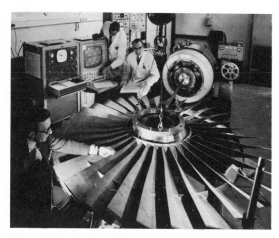

Just a big 33-bladed propeller! Secret of the RB.211 is huge frontal fan which generates high-bypass ratio inside nacelle.

their prototype exactly to where we wanted it, arrange the accessories the way we wanted them, and do the acoustics they way we wanted it. They did just that, and in this respect they had an advantage."

Out of it came the Rolls-Royce RB. 211, three shaft, turbo-fan, high by-pass engine. This, then, was the engine which Rolls proposed to Lockheed and the airlines in 1967 as its entry in the L-1011 engine competition.

"We chose the Rolls engine because we thought it would have three big advantages," Bill Hannan explained. These he cited as follows: (1) Some big technology advantages which seemed the start of a whole new line of engines that might revolutionize the commercial business. (2) Cost proposals which would "let us offer the engine advantageously in the U.S. and, certainly, outside the U.S. where it could be bought in pound sterling." (3) The Rolls-Royce background as the most experienced commercial jet engine manufacturer.

There probably was another reason: It was like going to a tailor to get your suit fitted instead of buying one off the shelf. Indeed, development of the engine paralleled development of the airframe.

What Lockheed wanted for the L-1011 was an engine capable of producing 40,000 pound thrust-power, improved fuel consumption over existing engines, a low specific weight, low noise level, improved smoke emission, simplicity of construction and maintenance. It was a big order. But Rolls accepted the challenge.

Fortunately, as far back as 1964 Rolls had started an "advanced technology exercise" from

which initially evolved the RB. 178 engine, a two-shaft turbo-fan with a 27,000 pound thrust rating. This design was seen as a suitable power unit for the stretched British Aircraft Corporation (BAC) Super VC10 or for possible new generation large transport projects.

It was about this time, one must remember, that airframe manufacturers both in the U.S. and abroad were beginning to think seriously of the so-called second generation, wide-bodied jetliners. Nobody was worried about big airframe structures, the "know-how" was pretty well established. "We can build an aircraft as big as the *Queen Mary,*" one design engineer is said to have remarked. "The question is getting enough thrustpower to achieve required performance, speed and weight lifting capabilities." The 747 and *"Galaxy"* and aircraft of their size were already "on paper" awaiting for the powerplants to come along.

Consequently, in 1965 a later version of the RB.178 engine—the RB.178-51—came into being having thrust increase up to 44,000-pounds. This bigger engine was intended for the Boeing 747 then in its conceptual stage. The basic layout and characteristics of the RB.178-51 were followed in a series of detail design studies, started in 1966 and from which evolved a new generation of propulsion engines for subsonic transport.

These studies centered around engines of about 10,000-pound thrust rating for small feeder aircraft, up to engines in the 40,000-pound to 50,000-pound thrust class for large "airbus" type aircraft. Out of this program in 1967-68 came the RB.203 *"Trent"* designed to meet the need of the smaller jetliners, followed by the RB.207 for the European A.300 "Airbus" and the RB.211 for the Lockheed L-1011. Interestingly, all three of these engines were high bypass-ratio turbofans employing the three-shaft principle—a revolutionary new concept for the gas turbine.

Since we are primarily interested in the development of the RB.211 selected for the *"TriStar"* a short technical description seems in order. From the Rolls-Royce people we learn that the RB.211 is a high-efficiency three-shaft turbofan with a bypass ratio of 5:1 which means that a large fan acting like a propeller produces over 70 percent of the engine's thrust from the air which bypasses the turbojet engine. Only one-sixth of the fan air goes into this turbojet, comprising compressors, combustion system

RB.211 nacelle dwarfs workman. It is almost eight feet in diameter. Note the numerous access doors to provide rapid maintainability.

and turbines. At the same time this turbojet or core engine low pressure turbine drives the fan, and the core engine efflux provides the remaining jet thrust of the engine. In this way the RB.211 combines the superior fuel economy of a turboprop engine with the ability to operate at the high speeds of jet airliners—speeds at which propellers become inefficient.

What we have here, then, in layman's terms, is a huge multi-bladed propeller (fan) seven feet, one-and-a-half inches in diameter providing tremendous thrust, the same as a propeller on the conventional piston-engine aircraft, PLUS added thrust of the jetstream from a gas turbine. Unlike the piston-engine-propeller aircraft propulsion system, in the high-bypass engine thrust from the fan or propeller is contained ("captured") inside a huge nacelle (which also houses the gas turbine) with no way to escape except through the small tailpipe aperture of the jet engine.

Inside the nacelle, in effect a large compression chamber, the airstream from the big fan (propeller thrust) swirls around (by-passing) the core engine (turbojet) expanding and escaping in a last minute surge of pressure—forward thrust-power. Thus, the name "high bypass engine" appropriately applies.

The high-bypass engine isn't new. Big fanjet engines that power the "Galaxy", the Boeing 747 and a whole family of smaller jetliners operate on the same principle. A second shaft, operating off a conventional turbojet engine with its turbine wheels and combustion chambers, drives a big frontal fan which is larger in diameter in relation to the other compression stages. Here again, we have the "bypass air"

generating the major portion of thrust forces, without any compromise to the gas generator section of the engine.

What *is* new with the RB.211 high-bypass ratio engine, is the addition of a third stage performing a similar cycle as with the two-shaft system. In the RB.211 three coaxial drive shafts independently connect the bypass fan and two compressors to their individual turbines. In short, three shafts run three systems, instead of two shafts for three systems as in previous fanjets. The result is 25 per cent fewer parts needed to generate required thrust, achieving the high pressure ratio and the high bypass ratio with a 25 per cent improvement in fuel consumption over the first generation two-shaft airline fanjets.

Furthermore, the three-shaft configuration allows reduction of the big fan speed thus, cutting down on noise. The RB.211's turbine exhaust jet is also slower-moving than on earlier engines because much of its energy is extracted by the added low pressure turbine to drive the big fan. The high rotating speed of turbines in the earlier jet engines has long been known to be the major source of "whine", probably the most disturbing noise factor.

To meet Lockheed's requirement for simplified maintenance Rolls designed its engine around seven basic modules, each an independent unit. This permits very rapid change of engine sections, and enables a service life to be set up for each module rather than for the complete engine. Each module can be removed and replaced individually with the engine still mounted on the aircraft and with minimum disturbance to adjacent engine modules.

This is the engine that Rolls-Royce offered to Lockheed and which today powers the growing fleet of L-1011 *"TriStars"* in airline service. The initial order which Lockheed placed with Rolls-

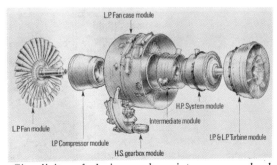

Simplicity of design and maintenance evolved from seven module concept. Here is breakdown of RB.211's modules.

The "S-duct" arrangement and fuselage mounting, complete with RB.211 engine during extensive noise tests at Hucknall, England.

Royce in 1968 was for 550 engines and spares totaling more than $450,000,000. The engines to be built at the Rolls-Royce Engine Division, Derby, England, and sub-assembly plants in Britain and Scotland with the engine pods and mountings to be built by Short Brothers & Harland Ltd. of Belfast, Northern Ireland. The engine itself was a bold step in advanced technology, but the decision to let Rolls-Royce build it, with many international political and economical implications was even bolder. Indeed, for better or worse, it marked the beginning of a new era. There were many problems ahead, technical, political, economic.

The first RB.211 engine ran on the test stand at Derby, England, on August 31, 1968. Subsequent development-type engines were tested on the ground in the high-altitude test facility of the British National Gas Turbine Establishment at Pyestock, England. There, the engine was put through rigid tests simulating most of the L-1011 flight envelope.

About the same time, extensive noise tests were being conducted at Rolls-Royce's Flight Test Establishment at Hucknall, England. These tests included the engine mounted in its under-wing nacelle and aft-fuselage "S" duct arrange-

Inside huge sound-proof chamber at Derby an RB.211 is about to start test run. Jet exhausts into metallic cave for noise suppression. Engine is shorter than powerplants on a 707 turbofan.

ment.

Meanwhile, Rolls had shipped complete engine mock-ups to Lockheed for study and familiarization by Lockheed and airline personnel. From these and volumes of written information and an interchange of technical personnel—Lockheed people in England, Rolls people at Burbank—there evolved a commonality of technical language and understanding between individuals which probably more than anything else contributed to success of the whole program.

The author will never forget a remark made by one of the Rolls-Royce engineers, who helped design the RB.211, during a visit to the Derby engine facility. This was in the fall of 1972 and things were going well for the *"TriStar"* program both at home and abroad. Everybody was in a good mood.

My host, in a tone of deep sincerity, explained: "This whole program has had its high points and low points. But from the very beginning, I believe it has produced a strong and moving relationship between the countrymen of our two nations. At all levels, government, management, engineering and the workers on the assembly line, through the interchange of personnel their ideas and ideologies, have resulted many life-long friendships, as well as a better understanding of each others problems!"

In a lighter mood, he added: "There's nothing that can bring two engineers together quicker than the hard cold facts of a slide rule or a computer. And when you put an engine together there's only one way—the right way."

Even though thousands of miles separated Derby from Burbank and Palmdale—the engine development from the airframe development—daily conferences via a direct "hotline" trans-Atlantic telephone and extensive use of computer data kept both fabrication and testing programs moving. During 1969 and the

British Aircraft Corporation VC-10 fitted with RB.211 installation served as Rolls' flying testbed. Normally the BAC jetliner is powered by four Rolls-Royce "Conway" engines.

early months of 1970 *"TriStar"* began to take shape in a new factory at Palmdale, California, as we shall see in the next chapter. While at Derby, England, the RB.211 engines moved from testbed on the ground to testbed in the sky and onto the production line. Things were running pretty smoothly. Then, something happened.

At their Flight Test facility in Hucknall, Rolls-Royce had modified a British Aircraft Corporation VC-10 commercial jetliner to be used as a "flying testbed" for the RB.211 engine. Two of the VC-10s rear-mounted Rolls-Royce *"Conway"* engines were removed and replaced by an RB.211 installation. On March 6, 1970, with Rolls-Royce chief test pilot, Cliff Rogers, at the controls the VC-10 made an 80 minute

A Saturn Airways "Super Hercules" built at Lockheed-Georgia Company accepts a canvass-wrapped RB.211 for flight to Palmdale L-1011 assembly plant. Saturn flies big skyfreighters around the world.

Rolls-Royce Choice

flight and for the first time the RB.211 engine was airborne. The flight-test program with the VC-10 simulated typical short-range flight plans extending over a period of 1000 hours.

It was during these flight tests that the RB.211 got into trouble, a near crisis that threatened the whole program. In the design of the engine Rolls-Royce had come up with a new composite material called *Hyfil* (carbon fibers bonded with resins) used to make the blades for the big frontal fan. Tests on the ground indicated the new material, replacing titanium, could save 300 pounds or more, and was far less expensive. It was a different story during the airborne tests of the engine.

After some flights in which the "flying testbed" VC-10 flew into rain and hail, it was discovered that the *Hyfil* blade tips were effected by erosion. Engineers tried remedying the situation with metal laminations on the blades.

Another problem developed: Too much stress weakened blade roots which had a tendency to break off upon impact with foreign objects (like birds), sometimes sucked in by the engine at high speeds.

"At this stage we had to go back to using titanium for the blades," said a Rolls engineer. "Fortunately, we had been carrying on a concurrent development along these lines. The expense was terrific, but it saved the project."

Concluding what probably represented the most extensive test program on the ground and in the air ever undertaken by an aero engine manufacturer, Rolls put the RB.211 on the production line. And as fast as the engines rolled off the assembly line, they were packaged for shipment aboard a Saturn Airways L-100 *"Hercules"* skyfreighter and flown to Lockheed's new L-1011 final assembly plant, built especially for the *"TriStar"* program at Palmdale, California, in the Antelope Valley.

CHAPTER SEVENTEEN

Star Factory In The Desert

When the decision was made to go ahead with the L-1011 program in mid-1968 Lockheed-California Company began construction of a space-age manufacturing facility to build the *"TriStar"* in an area ideally suited to aviation development. Excellent year-around flying weather and civic-mindedness already oriented toward aviation were major factors that prompted Lockheed to select the city of Palmdale, California, in Antelope Valley, for the site of one of the world's most advanced technology fabrication and assembly plants to produce the world's most advanced technology airliner.

Moreover, Lockheed and Palmdale were no strangers. During the production peaks on the

"T-Birds" and the F-94 *"Starfire"* series, at the height of the Korean emergency, Lockheed needed a supplemental field for flight testing of the planes as they rolled out of the assembly plant at Van Nuys, California. To fill the need, the company leased 225 acres at the Palmdale Airport, and built a $400,000 flight station there which began operations in 1951. The idea was to transfer the sometimes hazardous flight test work away from the growing air traffic, smog, unpredictable weather and the population explosion around the Los Angeles area.

About the same time, the company purchased 677 acres of land adjacent to a $30,000,000 facility the Air Force was building at Palmdale,

Star Factory In The Desert. This is aerial view of the huge Palmdale L-1011 assembly building, flight test hangar and surrounding installation. "TriStars" on flight line are being readied for delivery to various airlines.

Star Factory In The Desert

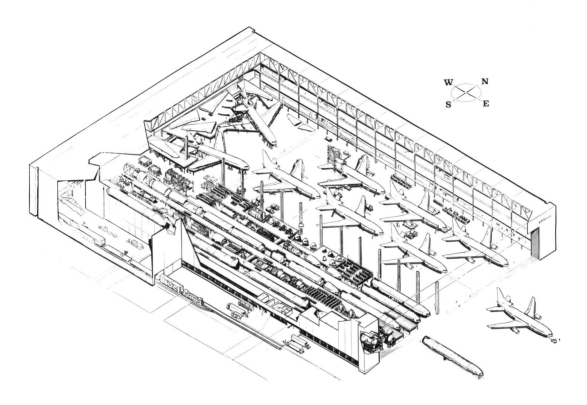

Artist's drawing shows interior arrangement of huge final assembly building at Lockheed-California Company's Palmdale plant. Build-up of L-1011 fuselages is in foreground with start of assembly at lower left. Wing mate is at upper left, and to the right is final assembly. Note: trucks and railroad bringing in materials and various subassemblies.

an isolated spot, where they would build the highly secret XB-70 supersonic bomber. Today, occupying slightly more than one-third of this Lockheed-owned property bordering Air Force Plant 42 and a U.S. Government airport with 12,000-foot runways, *"TriStars"* can roll out of the huge final assembly hangar at the rate of about ten a month. Appropriately, it has been called—*"The Star Factory In The Desert."*

Designated *Plant 10* the more than $50,000,-000 seven-building complex was designed specifically to incorporate the most advanced concepts in aircraft production and logistical support. *Plant 10*, surrounded by the Mojave Desert's joshua trees and cedars, encloses nearly 1,300,000 square feet of floor space under roof. It lies 42 airline miles north of Los Angeles, 20 minutes flying time, about an hour by motor car from Lockheed Aircraft Corporation's main office and plant at Burbank. More than 6,000 people work here. The payroll runs upwards of $1,-000,000 a day!

Indeed, the Lockheed-California Company's Palmdale final assembly and flight test complex

has changed the complexion of the whole area. As someone once remarked—"It has turned the desert green!"

Literally, this is true. One can see it as he walks up to the entrance of the modernistic Administration Building which accommodates offices for Lockheed personnel, customer airline representatives, and ground training facilities for future *"TriStar"* pilots. The once brown and barren desert floor has been transformed into green grass and flower beds!

The transformation, two years in the process, was a gargantuan task. Contractors—the William Simpson Co., Butler Construction Co. and the C. and I. Construction Co.—used 20,000 tons of structural steel to frame the buildings. Enough steel to lay 50 miles of railroad tracks!

Builders poured 183,000 cubic yards of concrete for factory floors and outside parking ramps and taxiways. Enough to build 15 miles of two-lane highway.

The steel, concrete, and 25,000 tons of additional building materials would fill 4,145 railroad boxcars. Such a train would stretch, cab

Lockheed-California Company President Robert A. Furhman.

to caboose, almost from Palmdale to Burbank.

But what goes on here is more important to this story. *"TriStar"* subassemblies and other production materials flow into the plant by truck, air, and rail, the latter along a spur line (which also had to be built) directly onto dual sidings inside a wing of the main assembly building. And what a building it is! You have to see it to believe it.

The structure towers 115 feet high, measures 900 feet by 590 feet, a total of 868,522 square feet on the first floor alone, exceeding the size of the famed Houston Astrodome by almost four acres. It is here that the pieces come together, with the factory floor divided about equally between the *"TriStar"* fuselage assembly and final assembly area.

Says Lockheed-California President Robert A. Furhman—"This building is big enough to turn out aircraft twice the size of the L-1011. One day that may happen."

What we saw on our first visit to this "aerie of the eagles" from a platform high above the factory floor was a sight to behold. Moving along the assembly lines were eight *"TriStars"* in

L-1011 "TriStar" jetliners in various stages of construction. At far left, fuselage sections are jointed together. At right the "TriStars" are in final assembly, near completion. Similar scene greeted author on his first visit to the Palmdale facility.

various stages of completion.

At the end of the line, about to move out through the mammoth hangar doors was one L-1011 structurally complete, out of the assembly fixtures, engines installed, painted in the bright and shiny red and white colors of TWA, and resting on its own landing gear. "They're installing avionics and flight test instrumentation and checking the functional systems," explained our guide, Ted Wilson, *Plant 10's* public relations representative. "When everything checks out they'll tow it over to the Production Flight Test hangar."

Behind the TWA *"TriStar"* was an Eastern

Airline's plane, the wings and empennage being mated with the fuselage. A third ship in *Delta's* markings was in a similar state. Further back, fuselage sections were mating. The amazing spectacle was that you could see the giant complex thing taking shape right before your eyes. At one station a complete fuselage. At another station sets of wings being moved into mating position. Here, the empennage, towering rudder and horizontal stabilizer moving into position. There, a nose section complete with Flight Deck. Here, the long circular main cabin section coming together, with workmen swarming over elevated platforms to reach the upper fuselage levels.

From high above factory floor one views wing mating and empennage mating on this TWA "TriStar." Engines will be added later. The vertical fin towers almost five stories high to give idea of size of building.

L-1011 TriStar and The Lockheed Story

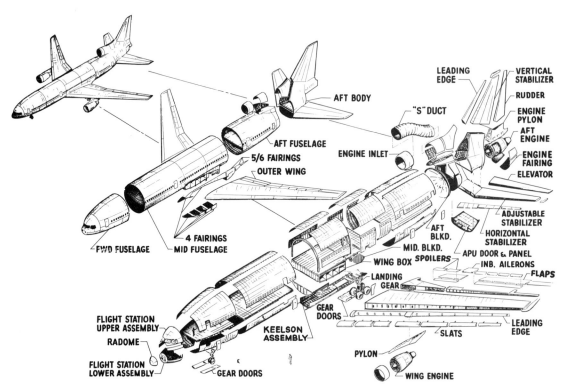

Artist's drawing shows "TriStar's" many sub-assemblies and how they come together. Sub-assemblies come from all parts of the world. (See below.)

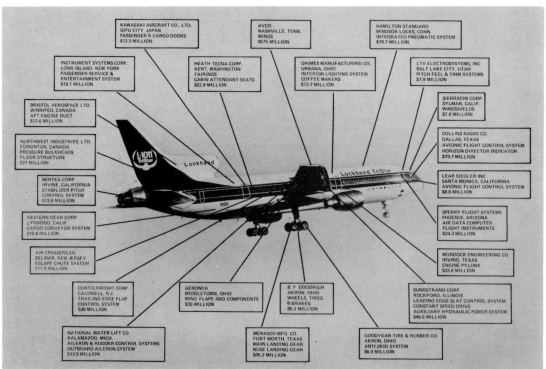

Sub-contractors for "TriStar" program are located in California, Canada, Japan, England and other places far from Palmdale. This breakdown shows major ones and dollar value of their contracts in initial phase.

Star Factory In The Desert

And the miracle is that everything fits, even though some of the subassemblies are manufactured thousands of miles distant from the factory in the desert. Cabin passenger and cargo doors, for example, are manufactured in Gifu City, Japan. The aft engine duct is built in Winnipeg, Canada. Wings for the *"TriStar"* come from the home of country music, Nashville, Tennessee. The secret is modern technology and computerization.

"Millions of bits of data arrived at from millions of hours of design and study are fed into computers and stored there," explained one engineer. "These data are fed into other computers to become 'guidelines' to run machines turning out precision parts to exact measurements. From a master template, one might say, the titan comes together. In technical jargon, they call it *computerized lofting.*"

Experience and "know how" also play a major part. Typical is Lockheed's relationship with Avco Aerostructures Division, Nashville, Tennessee, committed initially to build 350 sets of wings for the L-1011, including tooling for which Lockheed contracted to pay a whopping big $575,000,000.

Avco and Lockheed had first gotten together on the C-130 *"Hercules"* turboprop transport back in 1954. Ever since, the Aerostructures division has turned out vertical and horizontal stabilizers for this "work-horse" military transport. Then there had been the C-141, for which Avco Aerostructures built the wings; and it was followed by the C-5, for which Avco again won the wing contract in competition with other airframe builders.

With this record of successful, on-time performance behind it, Avco Aerostructures made an all-out effort to win the competition for the wings on the L-1011. It entailed some hard

TriStar wings in production at Avco Aerostructures Division, Nashville, Tenn. Six left wings for the Lockheed 1011 TriStar are shown here in the final stages of production. Another six right wings are in similar stage of completion in the plant area to the right (not shown). Jigs in which wing boxes are first built up can be seen in the background. Each wing is 88 feet long, 24 feet at point of attachment, and tapers to four feet at tip. Avco Aerostructures Division has a $575-million contract with Lockheed to produce wings for the new wide-bodied jet transport.

Main cabin with "wing box" and circular fuselage rings at start of fuselage assembly line.

management decisions, including the outlay of more than $110-million for the buildings, tooling, jigs and test equipment needed to perform on the contract. Boeing airplanes were still selling well, and the Douglas DC-10 program had been launched before Avco and Lockheed signed their contract. This imposed a risk on the project—for if insufficient L-1011s were sold, then both companies would be out a goodly sum of hardwon investment money.

In October of 1969, Avco Aerostructures Division dedicated new facilities in which it would build, test and load for shipment the wings for the L-1011. It added 500,000 square feet of space to its facilities next to Berry Field at Nashville, Tennessee, bringing the division's total plant floor space to about 2,100,000 square feet.

Work began immediately on production of the wings, each 88 feet long, 24 feet wide at the point

of attachment, and 4 feet wide at the tip. Each had 3,500 square feet of surface area and weighed in at some 20,000 pounds. A complete set of wings for one L-1011 required the fabrication and assembly of almost 15,000 detail parts.

The first wing was shipped by air aboard a Super Guppy air transport direct from Nashville to Palmdale, California, in the same day, April 27, 1970. A few days later the Super Guppy returned and airlifted the other side of the wing

Nose section in early stage of assembly. "Bars" on cockpit windows will be removed when glass is installed. Plane is famous for vision.

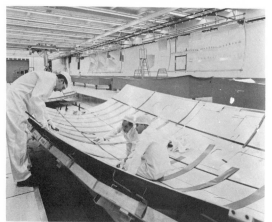

Workmen in dust-free clothing are applying titanium straps using adhesives before bonding in autoclave under heat and inert gas pressure.

Workers complete assembly of 80-foot long mid-fuselage segment. Note mobile platforms, ladders, like scaffolding in a shipyard.

to complete the set for the first L-1011 to come off the assembly line at Palmdale.

By the end of 1971, Avco Aerostructures had delivered 17 complete sets of wings to Lockheed, and during the same period made an economic decision that it would be better to ship the wings by rail rather than by air.

Putting *"TriStar"* together Lockheed had another advantage. The late Dick Fliedner, the first Director of L-1011 Manufacturing, put it this way: "Somebody once said it is impossible to build bridges and make movies. Some days we think it's that way with airplanes. But we've

Wings for "TriStar" await installation in big production hangar. In background, wings are being mated with aircraft fuselage.

got pros solving our production problems. They began building Lockheed airplanes out of wood, and they've been with us all the way to titanium. L-1011 design details, materials selections, manufacturing processes and development testing solved most potential production

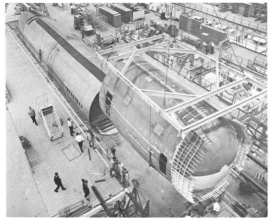

Attaching rear fuselage segment to finish assembly of L-1011's 147-foot long "pressure vessel". Note the aft pressure bulkhead. Empennage will be joined during wing mating.

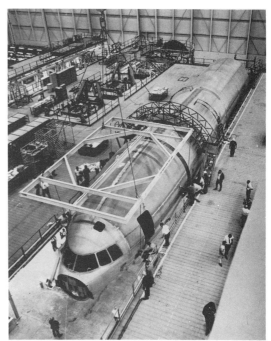

Nose section, moved into position by overhead crane with special cradle halter is mated with mid-fuselage segment.

difficulties with the *"TriStar"* before they could occur."

An example of the "old pros" at work is evidenced by the fact that major tooling for the L-1011 was designed and manufactured in Lockheed's Plant B-1 at Burbank, birthplace of the famous *"Electra"* line and the P-38. Typical was the huge jig for assembly of fuselage panels, a product of Plant B-1's machine shops. Wherever possible the jigs and special machinery needed to build the L-1011 was done "in house", and many times, design and development of the "tools" produced greater problems than final assembly of the plane itself.

Development of new and revolutionary fabrication techniques resulted. The side walls of *"TriStar's"* main cabin fuselage area, for instance, introduced a new type of construction. The barrel-shaped section of semi-monocque shell construction is comprised of tapered frames and thick skins—without stringers—rather than the conventional frame, skin and stringers. Forming of these large panels required special stretcher presses, and a new bonding technique. Lockheed pioneered both.

According to James B. Beach, Chief Engineer, L-1011 Production Design—"The extensive use of structural adhesive bonding of doublers, triplers and lapped skin panels into

Bonding adhesive which Lockheed helped to develop replaced riveting in large fuselage panels. Arrow points to one-inch square which supports car to show strength. Secretary Judy Tolly points to bonded strap. In background is world's largest autoclave.

Machined skin panel for center wing section is weighed in at 763 pounds, within ounces of design spec. Panel was machined from 1500-pound solid aluminum plate, at Burbank Plant B-1, then shipped to Palmdale.

Vacuum lift machine hoists contoured 37-foot long aluminum fuselage panel from giant forming roll at Lockheed Burbank Plant B-1. Sixty ton forming roll can curve high tensile alloy sheets in sizes that permit fewer fuselage joints in "TriStar."

large panel assemblies (up to 15 feet by 38 feet) is an important new development offering improved fatigue life, corrosion resistance and durability. Such large bonded panels are being used for the first time on the L-1011, and their production is made possible only by the use of

Huge jig for assembly of fuselage panels nears completion at Lockheed Burbank plant. Much of tooling for "TriStar" was fabricated in Plant B-1 at Burbank. "Constellations" were also built here. Skin panels are largest in aviation industry.

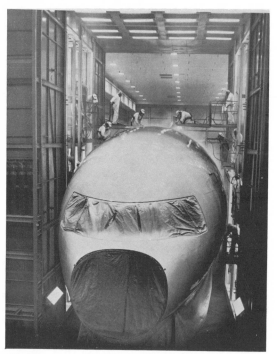

Painters spray "TriStar" using new mobile paint gantry, largest in the world. One coat of paint can be applied in just 40 minutes.

the largest autoclave in the aerospace industry."

At *Plant B-1*, Burbank, the autoclave is one of the major attractions. It is the world's biggest "pressure cooker". Interestingly, the process is remindful of the early days at Lockheed when fuselage halves of the first *"Vegas"* of plywood and resin went into their molds. The difference, perhaps, is progress catching up with progress. But in principle, there is great similarity.

Another revolutionary operation exclusive with *"TriStar"* is what goes on inside the huge paint hangar, third largest building at Lockheed's demand for advancement wherever possible in production of its new jetliner, the company early in the *"TriStar"* program launched an effort aimed toward the dual goals of a better aircraft paint and a better system of applying it.

The effort proved successful, resulting in development of a substantially improved polyurethane paint and the design and construction of a unique paint hangar that, among numerous other advancements, permits painting an entire *"TriStar"* fuselage with one coat in just 43 minutes. Under past methods, application of a paint coat to the big planes 8,632-square-foot

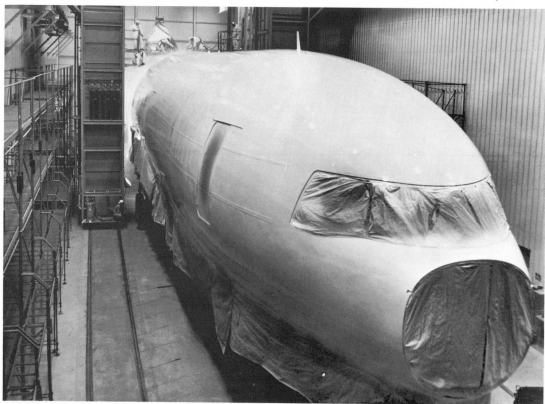

Huge paint hangar at Palmdale facility will take complete fuselage of L-1011—178-feet long. It takes 58 gallons of paint.

Star Factory In The Desert

fuselage surface would have required a minimum of four hours.

Concepts for design of the paint hangar, its equipment and the techniques of application were established following a year-long survey of aircraft paint systems currently used in the aircraft and airline industries. Results of this study indicated the most efficient way of painting "TriStars" would be to apply the fuselage coat following assembly of the aircraft body, then return the fuselage to the main assembly building for mating with its wings. Following final assembly and rollout, the planes go through pre-delivery test flight with wings still unpainted, and then re-enter the paint hangar for covering the wings and any required touch-up.

Key to the quick and evenly applied paint coats is the mobility of the painting platforms. In the fuselage booth, a high rate of production is achieved through use of the world's largest mobile paint gantry, a huge inverted U-shaped "room" that straddles the fuselage. With painters manning stations at four different heights on either side of the "TriStar" body, the gantry moves steadily down the length of the booth on four rails as the paint is applied.

The gantry, 36 feet long with a clear span height of 43 feet, weighs 93,000 pounds and is supplied with hot and cold deionized water, a pneumatic air supply and electricity. Breathing air is piped into the gantry's interior for connection with the painter's hood, and the entire booth is air conditioned. An elaborate exhaust duct system built into the gantry draws off the paint fumes.

The paint hangar's wash and touch-up section, which will house a complete "TriStar", occupies most of the structure's 67,000-square-foot floor space. This room is supplied with air at the rate of half-a-million cubic feet per minute.

Washing and painting is conducted from mobile platforms suspended from overhead rails. The painter can direct the platform anywhere along the length of the fuselage on one side or turn and move out over the wing. The wing underside is painted from fixed platforms. Horizontal and vertical stabilizers are painted separately on jigs prior to mating in the main assembly building.

Many other innovations are evident everywhere at the Palmdale facility. Small wonder Robert W. Bell, Production Manager for L-1011 structures at *Plant 10*, a veteran of more than 34 years with Lockheed should remark—"This is the best plant I ever saw. At rate we can handle 39 of the L-1011's in the jigs, on the floor and on the flight line, we can deliver an airplane every 2 days, if we go to our full production rate."

And at the official plant dedication ceremonies on July 20, 1970, California's Governor Ronald Reagan declared—"What an answer this facility is to those who feel only government can resolve our problems. Lockheed's L-1011 project is financed completely with private capital. It is an investment by the private sector in the future of the nation, state, and economic system in which they have total confidence and belief."

He added—"Here, we are dedicating a $50,-000,000 facility for the L-1011, one of the most sophisticated commercial jetliners ever produced by man."

Paradoxically, L-1011's began forming in the jigs and moving down the assembly line while the final assembly hangar was still under construction. And the first "TriStar" was ready for public display on the same day the building it was built in was dedicated.

Fabrication on "TriStar" No. 1 was started March 1, 1969. Work began, putting the pieces together on June 24, the same year. On April 29, 1970, the first sets of wings arrived from AVCO, and five days later wings and fuselage were mated. The big RB.211 engines from Rolls-Royce arrived in June and after a rigid test program they were installed in position in time for the plane to roll out on September 1, 1970. The roll-out met a schedule which had been established two and one-half years before! Right on the nose!

"TriStar" No. 1, painted white with red and orange stripes, was escorted from the final assembly building by a delegation of stewardesses representing the six airlines that had ordered L-1011's to date: Eastern Air Lines, Trans World Airlines, Delta Air Lines, Air Canada, Air Jamaica and Pacific Southwest Airlines. Also on hand were A. Carl Kotchian, president of Lockheed Aircraft Corporation; Charles S. Wagner, president Lockheed-California Company (now retired) and William M. Moran, vice-president commercial programs.

In its desert setting the "TriStar" paused for photographers outside the vast building where she was constructed. It was then rolled into the adjacent Flight Test Hangar for undergoing preparations to try its wings.

On November 16, 1970, with L-1011 Project

"TriStar" poses for her portrait. First plane shown here was about to start taxi run tests before maiden flight.

L-1011 'FRONT OFFICE'—First flight crew for Lockheed's L-1011 TriStar jetliner is pictured in flight station of the new trijet. From left are Rod C. Bray, research and development engineering team leader; H. B. (Hank) Dees, project pilot and aircraft commander; Glenn E. Fisher, flight engineer; and Ralph C. Cokeley.

Star Factory In The Desert

First "TriStar" minutes after take-off on maiden flight. Chase plane is North American F-86. Its pilot reported—"You're looking beautiful." L-1011 surpassed estimated expectations performance-wise.

Test Pilot H. B. (Hank) Dees at her controls, *"TriStar"* slipped gracefully off the desert runway and into her own domain on her maiden flight. Up front, on the flight deck, her only other occupants were crew members Ralph C. Cokeley, co-pilot; Glenn E. Fisher, flight engineer, and Rod C. Bray, flight research engineer.

The aircraft weighed 330,000 pounds before take-off, including 85,000 pounds of fuel and 40,000 pounds of test instrumentation. She got off the ground at a liftoff speed of 152 knots and after a takeoff run of only 5,300 feet. In accordance with its flight plan, the L-1011 reached an altitude of 20,000 feet and a speed of 250 knots on its first flight. She cruised the skies above the Mojave Desert for nearly 2 1/2 hours, an unprecedented long first flight (everything worked so well), before settling back to earth.

Observers were particularly impressed with the quietness of the *"TriStar's"* engines. "She

whispered off the runway, little more than a quiet hum," commented one newsman.

"It was a lovely flight," Pilot Hank Dees told reporters. "We had good control, particularly with the flying tail. The Rolls Royce engines ran fine. Pilots are going to like this airplane. Handling characteristics were better than our engineering simulations indicated."

He also revealed that the test program inaugurated by the first flight would include some 1500 separate flights totaling almost 1700 flying hours. "Six L-1011s will take part in the year long program," he said, "leading up to certification of the aircraft by the Federal Aviation Administration."

Before that day would arrive when she would get her certificate of airworthiness, *"TriStar"* was destined to face problems unrelated to her performance capabilities which threatened to bury the whole L-1011 program.

Ahead lie days of trial and triumph.

203

Roll-out of the first TriStar is accompanied by Lockheed officials and observed by the dedicated men and women who put it together.

Dedication ceremonies for Lockheed's Plant 10 or "Star Factory In The Desert", take place with the first TriStar as a backdrop.

On the flight line at Lockheed's plant at Palmdale, Calif., are 10 new L-1011 TriStars. The jetliners were rolled out of the nearby final assembly building.

CHAPTER EIGHTEEN

A Test Of Men And Wings

There was a bright new winged star atop the Lockheed family tree to greet the Yuletide season in 1970. *"TriStar"* had made its maiden flight about six weeks before, and the No. 1 aircraft was performing well in the early stages of an exhaustive flight test program which would involve the first six airplanes off the line. The test aircraft by Christmas Day were out of the factory at Palmdale and being readied for the flight test exercises, a year-long operation, said to be the most rugged program ever planned for a new aircraft. Hopes were running high that the first L-1011 would go into commercial airline service in the fall of 1971 pretty much on schedule.

All of this was a nice Christmas present for Lockheed Board Chairman Daniel J. Haughton, who could look back to four years ago when Christmas was a nightmare; when word had come that Lockheed had lost the billion dollar SST program (See Chapter Fifteen) and management had made the decision to go ahead in earnest with the "airbus" which became the L-1011 *"TriStar."* Certainly, the performance of the No. 1 aircraft on its maiden flight and others to date, were blessings worth counting and proof that management's decisions had been wise. Moreover, there were sure prospects for additional orders for *"TriStars"* from both

"TriStar" No. 1 leaves water-slick runway behind on takeoff during week-long series of wet runway tests in Seattle, Wash. Tests, which measured the plane's ability to takeoff, land and brake safely to a stop on wet runways, are required by British Civil Aviation Authority for operating the L-1011 in the United Kingdom. British (CAA) requirement is similar to U.S. Federal Aviation Administration's. The FAA certificated L-1011 "TriStar" on April 14, 1972 and the British CAA on June 30, 1972.

A Test Of Men And Wings

Lockheed Chairman Of The Board Daniel J. Haughton.

domestic and foreign air carriers. It was a good feeling, too, knowing that Lockheed which had given the airlines the *"Electra"* Model-10s, the *"Lodestar"* and this whole series of splendid, high-speed, luxurious airliners in the "thirties," plus the advanced design, pressurized *"Constellations"* and the second generation *"Electra"*—first U.S.-built jetliner—in the postwar decade, was building commercial airliners again. And *"TriStar"*, just about everyone agreed, was the most advanced technology airliner ever built, destined to become the brightest winged star of them all.

There were, however, as the year was coming to a close, problems at the corporate level that clouded up the sky and must be resolved to give *"TriStar"* a smooth flight into tomorrow. Biggest headaches were contractual disputes with the Department of Defense over the C-5A *"Galaxy"* the AH-56A helicopter and other military programs. In fact, on March 2, 1970 Haughton had written Deputy Defense Secretary David Packard outlining Lockheed's need for approximately $600-million in interim financing pending settlement of these disputes. Both sides would have to "give a little" to get things on a more even keel. If things weren't settled soon, there was danger that the *"TriStar"* and other Lockheed programs might

be in serious trouble.

Born September 7, 1911 in Walker County, Alabama about the same time that Allan Loughead (Lockheed) was "barnstorming around Illinois" in a Curtiss pusher biplane, and thinking about building the Model G—the first Lockheed—Dan Haughton had the background to face up to such problems and come out slugging. Graduated from the University of Alabama with a B.S. in Commerce and Business Administration (1933) and awarded an honorary doctor of law degree from his alma mater (1962) and George Washington University (1965) Haughton could handle himself well in the "ring" even if it was a five-sided Pentagon labyrinth.

Furthermore, there was a lot of "Lockheed" in this son of an Alabama farmer and storekeeper, inbred with integrity and unafraid to roll up his sleeves and get the job done. He had joined Lockheed in 1939 as a systems analyst. Right from the start his energy and ideas caught the eye of both Bob Gross and Courtlandt Gross—his future assured. Within two years he was made assistant to the vice president of Vega Aircraft Corporation, then a Lockheed subsidiary, a post he held until becoming works manager in 1943. Late that same year Vega merged with the parent Lockheed Aircraft Corporation.

From 1944-46 Haughton was Lockheed's assistant general works manager and then assistant to the vice president manufacturing until 1949. He served as president of two Lockheed subsidiaries, Airquipment Company and Aerol Co. Inc. from 1949 to 1951 when he became assistant general manager of Lockheed's Georgia Division (Now Lockheed-Georgia Company) and took over as Lockheed vice president and general manager of the Georgia operation a year later.

He was elected President of Lockheed Aircraft Corporation in 1961 and served in that position until May 2, 1967 when he was elected to the board chairmanship, succeeding Courtlandt Gross, who retired. He has been at the helm of the biggest U.S. aerospace firm ever since. Truly, "a captain of industry" charting the course of Lockheed through its two biggest programs—the building of *"Galaxy"* the world's largest aircraft and *"TriStar"*, each involving billions of dollars.

With him through his stirring career as a Lockheed man has been a long-time friend and associate A. Carl Kotchian, who came to

Lockheed President A. Carl Kotchian.

Lockheed in 1941 as a budget analyst, and who moved up to become President of the company in 1967 when Haughton became Chairman Of The Board. A native of Kermit, North Dakota (Born July 17, 1914) Kotchian, with degrees in economics from Stanford University and a CPA background prior to joining Lockheed, like Haughton, was a "favorite son" at Lockheed.

The two men were brought closer together in 1951 when Kotchian took on responsibilities as assistant director of financial operations at the Marietta, Georgia operation. He became director of financial operations there a year later. From finance, Kotchian moved over to manufacturing and then into general management, elected a Lockheed corporate vice president and general manager of Lockheed-Georgia Company, taking over in Haughton's footsteps.

As a "team" Haughton and Kotchian—possessed an aggregate of 60 years of Lockheed service in virtually every phase of the company's vast and complex operations. In 1970 with the *"TriStar"* program newly launched, we find them facing a critical period in the company's history comparable, if not far more difficult, than when Bob Gross salvaged Lockheed out of bankruptcy back in 1932.

What happened between February 2, 1971 and August 2 of the same year—six months fighting to survice is told in the following "chronology of

events" prepared by Lockheed and made available to the author. With a little poet's license, the story unfolds more like a Horatio Alger tale than the fact-filled diary of a great free-enterprise company fighting for its life. And winning.

February 2, 1971—Lockheed team headed by Dan Haughton arrives in London for joint program review with Rolls-Royce management on the status of engines for *"TriStar."* They get first indication that British Government has withdrawn financial backing and Rolls-Royce is contemplating possible receivership!

February 4, 1971—Rolls-Royce, citing losses on RB.211 engine development, requests appointment of a receiver and announces that it is not feasible for it to proceed with its RB.211 engine contract with Lockheed. British government states that it will acquire certain assets of Rolls-Royce but denies liability with respect to RB.211 engine contract. Portions of Rolls-Royce are subsequently being reorganized as a government-owned company—Rolls-Royce (1971) Ltd., with Lord Cole as chairman. Lockheed begins exploring various means of continuing L-l0ll program including availability of U.S. manufactured engines.

February 9, 1971—Haughton meets with L-1011 customers in New York. Airlines express concern over impact on delivery schedules caused by Rolls' collapse. Lockheed proposes no single course of action other than it will continue to explore all possible options.

February 11, 1971—British government announces interim financing to continue work on RB.211 engine pending exploration of possible continuation of the L-1011 program.

February 17, 1971—Dan Haughton is back in London again for initial conferences with Rolls and British Government officials regarding British terms for restoring engine program.

February 20, 1971—After conferring with British Defense Secretary Lord Carrington and Minister of Aviation Supply Frederick Corfield, Haughton returns to U.S. announcing he will resume talks with British government representatives early in March. He meets with Deputy Defense Secretary Packard in Washington to give status report on engine situation and then, on March 2, is back in London again for meetings with British government officials and Rolls-Royce management.

March 4, 1971—British propose a plan for a

While Haughton and Kotchian faced "battle of the billions" the L-1011 flight test fleet fought battle against the sky. Here "TriStar" No. 1 fitted with needle-nosed test probe is performing low speed stall tests. Insert shows plane with wing-tip flutter vane during required "flutter" or vibration tests.

joint Lockheed-British company to carry out the engine program; and engine price increase; British government funding of an additional $144 million, and a requirement for Lockheed to arrange that the British government would be repaid its investment if Lockheed should fail to carry through with the L-1011 program. Lockheed informs government it cannot accept elements of British offer. Haughton meets with L-1011 customers in New York and presents British proposals and results of Lockheed evaluation of availability of alternate General Electric and Pratt & Whitney engines for *"TriStar."*

March 9, 1971—Technical and financial representatives of customer airlines meet in Burbank for several days and receive detailed presentations from General Electric and Pratt & Whitney. They conduct comparative analyses of Rolls-Royce and U.S.-built engines.

March 13, 1971—Haughton sends message to Lord Carrington reporting that he has presented the British proposals to L-1011 customers, U.S.

During "cold dollar" days, L-1011 test aircraft was undergoing sub-zero temperatures equivalent to 58 degrees below at Canada's Winnipeg International Airport. Here Lockheed test crew prepares "TriStar" for an overnight 12-hour cold soak. During tests environmental control systems worked perfectly and despite cold treatment engines performed flawlessly during the round-trip flight between California-Canada.

L-1011 TriStar and The Lockheed Story

government, and banks. Reports that airlines also find the offer unacceptable and invites the British to present best offer for consideration by Lockheed and the airlines.

March 15, 1971—Haughton and Lockheed President A. Carl Kotchian meet with senior officials of L-1011 customers for status report discussions and also present status report to Secretary Packard, to Treasury Secretary Connally, and to Lockheed's lending banks.

March 19, 1971—Joint British government/Rolls-Royce team headed by Sir William Nield, British cabinet secretary, begins meetings with Lockheed in Burbank. Talks move to Washington where parties meet with Treasury Secretary Connally and with British Ambassador Lord Cromer.

March 24, 1971—Lord Carrington and Sir Peter Rawlinson, attorney general, fly from London to join negotiations. Before returning to London the following evening, Lord Carrington receives Lockheed's latest offer and meets with Secretary Connally.

March 30, 1971—Sir William Nield receives directions from London after Lord Carrington briefs Prime Minister Heath and other cabinet ministers. Following meeting of Haughton and Nield, statement is issued regarding "positions conditionally agreed to" by Lockheed and British. Lockheed briefs L-1011 customers individually regarding conditional agreements.

April 8 & 14, 1971—Lockheed meets with its lending banks to report on conditional agreements and L-1011 airline meetings and to discuss financing of *"TriStar"* program. Five days later *"TriStar"* customers, banks and Lockheed conduct joint meeting for review and discussion of positions. Those attending agree that significant progress has been made and to expedite resolution of the outstanding issues.

April 20, 1971—Prime Minister Heath says the British Government will not proceed with the RB.211 without guarantees as to future of Lockheed. Six days later banks provide additional $50,000,000 loans to Lockheed, bringing total bank financing to $400,000,000. Lockheed pledged additional security.

April 27, 1971—Treasury Secretary John Connally tells a Senate subcommittee that Lockheed will need a government loan guarantee.

May 5, 1971—Eastern Airlines signs a conditional agreement reaffirming its original purchase of 50 Lockheed L-1011*"TriStars"*with Rolls-Royce RB.211 engines. The next day

Noise tests, monitored by latest test equipment resulted in "TriStar" being declared quietest of the wide-bodied jetliners.

Secretary Connally announces that administration will support a government loan guarantee.

May 6, 1971—Trans World Airlines announces conditions that must be satisfied for it to continue with L-1011. One of the conditions is a government loan guarantee.

May 10, 1971—Lord Carrington tells Parliament the U.K. government has formally committed $240 million to finance completion of the RB.211 and that Rolls-Royce and Lockheed have reached a conditional agreement subject to U.S. government guarantee of additional Lockheed financing.

May 11, 1971—Haughton and Ian Morrow, with Lord Cole present, sign conditional Lockheed-Rolls agreement. Two days later Nixon Administration sends draft Emergency Loan Guarantee Act of 1971 to Congress, providing $250 million loan guarantee authority.

All through June and all through July, House and Senate Hearings dragged on. Lockheed had been forced to look to Washington as a last resort.

July 30, 1971—House passes loan guarantee bill with $250 million ceiling, 192 to 189.

August 2, 1971—Senate gives final congressional approval adopting House bill, 49 to 48.

A Test Of Men And Wings

During height of Rolls-Royce/Lockheed negotiations "TriStar" No. 3 made historic flight to Paris Air Show. This was scene at LeBourget Field, Paris, June 1, 1971 when thousands got first glimpse of L-1011's many features. Behind "TriStar" is another star of the show, a Saturn Airways L-300 skyfreighter, civilian version of famed "Hercules" C-131 military cargo aircraft.

Lockheed employees, many laid off because of work stoppage on L-1011 program, and with company threatened with bankruptcy show their concern in calm demonstration at Palmdale.

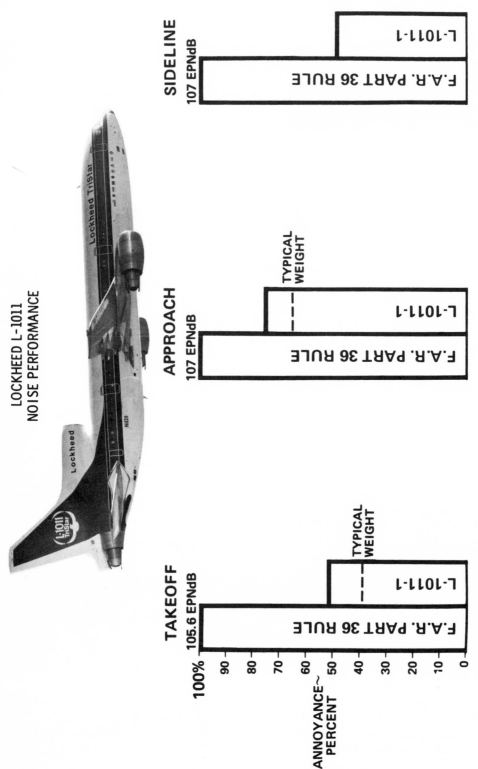

LOCKHEED L-1011
NOISE PERFORMANCE

TAKEOFF
105.6 EPNdB

F.A.R. PART 36 RULE

L-1011-1

TYPICAL WEIGHT

APPROACH
107 EPNdB

F.A.R. PART 36 RULE

L-1011-1

TYPICAL WEIGHT

SIDELINE
107 EPNdB

F.A.R. PART 36 RULE

L-1011-1

ANNOYANCE~PERCENT
100% 90 80 70 60 50 40 30 20 10 0

Lockheed's L-1011 TriStar is the world's quietest jet airliner, with sound levels well below the Federal Aviation Administration's limits for new jetliners. Left-hand columns show the FAA limits for takeoff, landing approach and sideline noise in effective perceived noise decibels (EPNdB). Right-hand columns show L-1011 sound levels at its maximum weights. Typical L-1011 weights, such as those used in medium-range missions, produce still lower sound levels. Percentage figues at far left indicate how relative annoyance of L-1011's sound is dramatically lower than FAA maximum.

A Test Of Men And Wings

Flight Test Data center aboard L-1011 test aircraft.

September 14, 1971—"Summit meeting" is held at the Federal Reserve Bank in New York to finalize Lockheed's expanded bank credit agreement made possible by the Emergency Loan Guarantee Act. Attending were representatives of Lockheed's 24 lending banks, the Treasury and Emergency Loan Guarantee Board, airline customers, Rolls-Royce, and the British Government.

"The agreement gave us the opportunity to prevent the bankruptcy that had been threatening Lockheed ever since the Rolls-Royce receivership in February," explained Dan Haughton. "It enabled Lockheed to continue the L-1011 *"TriStar"* program, and restore our corporate strength and position."

While all this was going on *"TriStar"* itself was going through an ordeal of a different kind— the toughest tests for wings. Five aircraft participated directly in the flight test program with a sixth held in reserve.

"The L-1011 flight test program," explained Lockheed-California Company Chief Engineering Test Pilot J. F. Woodman, "reflects the aggregate knowledge gathered by Lockheed Aircraft Corporation during some 40 years of aviation research and development testing. It utilizes the newest equipment and computer hardware."

A look inside *"TriStar"* No. 1 gives the layman an idea of what he was talking about. Instead of passenger seats, the cabin was filled with banks of electronic data acquisition and telemetry equipment and water ballast tanks. This electronic equipment, we were told, was capable of recording on magnetic tape up to 700 channels of data covering every detail of the aircraft's performance. The aircraft contained more than 275 miles of instrumentation wiring, 1,500 individual sensors measuring operating characteristics of the aircraft structure, flying

qualities, avionic systems and functional systems, altogether more than 7,000 pounds of test equipment. Each of the test aircraft was similarly fitted, each with special equipment for specific tests.

According to Woodman *"TriStar"* No. 1 was used to study takeoff, landing and cruise performance, propulsion systems, center of gravity tests and evaluation of the ship's unique "flying tail." Its flying envelope would also include maximum gross weight takeoffs and landings, high-speed runs, high-altitude operations.

"TriStar" No. 2 was assigned the task of evaluating the propulsion and Avionic Flight Control System (AFCS) as well as conducting early trials of the new Lockheed Autoland System.

"TriStar" No. 3 was assigned primarily to certify the Autoland System (which we will describe later) and in addition evaluate and certify all of the aircraft major functional systems.

"TriStar" No. 4 was used to test the aircraft's new navigation and communication systems and environmental controls systems.

"TriStar" No. 5 with no flight test equipment aboard was, in effect, "the airlines' airplane" flying around the country to major airports which *"TriStar"*would serve and demonstrating the plane's general performance and reliability characteristics.

In all of these tests totaling more than 1500 flights and more than 1700 hours aloft *"TriStar"* came through with flying colors. So confident were its builders that mid-way in the flight test program, on June 1, 1971 with Jack Woodman at its controls *"TriStar"* No. 3 took off from Palmdale and flew to LeBourget Field, Paris, France for appearance at the famed Paris Air Show. Flight time was 12 hours and 31 minutes. Most of the flight was made at 33,000

Water ballast tanks aboard test aircraft.

213

Second aircraft off the production line, No. 6 aircraft in the test fleet, is pushed into huge Flight Test Hangar at Palmdale for important Fatigue Test and Static tests. Before program is over, plane will be twisted, contorted and "flown" to ultimate destruction to test metal fatigue and structural strength far beyond airline operational requirements.

feet.

"The flight was a real test," Woodman reported. "To Paris and back, a total of 17,000 miles over every imaginable terrain—land, mountains, water, cities."

To facilitate its flight test program Lockheed built at the Palmdale Flight Center a special test hangar, a gigantic structure 500 ft. x 354 ft. (260,403 square feet) to house the most modernistic test equipment. Headquartered here are more than 400 flight test personnel amid the most sophisticated data acquisition and analysis equipment ever gathered together at one site. Among the latter are computers and data processing equipment capable of accepting telemetered information at the rate of one million bits a second!

The Flight Test Hangar's south bay is filled with huge steel frameworks to accept two complete "TriStars" for fatigue and static testing. The fatigue test program was designed to confirm integrity of the airframe by cycling it through some 52,500 simulated flights. The static test program was designed to determine overload capability of the aircraft's fuselage, wings and tail surfaces, and finally the ultimate strength of the structure.

Because of the importance of the fatigue test

program the second "TriStar" airframe off the production line was chosen for this purpose. This test airplane included flight control surfaces separately loaded to simulate actual flight conditions, the upper portion of both the nose and the main landing gear structures, pylons that hold the wing mounted dummy engines and the structure for mounting the center engine. This aircraft, we were told, would be subjected to 1,400,000 load cycles to test wear and tear and durability.

The basic objective of this gigantic test program (estimated to cost $20,000,000) is to simulate airline operational service loading so that any problem that might occur in the future is found by inspection, measured in its cyclic progression, corrected and repaired before a similar problem could occur in airline service. A second purpose of the program is to develop the inspection techniques and schedules that will be put into practice when the airplanes are in operations with the airlines.

One structures test engineer told us—"Throughout this entire program totaling over 52,500 separate simulated flights, all ground and flight loads are applied in their proper sequences. Loadings are actually in excess of normal operating conditions. Beginning

A Test Of Men And Wings

Fatigue Test aircraft (left) and Static Test aircraft (right) surrounded by maze of hydraulic jack and sensor test rigs. Facility at Palmdale is world's largest and newest employing many new testing techniques.

This "TriStar" may look as though she were "caged in" never to fly. But she will probably make more "flights" on the ground than any other. During important Fatigue Test she will make 36,000 separate simulated flights under every condition of airline operations.

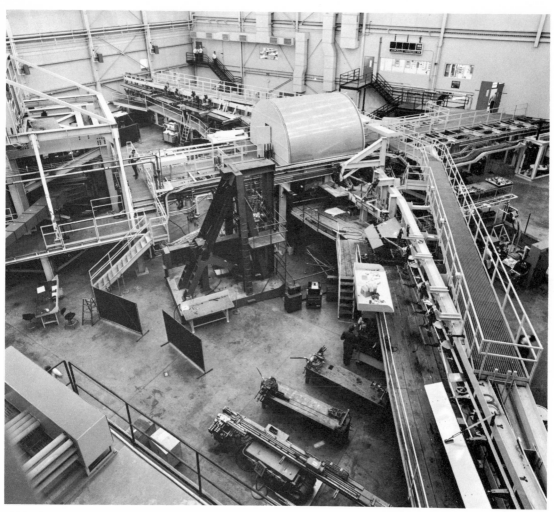

Vehicle Systems Simulator (VSS) or "Iron Bird" is example of expanding importance of laboratory testing for large new aircraft. Huge framework in the shape of a real "TriStar" is equipped with the aircraft's functioning system for integrated testing of all systems equal to lifetime of airline use.

Landing gear drop test tower at Rye Canyon facility.

with runway taxiing, then takeoff, climb, cabin pressurization, cruise, turbulance descent, depressurization and ending each flight with a landing and rollout, a total of more than 100,000 flight hours will be duplicated, equalling about 30 years of flying. This fatigue test program reached a successful conclusion in July 1973.

At another Lockheed facility, the Rye Canyon Research Laboratory in Valencia, California about 35 miles from Burbank, we saw various systems components of the L-1011 undergoing a variety of tests. There, multi-million dollar simulators—complete fuel systems, hydraulic and electronic systems, pressurization systems—are tested and tested again. In addition, the simulators are used to familiarize flight personnel and maintenance people with the various systems of the aircraft.

A Test Of Men And Wings

Windshield Impact Test rig. Cannon in foreground.

Among the more interesting tests are the Landing Gear Dynamics test and the Aircraft Windshield Impact test. The former constitutes a huge drop test tower which can simulate impact shocks on virtually any size or weight landing gear assemblies. It is interesting to point out that *"TriStar's"* main landing gear and nose wheel installations made "thousands of takeoffs and landings" before the first aircraft ever lifted off the ground.

For the windshield tests, at Rye Canyon they have set up the complete forward section (cockpit) of a *"TriStar"* to be fired at by a 5-inch-bore air gun. The gun shoots 4-pound birds at the "greenhouse" to insure the structure can stand the impact of such foreign objects.

There are, of course, many other tests. But never before has any new aircraft been subjected to such an extensive test program on the ground and in the air as that programmed for *"TriStar."* Certainly, never before have so many new monitoring devices and testing techniques—born of the computer and electronic age—so accurately and intricately recorded the anatomy of any single aircraft.

"We know more about this airplane than we ever had been able to know about any other," one engineer declared. "The test program itself is, indeed, as advanced in technology as

"TriStar" itself is representative of the most advanced technology aircraft."

The toughest test of all was yet to come.

On April 30, 1972 Eastern Air Lines substituted its first Rolls-Royce-powered L-1011 "Whisperliner" for the regular DC-8 service on its morning flight from Miami to Atlanta, Georgia and on to Kennedy International Airport, New York City. On this inaugural flight *"TriStar"* carried 214 passengers from Miami to New York in the morning and was then flown back to Miami to return with a full load of 226 passengers bound for New York the same evening.

"THE MIAMI-ATLANTA-NEW YORK-MIAMI FLIGHTS WENT PERFECTLY," cabled Eastern's President S. L. Higgenbottom to the Rolls-Royce people in Derby, England.

"TriStar" had come of age.

She was the quietest of any of the wide-bodied jetliners. She was the most luxurious, incorporating many new innovations—the below deck galley, the capability of automatic take-off and landing in all kinds of weather.

But come along, let's see for ourselves, what makes this airplane the "brightest star in the heavens."

The "Magic Numbers Game", it can be said has produced a modern magic airplane.

Airlines vary as to crew complement for L-1011's. Here is typical TWA flight crew: Captain, First Officer and Flight Engineer (above), and accompanied by seven Hostesses (below).

Trans World Airlines' first Lockheed L-1011 TriStar, Rolls-Royce powered jetliner. At lower right is a Lockheed Constellation, of which TWA was the largest user for more than two decades, beginning in 1946. The Model 049 Constellation shown here carried 81 passengers at 300 mph. The new TriStar, top, carries three times that many passengers at speeds above 600 mph.

The TriStar's wing mounted engine and main landing gear are shown in detail (above). Thrust reverser, in the "reverse thrust" position (below), is used on landing to reduce roll-out distance.

The "TriStar" on a test flight over some of California's mountainous terrain. Chase plane is another Lockheed, the "Jetstar".

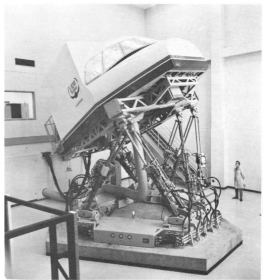

L-1011 flight simulator, a multi-million dollar pilot training tool, is supported on hydraulic arms to duplicate all normal flight attitudes of the TriStar. Use of the simulator greatly reduces the time and cost for pilot checkout.

CHAPTER NINETEEN

TriStar—Triumph In Technology

Back in 1929 the famous General James H. ("Jimmy") Doolittle, then a lieutenant, climbed into a modified Consolidated two-seater, strut-braced biplane at Mitchell Field, Long Island and proceeded to demonstrate to the world that a good pilot could fly, even if he couldn't see. The test was part of the Guggenheim Foundation's experiments in fog-flying. Doolittle, one of the best pilots in the world, was on loan from the Army Air Corps to perform the impossible—a "blind" flight from take-off to landing. He had an assistant, Lieutenant Benjamin S. Kelsey, the same Ben Kelsey who, ten years later, flew the first Lockheed XP-38 on its record-breaking flight across the continent.

Kelsey's job was easy. He was to sit in the front cockpit and see that everything went all right. If it didn't, he'd take over the controls, and fly the plane normally. But Doolittle's job was risky, and required unexcelled piloting skill and unwavering faith in the instruments in front of him. Doolittle, in the rear cockpit which had a tent-like affair over it, was in the dark. He had to rely solely on the illuminated instruments to guide him.

The husky Wright *"Whirlwind"* engine roared to life, and the plane started to move slowly over the grass runway. Kelsey sat there, both hands gripping the sides of the cockpit cowling, not touching a finger to the controls. In

"TriStar" on historic flight, May 25, 1972. With aircraft commander "Tony" LeVier in the left-hand seat monitoring her automatic flight control system, the plane takes off automatically from Palmdale enroute to Washington, D.C. for Transpo exposition. Flight was made all the way without a human hand on the controls, including a fully automatic landing at the end of the journey. Proof positive of the L-1011's claim as the world's "most advanced technology jetliner."

Piloting this Consolidated NY-2 "under the hood" famed pilot "Jimmy" Doolittle made first "blind" flight in 1929.

his "dark closet" Doolittle steered the plane straight and true as it bumped across the field, gained speed, and finally lifted its wheels clear and was airborne. He flew the ship, straight and level, south for about fifteen miles. Then, he banked gracefully and faultlessly, making a 180-degree turn, and came speeding back over the field.

North of Mitchell about fifteen miles he made another turn, and came back heading into the wind for a landing. On the ground, observers heard the plane's engine sink to an idling purr; they saw the ship sink lower and lower, until its wheels touched ever so gently. Then, it rolled to a stop within a few feet from where the machine had started its take-off run.

Doolittle had made a completely "blind" flight, taking off, flying a true predetermined course, and landing, without seeing the ground or sky. The secret was use of new Sperry Gyro Horizon and Directional Gyro instruments on the instrument panel in front of him. Linked together the instruments were his "eyes" providing an artificial horizon for judging altitude and a direction finder for maintaining a true course. Flight was a first step toward today's instrument landing system.

Three years later (May 9, 1932) another Air Corps' officer, Captain Alfred F. "Heggie" Hegenberger, like Doolittle, climbed into another biplane and took his position "under the hood" to test an improved version of the so-called blind landing system. At Wright Field, Dayton, Ohio "Heggie" took off, circled the field several times in a wide area, and then glided down to a perfect three-point landing. For the first time, without a "safety pilot" aboard, a pilot took off, flew a predetermined course, and

landed without once having seen his way.

The secret of success was the new radio compass invented by G. G. Kreusi, a Swiss-born American engineer. Receiving signals from transmitters on the ground "Heggie" was able to line up directionally true with the runway for his approach. Relying on another instrument, the Artificial Horizon Indicator and the Altimeter, he "flew" the invisible line, in normal descent to touchdown.

"It was tougher flying under the hood than flying in fog," Hegenberger later confessed. "In fog you can usually see down, if not ahead, for a few yards, anyway. In the thickest weather, you feel you've got a chance for a break at any instant, and that's consoling. But in that blacked-out cockpit you're really on your own, and God help you if you haven't got faith in those little dials in front of you!"

Captain Hegenberger had the faith and passed it on to others. Six years later, for instance, another pilot picked up where Al Hegenberger left off.

It was January 26, 1938. With Captain Jack Neale in the left-hand seat, a Pennsylvania Central Airlines' Boeing 247-D twin-engined airliner took off from Washington National Airport and pointed its nose north and west for Pittsburgh. The weather was clear in Washington, but on the other side of the Appalachians, things turned sour, and Neale found himself flying in a blinding snowstorm. He couldn't even see the wing tips. But Jack Neale was calm and confident, assured by the steady hum in his headset that he was "beaming" in on Pittsburgh with the accuracy of a homing pigeon. The radio compass was doing its thing, picking up guide signals along an electronic highway in the sky.

Near the Pittsburgh airport—blanketed by the blizzard—Neal turned a little knob on the instrument panel. That action actuated two needles on a dial, one of them swinging to the left of vertical. He pulled back and slightly to the right on the control column. The plane edged over to the right, the needle on the dial swinging back to zero. The instrument he was relying on was a modified version of the radio compass Hegenberger had used, more intricate, more delicate, but the principle was the same.

The second needle kicked up. Slowly it crept upward, but Neale let it get well past the center line until it had crossed the first needle at 90-degree angles. Then, pulling back on the throttles, easing the power of the engines, and

L-1011 TriStar and The Lockheed Story

pushing forward on the control column, he lowered the plane's nose. The needle on the dial came back to normal. He repeated the procedure several times, and these manipulations brought the airliner right to the boundary of the field, breaking through the snowflake visibility at fifty feet above the ground.

Seconds later the airliner was on the ground, rolling to a stop, turning around and taxiing up to the terminal where its passengers disembarked. The airlines, for the first time had tried and proved the instrument landing technique.

But flying "blind" wasn't enough. Man was not satisfied. There was yet another conquest to make, and it happened almost without recognition one day during the years that intervened between Hegenberger's first blind flight and the instrument landing of the PCA plane at Pittsburgh.

At Wright Field, down in the laboratories, Captain Carl J. Crane and Captain George V. Holloman and a civilian, Raymond Stout, had been working on an idea—to link the radio compass and the ground equipment of the Instrument Landing System with the Sperry gyropilot. (For years the Air Corps had been using Sperry's equipment which automatically operated a plane's control surfaces, holding it straight and level through various flight attitudes.) The trio didn't stop until they had tied the autopilot with the radio compass and another electronic "black box" which, they believed, would let them land without touching the controls.

Word got around on that hot Monday afternoon in August, 1937 that they were going to try it out in a modified Air Corps General C-14B monoplane. (It was really a Fokker-designed high-wing, single engine aircraft.) A small group of workers stayed overtime to see the plane take off and disappear in the distance.

When it returned about two hours later and made a perfect three-point landing, those who had waited it out were disappointed. Nothing really spectacular had happened. It was just another landing. But the fact is, they had witnessed history's first fully automatic landing.

This time, they had gone one step beyond the instrument flying technique used by Hegenberger and Neale. The Gyro Horizon Indicator and the Director Finder had been linked to the autopilot and "radio beams" emanating from ground stations to guide the plane down an invisible flight path to touchdown.

First automatic landing. The plane used was this Air Corps General C-14B equipped with Sperry Gyropilot coupled to Instrument Landing System (ILS) radio beams.

George Holloman described it this way to the author: "We took off and circled the field once. Then, we turned on the automatic pilot and tuned in an Indianapolis radio station. We flew for about an hour and found ourselves circling over Indianapolis. Then, we changed the station on the radio and tuned in on Dayton, and the plane flew without fault, "riding the beam", and before we knew it, we were back over Wright Field. Then, we tuned in on the localizer stations (transmitters A and B) put the radio compass and automatic pilot combination to work, and the plane settled itself to a smooth landing. About all we did was sit there with arms folded, and pray that everything would function right, and it did. That's all there was to it."

He added: "Someday, they'll put the system in reverse and planes will take off and fly and land without the pilot having to do a single thing except sit there and watch things and, maybe, turn a few knobs and push a couple of buttons."

BULLETIN

DULLES INTERNATIONAL AIRPORT, Va., May 25 (1972)—*A Lockheed L-1011 TriStar jetliner arrived here at 3:25 PM today after a completely automatic flight from its home base in Palmdale, California.*

Veteran Lockheed test pilots A. W. (Tony) LeVier and Charles R. (Chuck) Hall did not touch the control column of the big, Rolls-Royce powered trijet from the time of brake release on the Palmdale runway until after the

TriStar—Triumph In Technology

L-1011's fully automatic landing at Dulles.

LeVier, 59, who commanded the flight, said it was the first transcontinental flight by jetliner with the automatic pilot engaged from the start of the takeoff roll through the landing roll. He added that the 2,300-mile flight followed standard jet routes and was made under constant radar surveillance by Federal Aviation Administration air traffic controllers on the ground. The flight, with 115 crew members, Lockheed employees, newsmen and other passengers aboard, took 4 hours and 13 minutes, the plane averaging 545-mph ground speed.

LeVier, director of flying operations for the Lockheed-California Company, said the flight was made with the new automatic flight control system (AFCS) developed for the "TriStar" by Lockheed, Collins Radio Company and Lear-Siegler. Among the capabilities of the new system is an automatic landing, with pilots merely monitoring instruments as the aircraft descends to a runway (following the airport's

Instrument Landing System radio beams); it then touches down and rolls along the runway centerline.

Throughout the entire flight, LeVier said, from the time that the brakes were released prior to takeoff, he and copilot Hall simply monitored the instruments and systems and dialed course and altitude changes into the automatic flight control system. The new system did all the work, flying the aircraft all the way.

The day which George Holloman had prophesied 25 years before had become a reality. "TriStar's" unprecedented cross-country flight "without a human hand on the controls" was a flight into tomorrow.

Lockheed, Collins Radio and Lear-Seigler had put it all together: the pioneering efforts of Doolittle, Hegenberger, Holloman, Crane and Stout; the magic of radar that had come out of World War II; new electronic "black boxes," the offspring of the marriage of the science of electronics and the science of aeronautics, born

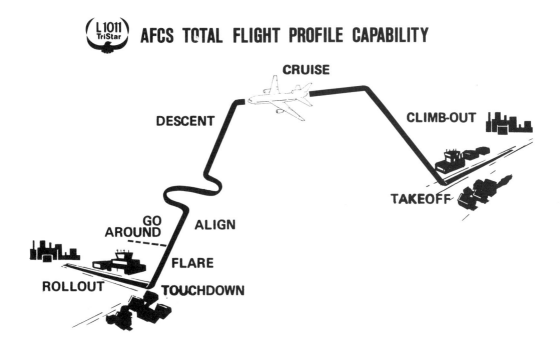

Artist's diagram shows "TriStar's" flight profile capability using Automatic Flight Control System. Plane can takeoff, fly predetermined course, and land without pilots touching flight controls.

to put a new word in the dictionary—AVIONICS; the miracle of transistors, computerization and minaturization, (a spin-off of the nation's multi-billion dollar space program). These are the things, all tied together, that make the L-1011—*"the most intelligent jetliner ever to fly."*

With its new AFCS autoland capability, the *"TriStar"* became the first aircraft to have certification for Category IIIA landings included in its initial Federal Aviation Administration type certificate. The FAA's Category IIIA rules allow landing with zero ceiling and only 700 feet of horizontal visibility on the runway.

What makes this possible? How does the system work? Lockheed engineering test pilot Bill Smith, who had charge of *"TriStar's"* autoland and autopilot projects is probably the best source to give us the answers.

"Actually, what we have in this equipment is two autopilots working side by side," Smith explained. "The system is fail-operational and fail-passive for a second failure. Dual command guidance signals from special autoland sensors—ILS receivers and radio altimeters—are combined with accelerometer input signals and processed in four identical autoland computation circuits. We take outputs from these, mix attitude rate signals from three vertical gyros. . .I suspect it's more than you want to write about. But the thing is, it works. . ."

"Along with this sophisticated electronics," Smith declared, "is a loud and clear annunciator panel in front of both captain and first officer that tells, step by step, what things are happening as the automatic landing proceeds."

"The annunciator panel uses prismatic electro-mechanical actuators for the indicator message displays. The messages pop into view, printed against a sharply contrasting background and edge-lit for maximum visibility under wide extremes of ambient cockpit light. As each step takes place, each mode of the guidance that the autopilots progress through during the approach and landing, key words (TRACK. . .ALIGN. . .FLARE) light up on the panel as the aircraft automatically passes through these stages.

"If anything goes sour along the way, it tells you that, too," Smith pointed out. "And in plenty of time to do something about it. It's the best autopilot system I've ever encountered—or even heard about.

"It puts you on the runway at a two foot per second rate of sink, exactly where you should be, and exactly the same, time after time after time. The thing makes the entire approach and landing the way we'd like to think we do it all the time."

(But come along and see for yourself. In the accompanying photographs Bill Smith and copilot Bob Schumacher take you through the six steps of autoland.)

Having flown "up front" in the jump seat right behind Tony LeVier as well as back in the cabin as a passenger, during several automatic landings (and take-offs) the author also has some observations. For instance, the entire approach is more like a smooth, even let down in an elevator than landing in an airplane. There is no sudden change in the cabin level, no sharp angle, pitching you forward straining against the seat belt. There is no 'sinking' feeling, and the back of your seat doesn't tickle your spine, like it does during a manual descent when the pilot must pull back on the control column to complete the flare-out just before touchdown. And during the whole approach there is no sensation of the aircraft "searching and feeling" its way to find the invisible guideline to the center of the runway. You have to experience it, to believe it.

And the beauty is that *"TriStar's"* autoland mode can be used at any airport equipped with a localizer and glidescope—the standard Instrument Landing System. For the air traveler it means fewer delays in airline schedules and fewer diversions to alternate airports caused by poor visibility at a flight's destination.

The "most intelligent jetliner" (L-1011) has another exclusive new system that aids in making precision landings. Called Direct Lift Control, this system automatically activates spoilers atop the wings during the landing descent. By increasing the amount of lift produced by the wings, the DLC system enables *"TriStar"* to track the glide slope with minimal changes in pitch, and to land consistently and softly on a specific spot on the runway.

There is also a new "built-in" automated navigation system which couples the autopilot with navigational aids to control both course and altitude. It allows *"TriStar"* to fly automatically over any course selected by the pilots, and merely identified by the airlines' flight number, using either standard airways or

Localizer (part of ILS system on the ground) is "captured" and copilot Bob Schumacher drops flaps to initial approach position. Autoland button on glare shield has been punched, both autopilots operating, airplane headed for airport.

Hands in lap, Smith and Schumacher watch "TriStar" approach inbound on glidescope for Palmdale airport. Autoland annunciator has not yet announced "TRACK" mode which occurs 1500 feet above the runway.

Bill Smith, in left-hand seat, points out second autopilot which must be engaged for redundancy on Autoland. Landing gear is now down and locked. Pilots await glidescope "capture." Glideslope is also part of the ILS.

Precisely aligned with the runway "TriStar" tracks down to the 50 foot flare point and autothrottles are reducing power of the engines as the autoland system readies the airplane for landing and rollout.

Smith adjusts indicated air speed on autothrottle system to slow down aircraft for approach. Indicated air speed is 158 knots so must be reduced. The autothrottle maintains the desired speed on approach.

Just at touchdown, autoland system flips over to "ROLL-OUT" mode, then uses nosewheel steering to guide the "TriStar" down the runway until aircraft comes to a complete stop. Pilot takes over for taxi to terminal.

the new off-airways "area navigation" routes. A tape recorded memory unit in the system can store all the navigational information required for a large airline's entire international route system. By giving the aircraft this automated ability to fly off standard airways, the system, developed by Lockheed and the Arma Division of AMBAC Industries, will help dramatically in reducing air traffic congestion.

How do pilots feel about all of this automation?

Listen to Captain John Thaddeus May, a 33-year veteran with Trans World Airlines: "The arrival of a new airplane on any airline always generates enthusiasm and great expectation for new long dreamed of capabilities," he confessed. "Influenced by the manufacturer, who is selling the product, the company sometimes gets a littled carried away when advertising these new capabilities. Experience has taught pilots to treat all new innovations with a mixture of enthusiasm and skepticism. This was es-

Veteran TWA Captain John T. "Thad" May in the left-hand seat of "TriStar" in docking position at Chicago's O'Hare International Airport. He was in command of Flight 24 which author flew in as passenger, non-stop Chicago to L.A. May called L-1011, "a true triumph in technology."

pecially true of the L-1011 since this airplane, we were told, would *'do it all'*—a complete automatic landing including cross-wind de-crab, touchdown, roll-out and even an auto 'go-around' if necessary.

"It was almost a year ago that I started training on the L-1011. Today, five hundred hours, and more than thirty autolands later, my skepticism is gone, but my enthusiasm remains. The L-1011 is truly a triumph in technology."

"It has been my privilege as Chairman of the TWA Pilots All-weather Committee," Thad told the author, "to have the responsibility of evaluating the autoland system and reporting the results to our MEC (Master Executive Council). This evaluation has included a survey of the opinions of other pilots also flying the L-1011. I am not privileged to give the details, but I can say that my confidence in the autoland system is shared by other pilots, almost to a man."

Even as we were talking, *"TriStar's"* electronic wizardry was working overtime. For we were sitting back in the luxurious lounge section of TWA's L-1011, Flight 24, westbound out of Chicago, non-stop to Los Angeles International Airport. The plane, Captain May explained, was on autopilot and using its automated navigation system, flying an off-airway course, the most direct line to LA. It was programmed for a completely automatic landing, even though the City of Angels was basking in bright sunshine and 74-degree temperature.

Another TWA Captain, who was "deadheading" back to L.A., joined us. What he said about autoland is probably the best compliment of all, even though he didn't want his name used, perhaps, for obvious reasons. "This system is just great," he remarked. "Frankly, I'm a little jealous. In this age of technology it's easy to accept the fact that an autopilot can be built to make an accurate automatic landing. But building one that manipulates the controls with the subtle anticipation of an experienced pilot, hell, that's a bit too much! I guess I can take heart, though, in that they still need us up there to punch the right buttons, to program the computers, and keep an eye on things. It's nice, too, that TWA still sends me the check and doesn't send it to 'George' (pilot's slang for the

Coach lounge on TWA's "TriStar" Flight 24, Ambassador Service, features stand-up bar and conversational-style seating along the windows. Since picture was taken airline has eliminated lounge, put in additional seats.

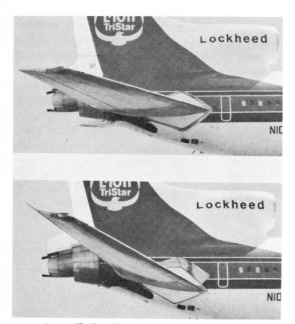

Another "TriStar" exclusive feature for added safety is the unique "Flying Stabilizer." Photos show how entire horizontal tail surfaces move up and down, giving the big aircraft, it is claimed, more sensitive and positive control during critical attitudes.

autopilot) who really does all the work."

The subject of another feature relative to the L-1011's "advanced technology" came into the conversation. *"TriStar"*, I was told, has an unusually effective wing with excellent overall airfoil efficiency, but it is the aircraft's *pitch control* and *trim systems* that together stand out as an innovation and true technical advancement for the new generation of large transports.

The reference was to the L-1011's unique "flying stabilizer" which gives pilots (and the autopilots) more positive control during critical flight attitudes. I learned that there had been a lot of concern about the pitch control and trim systems of the current generation jetliners, such things in pilots' jargon as *"runaway trim, stalled trim, mistrim,"* the potential loss of elevator effectiveness at high Mach numbers due to shock-induced separation, and the possibility of control ineffectiveness caused by certain load conditions.

The "flying stabilizer" is designed to overcome such hazards. What happens is this: Four large piston-type hydraulic cylinders actuate the "flying stabilizer," each powered by one of the aircraft's independent hydraulic systems, and each capable of furnishing adequate control force by itself to fly the aircraft safely. The actuators move the complete stabilizer in fixed

relationship to the pilot's control column, with the elevators geared so that they operate *automatically* as a function of stabilizer deflection. Through this system, the pilot achieves direct control over the entire horizontal tail surfaces, instead of just the elevators as with other aircraft.

In lay terms, the "flying tail" gives this huge jetliner unexcelled controllability, especially during takeoffs and landings. "She handles like a fighter plane," one pilot observed. "And that's a good feeling when you're holding the reins on a 200-ton leviathan."

On this note, our conversation broke up as Captain May left to go "up front" and we were met by Jon Proctor, Flight 24's Director of Customer Services (DCS) who took us on a tour of the aircraft to see some of its other outstanding features. Most innovative, perhaps, was our visit to the downstairs galley.

Located amidship, below the main cabin, this Lockheed patented galley (used on some Boeing 747s and Douglas DC-10s) is as roomy, if not more so, than the kitchen in most American homes. Featuring five high-speed, infra-red ovens, it is also equipped with refrigerator, freezer, ice-maker, and other restaurant-style accessories. Two elevators, each about the size

Jon Proctor, TWA's Director Customer Services (DCS) aboard Flight 24. The son of an American Airlines' captain who flew Ford trimotors in the early days of transcontinental airline operation, Proctor loves his work. Says "TriStar" is "the people pleasing airplane."

Meet the guys and gals who made up our Flight Crew aboard TWA's Flight 24 "TriStar" service. Standing left to right: Hostess Sally Steinhardt, Hostess Lois Young, Captain Thad May, Hostess Sandi Gomez, First Officer Doug Westlund, Hostess Cheryl Byron, and Flight Engineer Eugene Bridges. Seated, left to right: Hostesses Dee Pilgram, Sharon Hurley, Sandy Phillips, Marcie Kaczenski, Sherry Gutzler and Director of Customer Services Jon Proctor. It is interesting to point out that today's L-1011 carries more pilots and cabin attendants than the passenger capacity of Lockheed's first commercial airliner the ten passenger "Electra" Model-10, vintage 1933.

of a telephone booth, connect this food preparation area with the main cabin above.

Getting off one of the elevators, we were greeted by a sign which best tells how hostesses feel about the whole idea. The sign read—HOME SWEET HOME!

The signmakers were TWA hostesses Dee Pilgram and Sharon Hurley, who introduced themselves as "galley slaves."

"Seriously, though, I really like it down here," Dee Pilgram confided. She was one of TWA's first trainees for this new kind of hostess duty, and had been with the L-1011 from its mock-up stage. "You don't have to be so formal, and there's so much work to do that before you know it, the flight's over. Besides, I'm learning to be a gourmet cook, and you know the old saying about the quickest way to a man's heart..."

Watching the girls prepare meals for the 215 passengers "upstairs"—first-class and coach—one got the impression that this wasn't an airliner, at all, it was a restaurant with wings. On this day's menu there were lamb chops, filet mignon steaks, and breast of chicken.

"The food is prepared in TWA's own kitchens on the ground," Dee Pilgram explained. "It comes aboard in a chilled state in individual trays stowed in special serving carts that load directly through the galley's separate door, precluding interference with passenger loading, cargo loading and aircraft servicing.

"All we do is pop it into the oven, and presto, it comes out cooked to order, hot and ready to serve. Salad, roll, and dessert are added to the tray which is placed back in the cart (in a warming oven) and we send it upstairs for hostesses to serve to individual passengers."

"Galley Slaves" Sharon Hurley (left) and Dee Pilgram proudly show off their little corner of the world, the "kitchen sink" in the below deck galley of TWA's L-1011 Flight 24. The smiles tell us that KP isn't really such bad duty.

Sharon "pops" our filet mignon into the radar oven. On the tray are eight steaks. When done, she will put them into serving cart, send it upstairs via the elevator.

Stewardess aboard Eastern Airlines' L-1011 "Whisperliner" with serving carts loaded with "goodies." Note the two elevators. The below deck galley is 20 feet long.

This hide-away closet on TWA's L-1011 is new convenience feature. Once filled, hostess will press a button and coats and garment bags will be lifted out of the way into the airplane's overhead.

Spacious overhead storage bins make it easy and convenient for passengers on L-1011 to store hats, small bags and carry-on parcels. Bins also hold pillows and blankets for passenger comfort.

"The whole idea," she said, "is to take the food odors, and the noise and confusion of food and drink preparation, away from the main cabin.

"How do you want your steak, by the way?" she said with a wink. "Medium, rare or well done?"

"With a Jack Daniels on the rocks," I answered, joking.

"Here you are," interrupted Sharon, Dee's partner who had been busy preparing a cart filled with a lot of liquid goodies. And she handed me my drink.

Back upstairs, we joined Jon Proctor again, who took us from one end of the airplane to the other, explaining as we went along why *TriStar* was "the people pleasing airplane" as he called it. There are a lot of reasons as the reader can readily see from the accompanying photographs. But beyond all of this, in the eyes of this writer, at least, the L-1011 was something special.

On the ground at LA International, after Captain Thad May had brought her down for another automatic landing, we stood there a few minutes looking up at the towering tail and the sleek lines of this modern day "magic carpet."

If sun's glare is too harsh, "TriStar" has the answer. This three part sequence shows how special "sunglass-style" window is adjusted to control sun's rays and amount of light desired to suit personal comfort. Secret is polarized pane that has unique ability to harness light rays in one direction.

TriStar—Triumph In Technology

TWA's first "TriStar" which was our Flight 24, took time out to pose for this picture with a Vintage 1929 Lockheed Vega, a replica of Wiley Post's famous "Winnie Mae." It made one think of the many things that came out of Lockheed planes of the past to give us today's brightest star of them all—The L-1011.

And suddenly, it dawned on us, *"TriStar"* wasn't a thing of cold metal, electronic systems, the end product of science and machines.

No, indeed, *"TriStar"* was and is the shining symbol of the spirit of Lockheed.

There was the "flying stabilizer," for instance. Allan Loughead (Lockheed) had tried that on the Model-G, sixty years ago. There was her pressurized cabin. They had pioneered that with the XC-35 substratosphere airplane. There was her luxurious, air-conditioned, cabin with its "living room" atmosphere and decor, shades of the wonderful *"Constellations"* which had introduced a new kind of luxury aloft. There was her automatic landing system and, one remembered, Holloman and Crane and Stout, had used a Lockheed *Electra Junior* (the Model-12) in their later experiments pioneering automatic flight. There was her size, and one could recall the 'know-how' gleaned from *"Hercules"*, the *"Starlifters"* and *"Galaxy,"* the world's largest aircraft.

She was representative of all of these things and the men and women, tens of thousands, who had turned so many fantasies into fact.

One wonders, perplexed and puzzled because of an "uncomputerized" mind, what new horizons lie ahead.

What would Orville Wright say, and Allan Loughead, and Bob Gross?

This is how Agena Target Vehicle, developed by Lockheed for USAF and NASA appeared to astronauts from "Gemini" capsule as spacecraft approached the Agena for a docking maneuver.

CHAPTER TWENTY

Horizons Unlimited

Commercial aircraft maintenance and modification is speciality of the Lockheed Aircraft Service Company. LAS, wholly owned subsidiary was formed in 1946, beginning of company's broad diversification movement.

"There is a certain feeling of courage and hope when you work in the field of the air," Bob Gross once declared. "You instinctively look up, not down. You look ahead, not back. You look ahead where the horizons are absolutely unlimited."

Today it is more than forty years, the beginning of the fifth decade since Bob Gross and fellow investors brought his "forward look" to the faltering Lockheed Aircraft Company in 1932. During that time Lockheed has developed and manufactured nearly 35,000 air and space vehicles of more than 100 different types.

Today Lockheed Aircraft Corporation, the parent company headquartered in Burbank, California has divisions and subsidiaries spread world-wide, employing more than 65,000 persons. Its profile is that of a broadly based industrial complex highly skilled in translating the discoveries of science into advanced products,

systems, and services for human progress and national defense. It is the aerospace giant of the seventies.

The company's interests include missile, satellite, and space exploration and communication systems; military and civilian aircraft, electronics, propulsion; shipbuilding, ground support, heavy construction, air, ground, and shipboard materials handling; underseas warfare, ocean systems; bionics, nuclear products and services; military base operation, maintenance, and servicing; airport management, international business developments, computers, tracking base operations, and general industrial development and manufacture.

More specifically, some of these interests include design, development and production of (1). Poseidon underwater-launched ballistic missile and its successor the new C-4. Its experience in

"Poseidon" missile hurls skyward from submarine USS James Madison. Lockheed Missiles, & Space Co. is prime contractor and missile system manager for this project.

Lockheed's Deep Submergence Rescue Vehicle (DSRV) is the first of two such submarines which will be able to rescue crewmen from submarines stranded on the ocean bottom.

Solid propellant propulsion system for USAF short-range attack missile (SRAM), is test fired. SRAM motor was designed and developed by Lockheed Propulsion Company as subcontractor.

this sophisticated field of undersea deterrent weapons spanning 15 years, beginning with the famous Polaris missile. (2). The manufacture of the Agena satellite and space vehicle. (3). Continuing programs with improved versions of the C-130 "Hercules", the L-100 civilian counterpart and improved versions of "JetStars", the P-3 "Orion", land-based antisubmarine aircraft and the S-3A "Viking" a new carrier-based an-

tisubmarine (ASW) for the Navy; the C-5 "Galaxy" world's largest aircraft; the triplesonic SR-71 "Blackbirds". (4). Solid propellant rocket pulse motors for SRAM, short range attack missile.

In addition, for the past several years, Lockheed has been bringing its technological talent to bear on a wide variety of challenging social and environmental problems. Following

Navy/Lockheed S-3A "Vikings" carrier-based anti-submarine warfare aircraft, latest in long line of "wings for the blue and gold."

are some examples that typify the scope of the company's diversified research and development efforts.

OIL CLEAN UP—A Lockheed-developed and patented system, known as "Clean Sweep" literally scoops up oil from the surface of ocean and inland waters and deposits it in containers for later removal.

WEATHER WATCHERS—Contracts for four experimental, weather-watching and oceangraphic data buoys in two programs have been delivered by Lockheed to the National Oceanic and Atmospheric Administration. The buoys collect data on water and atmospheric conditions, and radio the results to shore stations. Measurements include wind speed and direction, water temperature, rainfall, ocean current speed and direction and wave height. The experimental weather-watchers will be the forerunners of a world-wide buoy network to constantly monitor and transmit meteorological and oceanographic data to shore stations thus enabling more precise weather prediction.

REMOTE HEALTH CARE—Lockheed is designing and testing a remote health care system which will bring hospital-quality care to a community at a distance from established hospital facilities. The system combines advanced medical instrumentation with com-

puterized data techniques and voice and picture transmission. In use, the system permits specially trained paramedics at remote locations to be able to send X-ray photos and other data to enable physicians at a central hospital to diagnose illnesses and prescribe possible methods of treatment. Lockheed also has developed a new X-ray intensifying screen which would reduce medical X-ray exposures by as much as 20 times—a significant reduction in the dangers of radiation exposure.

SMOG RESEARCH—Lockheed researchers have been studying smog in a specially-constructed chamber. The goal is to gain a better understanding of the complex reactions in smog production. This in turn, it is believed, can lead to practical solutions for reducing or eliminating smog.

SUBSEA PETROLEUM RECOVERY—Lockheed has developed a new approach to subsea petroleum operations. A system has been developed which eliminates the need for divers or remote manipulation of hardware from submersible vessels. Oil-field workmen can be transported from the surface to the wellhead (far below) in a transfer capsule, wearing ordinary clothes and carrying their own familiar tools to work directly on standard land-type wellhead

Lockheed's candidate for advanced attack Helicopter role. Full scale mock-up of the CL-1700, a small, twin engine aerial tank buster which has been proposed by Lockheed-California Company to fill U.S. Army requirement.

valve assemblies. The system, it is expected, will open up new and economical petroleum development in ocean depths down to 3,000 feet.

Lockheed is also engaged in the development of new type vehicles for exploration of the ocean floor. Indeed, Lockheed horizons are *unlimited, above and below!*

For purposes of this book, however, let us take a closer look at the future of the L-1011 "TriStar" and other commercial and private aircraft developments which are new goals of the Lockheed - California Company and the Lockheed-Georgia Company.

First, the "magic number airplane" L-1011 "Dash 385" which went into scheduled airline service in the spring of 1972, we are told, is just the beginning of a whole family of new wide-bodied jetliners. It is no secret that "TriStar" from its very concept was geared for growth.

Bill Hannan, whom we met earlier (Chapter 15) now Lockheed-California Company's vice president for airline requirements and product planning describes this growth factor in the following manner: "Any commercial airplane when it starts out has to have growth, and when you go to sell the design to an airline, the first question they will ask is—'Tell me how this airplane can grow and what growth plans are?' The airline is not going to buy an airplane that's at the end of the line, because the airline doesn't stop. Air transportation is a dynamic thing, itself. It gets bigger and the ranges change and the traffic goes up. The airline president wants to know that your airplane is going to keep pace with his requirement as time goes by. . . So, when we conceived this airplane we had already studied reasonably well the whole family."

Some details of significant design refinements in the proposed extended-range L-1011 were

HORIZONS UNLIMITED, above and below. Lockheed's deep-diving submarine "Deep Quest." Four-man sub, designed and built by Lockheed Missiles & Space Company is engaged in various oceanographic explorations.

Lockheed Shipyards on south shore of Seattle's Elliott Bay. Part of diversification program, Lockheed Shipbuilding and Construction Company is engaged in building amphibious assault transports (shown here) and destroyer escorts for Navy.

revealed at the 1973 Paris Air Show. "We have held discussions with major world airlines about the long range *TriStar*," explained A. Carl Kotchian, President of Lockheed Aircraft Corporation. "These talks include a version of the aircraft which can fly its full complement of passengers more than 6,000 statute miles."

Called the L-1011-2, the plane Kotchian was talking about will be powered by the newly-announced growth version of the Rolls-Royce RB.211-524 engine rated at 48,000 pounds take-off thrustpower, almost 15 per cent more powerful than the *TriStar's* present engines. Increases in both fuel and payload would raise the *TriStar's* maximum gross weight from 430,000 pounds to 516,000 pounds. Result would mean about 50 per cent more fuel capacity for the basic L-1011-1 design.

Although this aircraft would have the same exterior dimension as the first production *"TriStar"* the added power and fuel load would permit the plane to fly longer routes, opening up new airline markets. The extended-range *"TriStar"* for example, would be capable of intercontinental service between, say, Sydney-Singapore, Chicago-Frankfurt, or Teheran-London. The plane also would have the range capability of non-stop transcontinental operations.

Aboard a specially-fitted, high-density (400 seats) Court Line Aviation *"TriStar"* on a demonstration flight over Paris, Carl Kotchian told the author that there are two versions of the extended-range aircraft being considered, grossing 516,000 pounds and powered by the same new engines. A second proposed version, he called the L-1011-2LR which is tailored to meet specific airline interests in a longer range, wide-bodied jetliner with a smaller passenger complement. The passenger cabin of this version, it was pointed out, would be shortened and the galley relocated on the main deck to allow additional cargo capacity in the belly. Primarily, the plane would be used to replace aging first generation jets (like the 707s and DC-8s) on the so-called "thin routes." The shortened fuselage/cabin would be the principal distinction between the two extended range versions.

Key to the long-range *"TriStar"*, Kotchian said, was its commonality with the L-1011-1 ordered by TWA, Eastern Air Lines, Air Canada, Court Line Aviation, British Airways, Delta Air Lines, All Nippon Airways, Pacific Southwest Airlines and LTU (Lufttransport Unternehmen) the German Airline. When the new versions would be available, it was pointed out, would depend upon the interest of various airlines and the availability of the new, higher thrustpower engines.

Based on splendid performance records of the L-1011 *"TriStars"* during their first year of operation, flying domestic routes in the U.S. and to San Juan, it is likely present users and others will want the long-range version. Interestingly, figures compiled through February, 1973—nine months after the first Eastern Airlines *"TriStar"* went into service and seven months after TWA introduced its *"TriStar"* service—show the planes had accumulated 22,250 flight hours and approximately 1,160,550,000 revenue passenger miles with good passenger acceptance. Reliability of the planes during this period of introductory airline service has been comparable to that of other wide-bodied jet transports.

This splendid record was marred when a *"TriStar"* crashed in Florida's Everglades, December 29, 1972, enroute to landing at Miami. But a detailed investigation by the National Transportation Safety Board did not attribute the accident to any malfunction of the airplane or engine. The accident recalled to the author other similar tragedies that hit the *"Constellation"* the Douglas DC-6s, the Boeing 707s and other planes during their early operational periods—all of which went on to become the great airliners they are today. And *"TriStar"* appears to be the brightest star of them all.

Talking with Rolls-Royce people in Paris, it was learned, that the new and more powerful engines will be available when the long-range L-1011-2 program is launched. "The higher thrust-power engine is now under development at Derby," a Rolls engineer declared. "This engine will be externally similar to the RB.211, but it will have between eight and ten per cent greater climb and cruise thrust and an improved specific fuel consumption. Rig performance testing of major components has already been carried out and the results are substantiating predicted performance."

"Rolls-Royce has always been accustomed to the provision of thrust growth once a new commercial engine enters service," the engineer pointed out. "A typical example is the *Spey* turbo-fan engine, which, five years after service, had increased its takeoff thrust on a hot day by approximately 40 per cent!"

The engineer also revealed that there is prospect of a thrust upgrading to 55,000 pounds

Future plans for "TriStar" if market prevails include this short-range twin-engined design.

at take-off in a "dash 56/57" series RB.211 engines. Admittedly futuristic, it was explained that this might be achieved by using a larger gas generator producing virtually the same pressure-ratio in the same number of compressor stages. The bypass-ratio would be maintained at the RB.211-22 level by increasing fan airflow, involving a small increase in the fan diameter. The thrust and specific fuel consumption might further be improved by the addition of a fourth stage to the low pressure turbine.

With the prospect of such increased power, there is the possibility of yet another version of the *"TriStar"* which would take an entirely different approach. There would be, perhaps, 30 feet added to the present fuselage length and possibly some wing changes. This "stretch" L-1011, envisioned by Bill Hannan, would provide for approximately 70 more passengers, a total capacity wide-bodied jetliner of some 400 seats with conventional first-class and coach configuration. The plane would also have transcontinental range, competitive on such routes with the 747.

Because of the additional power available in the RB.211-524 engines, Lockheed has also been working on design proposals for yet a fourth member of the L-1011 family. It would be a twin-engined design, probably the same wide-bodied fuselage and wing planform, but of smaller dimensions, capable of carrying 200-250 passengers in big jet comfort on short-range, high-density routes.

Discussions about the twin-engine airplane have centered around proposals for an international consortium which would make the project more financially feasible. The "TwinStar's" future depends upon many things.

"But," says Bill Hannan, "there's a big market for these twins if you project your thinking out to 1985. Nobody seems to have figured out yet a good money-making short-haul airplane, conventional design, STOL or VTOL. We do know the airlines want it."

It may be that Lockheed one day will go back to its original design for the "Airbus".

Another member of the Lockheed family which we have neglected to mention is the Lockheed Service Company (LAS) which today is a world leader in aircraft maintenance and modification operations. Prime role is supplying aviation and ground services to foreign countries in their efforts to achieve technical superiority and economic security.

Overseas production, maintenance, service and management activities began on a large scale 35 years ago when LAS, then the Customer Service Division of Lockheed Aircraft Corporation, was requested by the British government to establish a facility and organization in England to reassemble the *"Hudson"* bomber. Ever since, at home and abroad, LAS has been performing a variety of tasks including operation of a C-130 *"Hercules"* airline in Zambia to transport copper, and a remote maintenance base for *"Herc"* airlift between Anchorage, Fairbanks and Alaska's North Slope. Today large-scale operations are being performed in Saudi Arabia and Singapore.

With two major U.S. bases of operation, one at Ontario, California, the other at John F. Kennedy International Airport in New York, Lockheed Aircraft Service is one of the largest—if not the largest and certainly the first—independent aircraft maintenance facilities in the world. At Kennedy, for example, 25 commercial airline customers, both U.S. and international carriers, utilize the LAS facility for gate-handling service, turn-around-service and heavy maintenance.

Typical of LAS activities is the modification of an L-188 *"Electra"* turboprop for the National Center for Atmospheric Research. Containing an assortment of sensors and measuring devices, this *"Electra"* will be used for meterological studies in the Global Atmospheric Research Program. A number of nations are participating in this effort, scheduled for the summer of 1974. Basic objective of the project is to obtain a better understanding of the large-scale physical process controlling atmospheric behaviour. Eventually, the knowledge gained will lead to more accurate, longer range weather forecasts.

Another highly specialized modification program nearing completion at the LAS Ontario, California facility is the installation of the world's largest airborne telescope system—weighing over 15,000 pounds—in a NASA *"Starlifter"* C-141 aircraft. This work is being carried out in cooperation with Fecker Systems Division of Owens-Illinois, Inc., the manufacturers of the telescope.

Flying missions at 45,000 feet, above 85 per cent of the earth's atmosphere and 99 per cent of the water vapor, astronomers will be able to make observations in the infra-red region which will be 1,000 times more effective than if taken at ground level.

Over the years, LAS has become a leader in high-technology aircraft modifications. Recent

Horizons Unlimited

Artist's concept of STOL (short take-off and landing) aircraft now under test at Lockheed-Georgia Company under NASA contract.

advanced modification programs have encompassed the installation of microwave guidance systems, stellar inertial guidance systems and complex radar systems.

Meanwhile, Lockheed-Georgia Company on its "new horizon" has another approach to the short-haul operation. The idea centers around a modified "Hercules" C-130 to make it an amphibian aircraft designed to meet the requirements of a STOL (Short Take-off And Landing) transportation system in specific areas.

Excerpts from a company press release tell the story: "Studies have shown that the principal areas requiring this mode of transportation are the Northeast Corridor; Atlanta southward to Miami-Orlando; the Detroit-Cleveland-Chicago triangle; the Dallas-Fort Worth-Houston triangle and the West Coast Corridor—San Diego to Seattle. Lockheed points out that all of these centers are located on water.

"The acquisition of land for land-based STOL ports is likely to be prohibitively high in some areas and such projects will undoubtedly meet opposition from citizens, and those concerned with environmental problems. For these reasons Lockheed is of the opinion that an amphibian aircraft is the logical answer. The adaptation of local resources would be comparatively easy and cheap and would allow a full city-to-city service to be operated which would be environmentally acceptable, quiet, inexpensive, would relieve airport congestion, and which, by using the modified C-130 "Hercules" aircraft could be quickly available."

The announcement goes on to say: "The modifications to be made to the basic C-130 would be the addition of a hydro-ski; the installation of auxiliary floats and of a false hull; the inversion of the engines (as in the Navy P-3 "Orion") to allow over-the-wing installation to provide better propeller tip clearance. In practice this would only require the gear box to be inverted.

"To give STOL capability, double-slotted, compound Fowler flaps would be installed together with spoilers; the rudder, dorsal fin and stabilizer would be increased in size. In addition, there would be a fully-powered flight control system and a stability augmentation system. These components have already been designed.

"The "Hercules" amphibian would seat 70 to 100 passengers (depending on the stretch of the fuselage) with a basic 6-abreast seating arrangement."

Performance-wise, the plane would have a gross take-off weight of 126,000-pounds, cruise at 300 knots and have a range of 600 miles. For land operations it could take off in about 1,750 feet and land in 2,450 feet. The plane would be equipped for instrument landing capability, and advanced technology would enable the plane to taxi or locate the ramp in zero-zero conditions.

For the ground facilities, suitable ramps, leading from the terminal buildings to the water are cheap and easy to construct, Lockheed points out. A complete facility requirement, consisting of navigational aids, ramp, terminal buildings, fire/crash boat, channel markers and

"Hercules" amphibian. Lockheed-Georgia Company is offering proposed design of famed C-130 cargo plane in amphibian version for STOL operations. Shown here is model of plane that could keep "Herc" production line going into third decade.

lights plus utilities and support services could be set up for as little as $500,000. Although the Lockheed study has concentrated on the use of the amphibian in the U.S. and Canada, it could well be that it would have applications in many parts of the world.

In addition to studies for the "Herc" amphibian, the Lockheed-Georgia Company is also working on other STOL aircraft studies for NASA. One of these is the design of a quiet-lift propulsion aircraft.

Although no work is planned for the im-

Experimental VTOL aircraft, Army's XV-4A "Hummingbird." Using thrust from twin jet engines, diverted through ejectors, the craft rises straight up, then starts transition to forward flight.

mediate future for VTOL (Vertical Take-off And Landing) aircraft it is known that Lockheed has had previous experience along these lines with the XV-4A *"Hummingbird"* designed to rise straight up, land straight down, hover and dash ahead. The XV-4A is a two-engine jet developed by the Lockheed-Georgia Company.

In an entirely different approach to vertical flight, Lockheed-California Company for several years has been engaged in the development and testing of rigid rotorcraft, the experimental vehicle being the winged XH-51A helicopter. This helicopter is 32 feet long and has a rotor blade diameter of 35 feet. Its stub wings have a 17-foot span.

The XH-51A uses a Lockheed-developed rigid-rotor system that provides both "hands off" stability and high maneuverability. An auxiliary jet engine on the left wing supplements the helicopter's regular turbine engine. This experimental research compound helicopter exceeded 200 miles per hour, faster than any other

rotorcraft, while at the same time being able to take-off and land on the proverbial dime.

Tests are continuing with improved versions of the rigid rotor, fixed-wing principle for the helicopter. Presently, however, there are no plans for any commercial adaptation.

What about a second generation SST? Is Lockheed doing anything along this line?

Nobody really wants to talk about any plans with regard to any revised Supersonic Transport designs or proposals. Lockheed-California Company is, however, under contract to NASA to do some design studies and perhaps even wind tunnel testing of the Space Agency's radically new supersonic concepts.

Celebrating the 60th anniversary of the first flight of Allan Loughead's Model-G (June 13, 1913) the company he actually founded so long ago is "keeping a watchful eye on" the progress and acceptance of the British/French "Concorde" and the Russian TU-144 supersonics. What happens in the next two or three years

PRESENTING: JETSTAR II—Artist's concept with Paris background depicts the JetStar II, an advanced model of Lockheed-Georgia Company's business aircraft with transcontinental range, improved fuel economy, and quiet, smoke-free turbo-fan engines. Lockheed-Georgia said it now offers the JetStar II fitted with four Garrett AiResearch TFE-731-3 engines for delivery in mid-1975. The new powerplants will make possible nonstop flights across the United States and one-stop flights to Europe from Denver and Chicago. An updated version of the service-proved Lockheed business jet that commerce and governmental leaders fly all over the world, the JetStar II will retain spacious accommodations for 10 passengers and a crew of two. The TFE-731-3 engine meets all state and federal noise and smoke emission standards.

L-1011 TriStar and The Lockheed Story

Different helicopter approach. With rigid rotor providing built-in stability, Lockheed winged helicopter has auxiliary jet engine and has set speed marks for rotary wing aircraft. It is easy to fly and simple to maintain.

after these foreign-built SSTs go into scheduled airline service, could well decide Lockheed's future venture into this area.

Then, there is this remark made recently by "Kelly" Johnson surveying the field of general aviation: "I foresee an increased growth in the field of general aviation, the use of corporate jets, and a revolution in terms of applying turbo jets to small private planes."

"Perhaps even small SSTs for corporate use," the designer of Lockheed's triple-sonic SR-71 declared.

And who knows what's going on at the SKUNK WORKS these days?

Beyond this is the question of the year 2000 airplane as seen through the eyes of Lockheed's "Bill" Hannan.

He says: "This is not a 'blue sky' idea but a situation for which we are developing some concrete answers right now!"

He described one of these future aircraft concepts which Lockheed is investigating as "a nuclear-powered airplane that will fly 600 passengers in comfort at just under the speed of sound, non-stop to any city in the world." Its nuclear propulsion system would result in smoke-free operations and unlimited range. This future Global Airliner would have the comfort of today's new wide-bodied jetliners, and also have the flexibility of the Lockheed L-1011 to operate from existing airports.

"Such an aircraft," Hannan stated, "would have a 350-foot long fuselage, 199-foot wing span, maximum length of 25 feet, and a gross take-off weight of 850,000 pounds, only slightly heavier than the largest plane flying today."

"New aircraft of this type," he concluded, "will be possible because of advancements in new composite materials which will result in improved strength and reduced weight. Composite materials, such as carbon fiber, titanium alloys, and others will permit aircraft manufacturers to increase payloads by 20 per cent while maintaining present weights."

Indeed, such a plane may come sooner than we think. Lockheed's pathway to the stars has been filled with many fabulous "impossible" achievements.

L-1011 "TriStar" is just one shining example.

Ten years ago before the advent of the advanced technology and big fan powerplants few people dreamed there would be a plane like the L-1011.

Perhaps, that's what Bob Gross meant about never looking backwards.

Wings for tomorrow. Here is artist's drawing of atom-powered 600-passenger subsonic airliner. Plane would have unlimited range. It could operate from airports that serve today's jets.

INDEX

INDEX

Index

Index

255

Index

BRANIFF

 SOUTH AFRICAN

 NORDAIR

 JAPAN

 PACIFIC SOUTHWEST

 ALOHA

 PAKISTAN

 BRITANNIA

 CALEDONIAN

 MALAYSIA-SINGAPORE

 SAUDI ARABIAN

 EASTERN

 ETHIOPIAN

 ALITALIA

 BRAATHENS

 OLYMPIC

 AMERICAN FLYERS

 TRANS CARIBBEAN

 TRANS-AUSTRALIA

 DELTA

 ARIANA

 LUFTHANSA

 CP AIR

 TRANS WORLD

 LAN-CHILE

 EXECUTIVE JET

 AMERICAN

 NORTHWEST

 TRANS INTERNATIONAL

 GERMAN GOVT.

 SOUTHERN AIR

 WIEN CONSOLIDATED

 NATIONAL

 SABENA

 TRANSAIR LTD.

 ROYAL AIR MAROC

 VARIG

 TAP

 NORTHEAST

 CONTINENTAL

 PACIFIC WESTERN

 ALL NIPPON